TOPEES & RED BERETS

Saga of a Suffolk Officer 1914–1975

Topees & Red Berets

Saga of a Suffolk Officer
1914–1975

Silvanus Bevan

A SQUARE ONE PUBLICATION

First Published in 1995 by
Square One Publications
The Tudor House
16 Church Street
Upton-on-Severn
Worcestershire
WR8 2HT

ISBN 1 872017 96 7

British Library Cataloguing in Publication Data

Bevan, William Silvanus
Topees and Red Berets: Saga of a Suffolk Officer, 1914–75
I. Title
355. 322092

Typeset in 11 on 12pt Palatino by
Avon Dataset Ltd, The Studio, Bidford on Avon B50 4JH

Printed in Great Britain by
Antony Rowe Ltd, Chippenham

For
Richard, Charles and Alice
'Down Under'

ACKNOWLEDGEMENTS

I would like to thank Major Tony Bridge, late The Dorset Regiment and H.M. Colonial Service for ploughing through the draft manuscript, noting errors and making helpful suggestions. I am grateful to both Colonel John Waddy, late The Somerset Light Infantry and The Parachute Regt., and Lieutenant Colonel Reggie Steward, late The Frontier Force Rifles, Indian Army, and 50 Indian Parachute Brigade, for reminding me of names I'd forgotten. I'm indebted to my friend Major Bob Godfrey MC, MA late The Suffolk Regt., for permission to quote from his book 'The History of The Suffok Regiment 1946–1959'. I would also like to thank both Lieutenant-General Sir Michael Walker, KCB, CBE, Colonel The Royal Anglian Regiment, and Colonel Christopher Dale, Regimental Secretary, The Royal Anglian Regiment, for their interest and help. I am most grateful to my step-daughter-in-law, Valerie Lawrence, for her assistance, especially in re-typing part of the book, and my wife for her encouragement, valuable criticism and forebearance over the past two years.

Milford-on-Sea.
Summer 1995

W.S.B.

CONTENTS

List of Illustrations

List of Maps

Introduction

This book has been written for the benefit of my son, daughter and stepson in Australia. They all have a rough idea of why I was born in Cyprus, then an unimportant colony of the British Empire inconspicuously tucked away in the north-east corner of the Mediterranean. However, unless I record the circumstances leading up to this momentous event, and how I met and eventually, after many years, married their mother – before long neither they, nor their Australian offspring, will know much about their parents or their origins.

I have lived through two of the most terrible wars in the world's history, and in spite of being actively involved in the last one, have survived more or less unscathed. As a regular army officer much of my service was spent overseas. I've seen the British Empire dwindle from almost its zenith to virtual extinction; soldiered in India in the days of the British Raj; was wounded on India's famous North-West Frontier and was one of the earliest paratroop volunteers. After the war I was involved in many troubles and emergencies overseas. Uniquely, I was the last officer to command The Suffolk Regiment in action – the 'Old Twelth of Foot' – famed for its steadfastness at the battle of Minden in 1759.

So I've got a tale to tell, most importantly about the twenty-eight and a half years I shared with my dear, beautiful wife Murna, who died twenty years ago. My desire to keep her memory evergreen has, above all else, motivated me into writing the story of our lives.

Summer 1995.
Milford-on-Sea,
Hampshire

SILVANUS BEVAN.

Chapter 1

Childhood Days in Cyprus and England 1914–1924

My parents were married in 1901 by my maternal grandfather, the Rev. J.G. Gibbs, the Rector, in the Berkshire village of East Hendred. Later that year my father, Willie Bevan, aged thirty-seven, left for Cyprus to take up the position of Private Secretary to the High Commissioner – in the days before there was a Governor. My mother, Alice, followed him several months later.

I came on the scene in Nicosia on 25th February 1914, seven months before the start of the Great War. My father was then overdue for home leave, but as he couldn't afford to take the whole family (no free travel in those days) he accompanied my mother, my sister Betty and me, as far as Alexandria, where he left us and returned to Cyprus. We went on to England in a larger ship.

On arrival in England we stayed with Granny and Grandfather Gibbs and our aunts, Audrey Heywood and Cicely Gibbs, at Upcross, a large rented house (now a hotel) on the outskirts of Reading in Berkshire, my grandfather having retired from the Church. I think the plan was that we would stay with them for a month or two then return to Cyprus. However, soon after our arrival war was declared with Germany, which upset all my parents' plans. My mother, anxious to rejoin her husband, decided to return to Cyprus, leaving Betty and me at Upcross until hostilities had ceased – no one thought the war would last more than a few months.

Aunt Audrey had trained as a nurse at St. Thomas's Hospital in

London, at the time very enterprising for someone of her social standing. Presumably that's where she met her husband, Dr. Willie Heywood, who, on the outbreak of war, immediately gave up a thriving practice in Newbury and joined the Royal Army Medical Corps, serving for four years in forward hospitals in France. Tall and rather dour, he didn't suffer fools gladly. I remember him with affection tinged with respect.

Aunt Cicely, the youngest Gibbs girl, remained a spinster all her life – I was very fond of her as I was of her sister, dear Aunt Audrey. Betty, cousin Mary and I remained at Upcross for the best part of five years – during nearly all the First World War – wonderfully looked after by our aunts and Gladys, our nanny. It wasn't too bad for me as I was so young, but Betty, having lived for four years with our parents in Cyprus, was deeply upset at being separated from our mother, especially when she was sent to a boarding school where she was terribly homesick. A most disturbing period in our young lives – I don't think our parents ever realized this. (Years later, my son Charles, suffered in the same way and still considers he was insensitively treated – at that time it was normal practice, anyway there was no alternative).

As the wife of a Government Official, my mother managed to wangle a berth on a troopship from Cyprus to England in late 1919. Her passport shows that she was authorized by the Foreign Office to travel back to Cyprus on 2nd February 1920, direct or via Egypt – accompanied by her two children. This entry is over-stamped in English & French – 'This passport is not valid for the zone of the armies'. I think we got priority in obtaining a passage so soon after hostilities had ceased – the Middle East was still full of troops awaiting de-mobilization.

We sailed from Devonport on board the *S.S. Czaritza*, a re-named captured German liner, arriving at Alexandria on 10th March 1920. I can just remember chasing Betty around the decks and getting very thirsty in the process – a steward told me "You'll drink the Captain out of water" much to my mother's amusement. On disembarking at Alexandria, I was fascinated by shoals of small fish which I thought were sardines, swimming around the ship's sides, I'd never seen anything like that before, it stuck in my memory.

We crossed on 11th March on the small, scruffy ship *Tanlerh*, plying regularly between Cyprus and Alexandria, arriving at Famagusta on 14th March where we were met by my father. I have a vivid memory of the journey, some 45 miles of un-metalled road from Famagusta to Nicosia in a T-model Ford. In every village we went through the car was surrounded by packs of barking, snarling, vicious dogs; they chased us a long way – I was scared that they might leap into the back of the car where Betty and I were huddled.

After a separation of six years, my father was reunited with his family. I think he was content in his job as Director of Agriculture – from letters and documents it's clear he was popular with the Cypriots. The Governor, Sir Malcolm Stevenson, I remember as a fat, gruff, rather un-pleasant character. He lacked the vision to appreciate the immense potential of the island's agricultural products and did nothing to encourage my father's efforts; the Chief Secretary was of much the same ilk. Despite my parents' obvious parlous financial situation, and the lowly status of Director of Agriculture in the official 'pecking-order', I think some of the senior officials were jealous; my father was so patently an upright, dedicated, courteous and well bred man – what's more he had an attractive and clever wife.

Before leaving my Cyprus days, a bit about life there at that time may be interesting to future generations. We had no modern conveniences whatsoever. My mother took out quite a lot of bits and pieces, pictures, crockery, linen and so on. There were

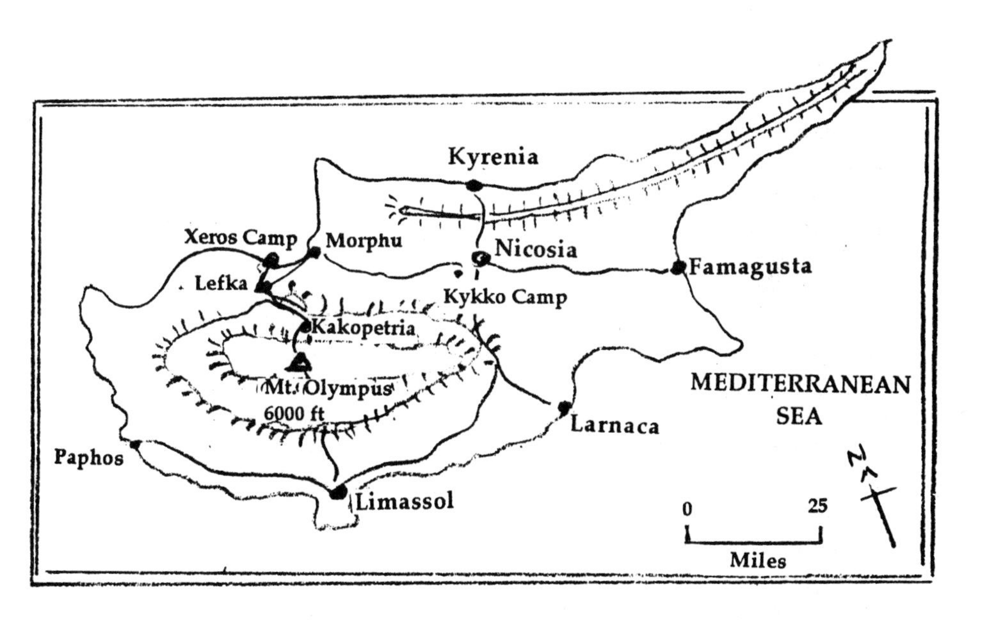

Map of Cyprus

Willie and Alice Bevan. Cyprus, 1919

Willie Bevan on tour in Cyprus, 1918

disasters – 'silver-fish' bored holes in the pictures, which also suffered in the wet season as roofs were anything but water-tight – I remember my mother sitting up in bed under an open umbrella! We had no car, anyway there was no road to our house, only a track. We walked to visit friends, sometimes hiring a Victoria carriage drawn by two horses – rather fun.

During the hot season we went on the single-line narrow gauge railway (discontinued in the early 1930s) to the foothills of the Troodos mountains dominated by Mount Olympus (over six thousand feet), completing the journey to a Government leave cottage by mule and donkey – Betty and I in canvas bags slung on either side of a mule; my mother often rode holding an open parasol to protect her from the sun.

After the heat of the Mansourian plain it was wonderful up there in the cool air, amongst the resin-scented pine trees. Streams in the valleys springing from fern-fringed grottoes, fringed with anemones, cyclamen and wild strawberries. There were other Government Officials' families on holiday, so we had children to play with.

Miss Young, a pioneer in camping holidays, ran one for small parties on Troodos – they became popular and quite well known throughout the Middle East. One year some of the comfortable tents, lined with coloured panels of Egyptian cotton, caught fire; our mother took Betty and me to see the damage, it made a lasting impression. Over thirty-three years later I remembered this incident when Eoka terrorists deliberately started a forest fire, which roared up a valley engulfing eight soldiers on a mountain track, burning them to death.

Occasionally we took holidays in Kyrenia (today in the Turkish sector of the island) a picturesque small harbour-town twenty-five miles north of Nicosia over the rugged Kyrenia mountains, the haunt of eagles. We stayed at a house belonging to the Petrides family; I slept in a small room right at the top known as a 'bella vista' with windows facing Asia Minor and the Turkish coast about forty miles away across the Mediterranean. A wonderful place from which to watch the thunder storms gathering and the fantastic sunsets, but frightening for a young boy on his own at night with thunder and lightening crashing and flashing around – I used to slip down the ladder and take refuge in Betty's bed!

I've mentioned that the house belonged to the Petrides's family. From the name one would imagine that they were Greeks, but this was not so. Cecil Petrides was of Athenian Greek descent, educated at Dulwich College in south London, to his dying day more English than the English. I have many happy memories of him and his family, not only when we lived close to them in Nicosia, but also many years later when he farmed near us when we were living at Northiam in Sussex. Cecil and Olive Petrides, although a lot younger than my parents, became close friends. Betty and I thought of their children – Molly, Daphne and Meriel as cousins – the only son, Basil, was killed during WW2 serving with the RAF. Meriel married my friend, Major Jack Prescott MC, of my Regiment; their eldest son John is my godson. Jeremy, the younger son, is a Lieut. Col. in The Royal Anglian Regiment, the successor to The Suffolk Regiment – Daphne was my daughter Alice's godmother. My ties with the Petrides have been close all my life.

Near us in Nicosia was an Armenian farm of single-storied mud-brick buildings, cattle sheds, barns and a sun-baked threshing-floor on which wheat sheaves were spread out to dry. The corn was then separated from the straw by a sledge with sharp flints in its under-side, drawn round and round by a bullock driven by an old crone sitting on a chair on the sledge – not changed since biblical times. There was also a potter who cast amphorae – two-handled pottery vessels – locally known as chatties, used for holding water, wine and olive oil. I still have two which I saw him throw on his wheel. The clay being porous, water kept surprisingly cool.

An unusual episode in my father's official duty is of historical interest, particularly as his great grandchildren are half-Russian. When the Russian Revolution took place in 1917, the aristocrats and bourgeoisie fled, some to China – to Shanghai and Harbin amongst other places (I think this is what my son-in-law's family the Kouznetsoffs did). Some escaped to Europe, others across the Black Sea to Constantinople, thence to Egypt and Cyprus. So many arrived in the island that the Government established a refugee camp in Famagusta, my father was given the job of running it. Being almost as fluent in French as in German, he was an ideal choice – French being the language in Tzarist Court circles.

Although the refugees had escaped with their lives, many were destitute. Some managed to hang onto their jewels and things easily portable. My parents bought several Caucasian rugs from them – two eventually came to me (I lost one in India when I had to leave my kit in The Red Fort in Delhi on moving to the Middle East – the other I still have, after eighty years it's still in good nick).

My parents had quite a social life. The Nicosia Club had tennis courts, a nine-hole golf course – 'browns' not 'greens' – and held frequent events, including the popular amateur dramatics, for which Willie and Alice Bevan were always in great demand. They must have enjoyed themselves, as much as my father's slender purse would permit.

By 1922 my father was approaching sixty, the retirement age for Colonial Service officials. Presumably my parents had been thinking about schooling for Betty and me, we were twelve and eight respectively. They decided that my mother, Betty and I should return to England, my father would remain in Cyprus until he retired in eighteen months time.

Arrangements were made for our passage home. From my mother's passport, the original plan was for us to travel via Rhodes, Greece, Constantinople, Italy and France, but for some reason this was changed. On 3rd April 1922 we motored to Larnaca, a small town on the south coast. I remember clearly arriving at the jetty and seeing a ship riding at anchor about a mile off the coast – there was no harbour.

It was wet and windy. The ship looked small, as indeed she was – a Norwegian tramp steamer of perhaps 700 tons. We got into an open rowing boat with four Cypriot oarsmen, and set off for the *Carvella*, pitching and rolling in a distinctly choppy sea. When almost alongside, my new Panama hat, of which I was inordinately proud, blew off. The boatmen started rowing away from the ship to retrieve it, my father told them sharply to leave the wretched hat and make for the ship. When finally alongside, the burly Norwegian First Officer standing on the grating at the bottom of the companion way, grabbed each of us in turn and bundled us unceremoniously up the steps onto the heaving deck, the proceeding being watched with amusement by the crew.

I clearly remember watching through the cabin porthole as my father was rowed back to the shore. Betty and I were sad to see him go, but being on board was exciting, so we didn't grieve for long. My mother must have been desperately upset, she'd had so many separations, rotten for her being on her own again – a brave woman.

It was an exciting voyage. I saw a deserter slipping down a stern hawser when we were alongside in Alexandria, and I remember an Egyptian stevedore trying to steal a loaf from the galley and getting a finger cut off by the ship's cook with a cleaver for his effort. The weather after Malta was stormy, our cabin was right aft over the screw, which in the heavy seas was constantly out of the water causing shattering vibrations. The Captain moved my mother and Betty to his cabin on the bridge and bunked down in the chart room with me. Every morning he took me aft to have a sulphur bath in our cabin, this was supposed to cure my eczema – in fact it made it worse.

One night the deck-cargo of carobs and onions stacked over the two holds worked loose and shifted, causing the ship to list – very alarming. The crew were up most of the night securing it. A stowaway, a heavily tattooed Pole, was discovered in the fo'c'sle; the Captain had him thrashed a few times, then given a meal and put to work chipping rust off the funnel. We passed a ship with whales lashed either side – rarely seen in the Mediterranean these days.

We were on the bridge when passing through the Straits of Gibraltar. The Captain – I think his name was Anderssen – let Betty and me have a look through his telescope, he said something to the effect that ... "The Rock of Gibraltar belongs to England, you should be proud." Coincidentally, for twenty-eight years I wore the badge of The Suffolk Regiment incorporating the name 'Gibraltar' – the 'Old Twelth of Foot' took part in the Great Siege of 1779–82.

After an easy passage along the coast of Spain, through the Bay of Biscay and up the English Channel, on entering the North Sea we ran slap into a solid, all-enveloping sea-mist, making progress impossible for several days. Our fog-horn blasting out incessantly, muffled answering wails from invisible ships all around made everything seem eerie – this was before the advent of radar – I doubt whether the ship even had a reliable radio.

Having survived something of an epic voyage, or so it seemed to us, we entered the Humber, steaming stern-first past endless shabby wharfs up the river to the port of Hull; we finally docked by vast rusty cargo sheds. A very concerned Uncle Charles was the first aboard. He'd been so worried at not having heard anything for several weeks, that he'd gone over to France to try to get news of the ship's whereabouts. We went ashore in a rowing boat. As Betty climbed the steep slippery landing steps, the Persian cat she was clutching, which we'd brought all the way from Cyprus, took fright, jumped out of her arms and made off – the last we ever saw of it; doubtless it found a berth as a ship's cat on another boat. Betty was in tears for much of the train journey to London.

We put up in rooms close to Uncle Charles's school 'Gibbs's' in Sloane Street. Within a few days I was admitted to the childrens' ward of Charing Cross Hospital, where I remained for three weeks. The ward was full of Cockney kids, so I quickly picked up their accent, much to Granny Gibbs's horror when she came to visit me with my mother!

When my eczema was better, I joined my mother and Betty in a maisonette Uncle Charles had prepared for us in the top floors of 135 Sloane Street, my mother must have fixed this up with him before we left Cyprus – 'Gibbs's' school occupied all 134 and most of 135 Sloane Street. I started at my Uncle's school, Betty went to Francis Holland School for Girls close by, off Sloane Square.

My father returned to England in mid-1924 and joined us in the maisonette. He was then almost sixty and due for retirement, but mercifully was employed for another couple of years, first as the Director of the Cyprus Pavilion at the British Empire Exhibition at Wembley in 1924–1925, and subsequently as the first Commissioner for Cyprus, setting up a modest office in London. Mr. Kelly, a pleasant but rather down-at-the-heel fellow (there was a terrible lot of unemployment) was his assistant and general factotum.

I have letters to my father signed Edward P (the Prince of Wales later King Edward VIII) and Albert (later King George VI) dated November 1924 and 1925 respectively, in their capacity as President of the Exhibition, congratulating him and his staff on their splendid work. My father was appointed an Officer of the Order of the British Empire (OBE, Civil Division) in June 1925, his scroll is signed by both King George V, and 'Edward P' the Grand Master of the Order.

We went to the opening ceremony in the stadium specially built for this purpose at Wembley, now the venue for major sporting events. It was a memorable occasion, I came away feeling very proud of being an Englishman – so obviously the 'top-dog' nation – just look at our Empire!

The culmination was a display of imperial might which made a deep impression on me, perhaps influencing my choosing the army as a career. I'll describe it:

> To the right a native village with palm trees, complete with Blackamoors in grass skirts, feathers in their fuzzy air and bones through their noses, shouting and brandishing spears, apparently just about to pop two white missionaries into a huge caldron over a blazing fire. Suddenly – to the left – enters a platoon of British soldiers in scarlet jackets and white topees. The young officer waves his sword in the direction of the native village – the soldiers advance, section by section, giving each other covering-fire in the correct military manner – lots of blank ammunition, bangs and smoke. The Blackamoors take to their heels – the missionaries are saved in the nick of time.
>
> Three Cheers for King and Country!

Chapter 2

In England 1925–1934

My father became Master of the Worshipful Company of Ironmongers in July 1926 when we were still living in Sloane Street, his term of office ended in July 1927 – he must have found it a strain to meet the considerable expenses the Mastership involved. In late 1926 we moved to a small house in the East Sussex village of Northiam, known as Forge House; as its name implies it had originally been the village smithy, it had a good sized garden and an orchard. It can't have cost much, perhaps £500, my father was by then retired and money very tight. I imagine my mother's Marriage Settlement was dipped-into to raise the necessary – its terms might have allowed this as she obviously benefited, but more likely Uncle Charles Gibbs lent the money, my father certainly couldn't have raised it.

Northiam was a typical East Sussex village, with two fine Tudor houses at either end of the long road running through it. At one end was Brickwall, a superb Elizabethian mansion with a deer park (later to become a private girls's school), owned by the Frewen family, well known landed-gentry, who held the parish 'Living'. The vicar, the Rev. Frewen, a splendid boozy bachelor, with a runny purple nose, which he mopped constantly with a large silk bandanna handkerchief tucked up his sleeve when not in use, gave me coaching in Latin during the school holidays which I enjoyed, but I don't think I learnt much! An earlier Frewen had beguiled wealthy titled folk into investing in cattle ranching in

Canada in the late 1800s, becoming a millionaire in the process – only to lose it all gambling. A colourful character, famous for an epic journey he made in Canada through deep snow to seek help – several books have been written about him. Dixters, a perfect Tudor manor house with a famous garden, was at the other end of the village.

Forge House was opposite a pub, my parents found this distasteful, I can't think why as the owners were pleasant helpful people and the pub stood well back from the wide road, so they decided to move to Suffolk, presumably because property was cheaper there. This move upset both Betty and me; Betty because she had made friends in the neighbourhood, and I liked it as the Petrides lived at Boyces Farm, Staple Cross, about five miles away, an easy bike ride – I often rode over, stayed with them, and helped on the farm.

We became the proud owners of a second-hand open tourer car, a Clyno (doors on the left side only). While watching from the dormer-window of my attic bedroom as Betty was just about to go back to boarding-school, I heard my father call out – "Hurry up Betty, I don't want to have to drive at thirty all the way". Lacking mechanical aptitude and road-sense, he was unhappy at the best of times when driving, so viewed the prospect of having to cover the ten miles to Robertsbridge station at thirty mph with considerable trepidation. No driving tests in those days.

My parents were always at a loss to know what to do with Betty and me during the long summer holidays – there were no package holidays' for families in those days. The problem was resolved by my aunt Audrey Heywood, cousin Mary's mother, who suggested that Betty, Mary and I should go to a sort of camp, run by a Miss Weldon, an eccentric, wealthy and intensely religious spinster, affectionately known as 'The Bish'. Mary's father's family, the Heywoods, were Christian missionaries in Africa, one was a bishop – Aunt 'Audy' heard of these camps through them.

We three duly attended our first camp, held in a boys' Prep school, Furzey Close, at Barton-on-Sea, near where I now live. About a hundred attended these Officers Christian Union camps, often whole families, including Service people on leave from overseas – there were plenty of pretty girls. In spite of the tedious morning and evening prayer sessions and hymn singing, it was quite good fun. The following year the camp was held in The Felixstowe Ladies College, a magnificent place originally belonging to the Cobbolds, wealthy East Anglian brewers (my godmother, Sybil Porter, neé Cobbold, was born there). Felixstowe was, and still is, an up-stage seaside resort on the Suffolk coast.

There were ten of us in my dormitory, one of whom was Tony Crosby-Warren, two years my senior and all of six foot five and a half inches tall, he was still at Clifton College. He and I got on well together, but I'm afraid we behaved badly. Tony had a crate of beer under his bed, he'd have been slung out on his ear if this had been discovered, fortunately, my sister succeeded in persuading us to toe-the-line – Tony had a crush on her.

One afternoon while walking along the promenade Tony and I spotted the Cork Lightship, marking the entrance to the shipping channel into Harwich harbour. Painted red with Cork in large white letters on either side of the hull, and a lantern at the top of a squat central mast, it appeared to be quite close to the shore, hardly any distance away – or so we thought. Tony said "Let's get a boat and row out to it". I naturally agreed. So we hired a small rowing boat with two sculls, to be paid for on return in a couple of hours, and off we set for the lightship. "Shouldn't take us long – I can almost see the chaps on it" I said. We started off rowing together with one scull each, I was in the bows behind Tony.

The sea was calm, no wind to speak of, as we watched Felixstowe glinting attractively in the sunshine gradually recede, to use a modern expression – 'no problem'. But there was a problem, with capital 'P'!

It gradually dawned on us that we couldn't see Felixstowe, nor the coast-line, and what was more, we both began to catch crabs – several times I slipped off the thwart landing flat on my back having missed putting my oar into the water. The sea had imperceptibly become choppy, the wind had freshened and we were a long, long way from shore.

"Where's the lightship?" I called out to Tony. "Where do you think? Behind us of course." he replied. "Can't see it. Oh yes, I can just make it out, we're miles off course" I shouted out. By then the palms of our hands were skinned raw – I was suddenly very tired. Tony tied his hanky round one of his hands and mine round the other, grasped both oars and rowed furiously for a long time, being so tall he could put his feet on the stern thwart and get a good purchase. After what seemed ages, I took over both oars while Tony rested, but we decided we'd get on best pulling together with one oar each, taking it calmly – or trying to. The tide in the shipping channel had carried us far to the north, we could just make out the lightship due south of us.

Eventually, after five hours, when it was just beginning to get dark, the tide turned and helped us. By then rowing with desperation we hove in sight of the lightship which suddenly loomed out of the mist almost on top of us. To our great relief the crew gave us a cheer, lowered a rope scrambling-net over the side for us to climb up and pulled us aboard.

After a meal of baked beans, fried eggs and bacon in the tiny saloon, the skipper told us we'd have to stay aboard over night – he'd get a pilot cutter to take us into Old Felixstowe Harbour next morning with our boat in tow. Meanwhile we were to kip down. Easier said than done – it was blowing quite hard, the vessel being anchored from the centre of the keel rolled and pitched in an alarming manner, I was beginning to feel distinctly queazy, and for good measure, the fog-horn immediately above us was blasting out every ten seconds – any chance of sleep seemed out of the question but being utterly worn out – we slept.

Next morning, after putting a pilot aboard a ship entering the Harwich channel, a pilot cutter came alongside and took us off, towing our rowing boat astern. We waved 'Good bye' to the crew who'd done us proud. We sent them some tobacco and chocolates a few days later as a 'Thank you' for looking after us so well.

Needless to say, when our absence was realised, great concern ensued in the camp – prayers were offered for our safe return! Perhaps they were answered – like a couple of bad pennies we returned to the fold. Word of what we'd been up to somehow had filtered through, surprising as I don't think the lightship had a radio – by underwater telephone cable perhaps? Anyway, our little adventure ended without disaster – it might easily have been otherwise.

My parents bought Tye House, a fair sized town-house in the middle of Hadleigh, a small somewhat depressed little market town in Suffolk, ten miles from Ipswich. Hadleigh's claim to fame was, and still no doubt is, that it had a Dean – as opposed to a Vicar (or Rector), who lived in The Deanery near the large church. In ecclesiastical jargon this is known as a 'Peculiar'; there aren't many of them. Dean Bates had two sons, one became soft on Betty, and a daughter Mary, about my age, we got on well together. The Dean, considering himself rather a dab at tennis, challenged us to a game on the Deanery grass court, complete with sagging net. He was so confident he'd beat us that he not only played in his straw hat, shirt sleeves and braces, but didn't even trouble to stop smoking his pipe – but not for long. I hit a mighty return which connected with his pipe, ramming it down his throat! Needless to say I wasn't asked to play there again.

Tye House was a great change from The Forge House in

Northiam. The small back garden was dominated by an old mulberry tree, there was only the pavement between the front wall of the house and the main street, adjoining buildings on either side and a dreary outlook at mean shops opposite. The main rooms at the back, additions to the original building, were well proportioned – a large central hall with a skylight gave a feeling of space. A glass roofed loggia with a vine, spanned the length of the garden side of the house.

Mains electricity hadn't reached Hadleigh, however, we were rather grand in having our own petrol-engine driven generator, which was supposed to charge a bank of batteries; after about two months the engine packed-up and the batteries were found to be worn out. So, for the next two years we made do with oil lamps, and a couple of 'Tilly' paraffin pressure-lamps, giving a wonderful light but requiring constant pumping, their fragile mantles tended to disintegrate at the slightest jar – plus good old-fashioned candles to see us to bed.

Our move to Hadleigh coincided with the Great Depression of 1929; there was much unemployment and poverty in the town. My father organized a club for men on the dole, where they could meet, get advice and a bit of recreation. This gave him an interest. He was sixty five and beginning to realise how badly off we were – his pension of £250 a year remained unaltered till his death in 1952. He'd have liked to have got a job, but this was virtually impossible for someone of his age, especially as he'd been out of England for twenty five years and had no business experience. Poor old chap, I know he felt badly about not being able to provide better for his wife and children. In spite of everything, I was happy in Hadleigh.

In January 1928, just before we left Northiam, I started at Sherborne School in Dorset. I think Uncle Charles helped with the fees, I know my mother's Marriage Settlement was raided again, because '£450 for school fees' was subsequently deducted from my share in my father's Will! I was lucky enough to get into Westcott House. My Housemaster, Geoffrey O'Hanlon, a bachelor, had converted the house to hold some forty five boys, naming it after a previous headmaster. 'Teacher' – as he was always known – was a man of great charm and many talents, he could have become headmaster of any public school in the country – but his heart was in Sherborne. He had a fine record in the Great War, winning the MC while serving with the Dorset Regiment. He could be very fierce when the occasion demanded, but was always fair, approachable and kind hearted.

On first arrival, before getting a study, one had a desk in the Day

Room, progressing after a term or so to a 'horse-box', fitted with a table, chair, shelves and a cupboard with sliding doors below; low wooden partition walls affording some privacy – a great improvement. After two terms 'Teacher' appointed me Head of the Day Room, my first taste of responsibility.

John Bennett and Peter Hogg, two senior boys, were keen ornithologists and kept falcons and owls in an annex to the bicycle shed. They had permission from the Wingfied-Digby family to roam about Sherborne Castle grounds to study wildlife. I got friendly with them and discovered that they weren't above doing a bit of poaching with double barrelled .410 pistols, easy to conceal down a trouser leg. I acquired an old Webley air-pistol, not a very lethal weapon, which I kept in the cupboard in my horse-box (sadly John Bennett died from exposure while on a solo trek in British Colombia soon after leaving Sherborne; Peter Hogg rowed twice for Oxford in the Oxford and Cambridge boat race then joined the Sudan Political Service). A 'flu epidemic put me in the sanatorium; while there 'Teacher' for some reason had a look through my horse-box and, alas, discovered the air-pistol. I was demoted without ado, and was extremely lucky to escape a beating.

Having started off by marking in the butts on the ranges, I quickly progressed to the firing-point and soon proved my prowess with a rifle, representing the school at Bisley in the Cadet Pair and in the Shooting VIII in 1930 and 1931, getting tolerably good scores and winning respectable cash prizes – far better than sweating away on the cricket field with some fearsome chap hurling a very hard ball at you, which you were supposed to hit with a totally inadequate bat.

My time at Sherborne was undistinguished, I was a poor scholar, never rising beyond the Upper Fifth and failing the School Certificate, but I made lasting friends and still hold much affection for the school in its marvellous medieval setting. 'Teacher' O'Hanlon kept in touch with me up to the time of his death when he was in his nineties; I rather think he felt the school should have done rather more for me.

My sister Betty who had become 'Elizabeth' – more fitting for a somewhat superior young lady – was vaguely studying Art in London, a heavy drain on my parents slender resources. We hadn't got a car, but when I reached fifteen – old enough to get a driving licence, I managed to scrape up enough to buy a motorbike, a BSA with a round tank and two-speed gear box; I bought it off a chap at Sherborne for £11 – life then began!

Some of the 'Bright Young Things' in the neighbourhood – Elizabeth being one – organized an Invitation Subscription Dance, to be held at Christmas time in the Hadleigh Corn Exchange. About two hundred local folk, many of them friends, were invited on the old-boy network, tickets £3 each. A London band was booked, a buffet supper provided. It promised to be quite a do, eagerly looked forward to by all the young folk roundabout.

I was almost seventeen and considered old enough to attend the dance – but how was I to find a partner? My parents heard of a Mrs. Rolleston of Stoke-by-Nayland, a village some five miles from Hadleigh, who had two daughters: Kathleen, my age, and Murna four years younger. After enquiries, it transpired that not only would Kathleen love to go to the dance, but also Mrs. Rolleston approved of her going with me. Marjorie Rolleston was a bit of an enigma; it wasn't clear whether she was a widow or a divorcee – there certainly wasn't any Mr. (or was it Commander?) Rolleston – no one seemed quite sure. I couldn't have cared less, all I wanted was a partner, and I'd heard on the grape-vine that Kathleen was quite a gal.

The great day arrived. Kathleen was delivered to Tye House by friends, and round we went to the Corn Exchange, quite close by. She was a spirited girl with pretty bobbed brown hair, a good figure, full of fun – clearly a bit of a Tom Boy. No great beauty, perhaps too prominent a nose, but far from unattractive – I liked her. The dance was a great success, we pranced round, she was a better dancer than me, at least until I'd had a beer or two in the pub opposite which had an extension that night, after which I seemed less inhibited and in altogether better form on the dance floor.

A few days later, Kathleen rang to ask if I'd like to take part in a mixed-hockey game at Stoke-by-Nayland the following week. It sounded as if it might be fun, so I said "Yes, I would". I duly rode over on my motorbike to find we were playing on what was little more than a grass field – the cattle had been shooed away and there weren't too many cowpats – so we bullied-off, Kathleen being very much in command. The game was fun, and I didn't suffer much damage from the girls, who were jolly fit and terribly keen. After the game we all went for tea to Kathleen's home, Hill House, just below Stoke church on quite a steep hill.

When the others had left, Kathleen, another boy and I went upstairs to what was called the school-room, where in the past Kathleen and her sister had had lessons from a governess. It was a cosy room in the front of the house, facing down the hill. We sat at table before a glowing fire and played rummy, a popular card game. It was winter and quite dark by five thirty, Kathleen suddenly said "There's the bus, Murna will be here in a minute" – she hadn't mentioned her sister before.

Listening – I heard the grinding of gears as the bus drove off up the hill, the squeak of the hinge of the wrought-iron garden gate being opened – a clang as it shut, quick light footsteps on the brick path below the window, the front door opening and closing. Moments later the school-room door, which I couldn't see as I had my back to it, was pushed open – and Murna came in. She dumped her books and black velour school hat on a desk behind me, then came round and stood in front of the fire where I could see her – that moment my life changed for ever.

There she was – in a dark blue gym dress with a velvet yoke, black shoes and stockings – the most beautiful girl I'd ever seen. Large deep-blue Irish eyes, long smudgy black eyelashes, dark eyebrows with an unusual upward slant at the ends, a wide forehead, bobbed dark brown almost black wavy hair with a fringe – shining where the firelight caught it, soft pink cheeks and full red lips, which seemed to be smiling at me – or so I liked to think. She was well developed for a girl of just under fourteen – very female. Even at that age she was stunningly attractive, quite unconsciously sexy. Shy and quiet, but smiley with a slightly husky voice – obviously taken aback at finding two young men in the school-room.

With my head in a whirl and a pounding heart, I somehow managed to get myself safely home along the five miles of dark winding narrow Suffolk country roads, my motorbike's acetylene head-lamp feebly lighting up the hedgerows as I shot by – in a daze. I got to know every inch of those five miles in the next few years.

Murna went daily by bus to the Colchester High School for Girls. As I was still at Sherborne there wasn't any chance of seeing her except during school holidays, anyway her mother kept close tabs on her, considering it improper for a girl of her age to come over to Hadleigh on her own. My bike didn't have a pillion, so it'd have been impossible anyhow.

There was always a lot going on. In the summer tennis competitions in private houses were good fun, provided not taken too seriously. I was a poor performer hitting the ball too hard, sometimes my partners got in the way with painful results, so no one was keen to partner me. Then there were village fetes and travelling circuses, not as sophisticated and commercialised as today. Mrs. Rolleston hired a beach hut at the exclusive seaside

Murna Rolleston, 1932

Murna and Silvanus, with Kathleen and a friend. Frinton, 1934

Murna skating at Villars. Switzerland, 1936

resort of Frinton, an hour's drive away, where we all bathed and enjoyed ourselves; I'm sure I showed-off horribly, trying to impress Murna.

The time had come for me to decide on a career – difficult as I'd fluffed the School Certificate exam. So I left Sherborne when I was seventeen, about a year early, and went to a crammer, Vinny Ransome, an old friend of Uncle Charles from his Oxford University days. I lived with Vinny and his wife in a minute house, Merle Cottage, on a steep hill in Marlborough and really worked very conscientiously, but Vinny wasn't much of a teacher – again I failed the exam!

By this time I'd decided to go into the army, influenced by my getting into the Sherborne Shooting VIII – membership of the school's Officers Training Corps (OTC) was compulsory. I had become a good rifle shot, perhaps the result of all the scatter gun shooting I'd done with Uncle Charles since I was a boy. The vital step was to pass the School Certificate, the sine qua non for admission into The Royal Military College at Sandhurst. My parents, who must by then have been getting desperate, arranged for me to go to yet another crammer, this time the Rector of Cockfield, a straggling village ten miles from Hadleigh, who tutored about half a dozen dunces like me for the exam; I rode there every morning on my motorbike.

The exam was held in Oxford. Fortunately my parents knew an ex-Cyprus widow, Mrs. Scott-Moncrieff, who lived there with her very pretty daughter, Jeannie, I knew them as we'd stayed there before – Jeannie was also taking the exam. This time I defeated the examiners, getting respectable marks in all subjects except Latin, which I just scraped through – all subjects had to be passed in one go. I don't know why I did so badly at Latin as I've always been interested in the language – I suppose I got rattled and lost concentration.

At last, equipped with the necessary academic qualification, I applied for a vacancy to Sandhurst. In due course I attended a Selection Board in London – four senior officers, asked tricky questions (rather stupid ones actually). Having passed this hurdle, my father was notified that I should report myself to Sandhurst for the term beginning in February 1932, complete with an imposing list of clothing – but fate was to dictate otherwise.

Feeling rather pleased with myself, I decided to ride down to Sherborne for the Old Boys' House Supper, an event held annually at the end of the Winter term in each of the eight school houses, generally resulting in much horse-play and beer drinking. The following morning, after attending the traditional service in the school chapel, I set off on the homeward journey of over two hundred miles.

Crash helmets and protective waterproof clothing were unknown then; I wore a cloth cap and ex-army greatcoat, the pockets full of spanners – it weighed a ton when wet. I soon was damned cold. My bike was only capable of 40 mph down hill, so it was slow going crouched over the handle-bars, with no protection against the elements. All went well until I reached Bishop's Stortford, a small town two-thirds of the way home. I must have been jolly tired, momentarily lost concentration, took a corner too fast, went into a front-wheel skid, came off, bashing my head on the road in the process. Two days later I awoke in a darkened room; a man with a beard was bending over me, asking in a strange accent – Australian I later found out – how I felt. Obviously, I survived.

By the time I'd recovered I was nineteen, over the age-limit for entry to Sandhurst. The Army authorities '..regretted but...', so there was nothing for it but to think of another career. I'd absolutely no ideas what to do, nor had my father. With hindsight, I should have been groomed to take over 'Gibbs's' – Uncle Charles's school, I'm quite certain I could have made a go of it in spite of my poor academic showing to date. I'd had a good education, and although I say it myself, I was no dunce.

After much head-scratching, it was decided I should try farming (a repeat of my father's early disaster). With this in view, Uncle Charles, who always turned up trumps at critical moments in my life, contacted an 'old boy' of his school, one Henry Pott, a bachelor, farming in a big way in Northamptonshire – and arranged for me to be apprenticed to him for a year. I think this arrangement was as much to give me a chance of regaining my health as anything else.

For some time past I'd set my mind on getting a Morgan 3-wheeler car, my BSA motor cycle having been sensibly vetoed by my parents. A firm in Balham, south London, advertised a 'Family' model for £15. I had a look at it, and being very green, bought it for £12. I managed to get it back to Hadleigh – just! A few days later I set off for Henry Pott's place, The Home Farm, Barnwell St. George, my twelve-bore shot-gun and .22 Mauser rifle strapped on the luggage rack over the rear wheel.

The journey was a disaster. Both chains driving the rear wheel kept on riding off their sprockets. Darkness fell, the lights wouldn't work, so I was forced to keep to minor roads where there was little traffic – and got lost. Finally, having been unable to see the drip-feed oil gauge on the instrument panel, I didn't realise the air-cooled engine was being starved of oil, with the inevitable result that both cylinders seized-up, I came to an grinding halt.

There was nothing for it but to ditch the Morgan on the roadside and thumb a lift to Peterborough station, ten miles away. Of course my finances were, to put it mildly, parlous. I hadn't enough to buy a ticket to Oundle the nearest station to Barnwell – what to do? I explained my tricky situation to the station's Police Constable, borrowed five bob off him (which I refunded by post) I doubt if I could have done this today, the police were more accommodating then. Unable to afford a taxi, I had to walk the four miles from Oundle to the farm. When I eventually reached the house I found it locked and shuttered except for a narrow pantry window at the back, which was a fraction ajar. While climbing in, and nearly getting stuck in the process, a light was suddenly switched on and I was confronted by the housekeeper in her dressing gown, brandishing a poker; a sour body at the best of times, she was not amused. An inauspicious start to my farming apprenticeship!

Henry Pott, the elder of two brothers, both of whom had been to Gibbs's school, was a large man in his late twenties. His sister had run the school's Wolf Cub Pack – I'd been a 'Sixer', his younger brother Roger, had been Head Boy. Betty and I went to jolly good childrens's parties at the Pott's grand house in Cadogan Gardens – so Henry and I had much in common.

Barnwell St. George was a pretty village of thatched cottages with a stream running through it; a vicarage, a doctor's house and a pub. The ruins of Barnwell Castle (destroyed by Oliver Cromwell in the Civil Wars) were a short distance away; in the grounds stood a large stone house, Barnwell Manor, belonging to Major Cooper, chairman of the International Stores – until quite recently the home of the Duke of Gloucester.

Henry had a thousand acre mixed-farm. Cattle, sheep, pigs, wheat, root crops, chickens and so on. There were two tractors, a Fordson and a Massey-Ferguson, but Shire and Suffolk Punch cart-horses were still used for most jobs on the farm. Deep ploughing was done by contract; powerful steam engines stationed at either side of a field pulled a massive five-bladed plough backwards and forwards across the field by a steel cable attached to rotating drums under each engine's boiler, moving forward five furrows each time the plough reached a side of the field. Henry employed a foreman and eight farm workers. Agricultural wages were disgracefully low, a labourer got thirty bob a week, a tied-cottage and a few perks such as vegetables and wood for fuel – just above subsistence level.

I learnt a lot in the twelve months I was at Barnwell. How to milk by hand, to plough with horses and by tractor, to hoe rows of beans without cutting the young shoots, to drill potatoes, to castrate piglets and tup lambs, to shear sheep by hand and with powered clippers – in fact I did the full gambit of farming activities – quite hard going at times. I enjoyed the life but suffered terribly from eczema – especially when we were using the threshing machine, an enormous box-like monster on wheels, driven by a belt from a steam engine, creating clouds of dust, and making a tremendous rumbling, groaning, whirring noise in the process.

One afternoon, while cleaning my .22 Mauser rifle, I almost put paid to my career – the rod jammed in the barrel. To clear it, the oily-flannelette had to be removed through the breech. Quite simple – all one had to do was to press the trigger, release the firing-pin, allowing the bolt to be withdrawn. No problem, providing the weapon was unloaded – as it should have been – but it wasn't. The butt was on the ground, the barrel between my knees pointing upwards, I pressed the trigger – BANG. The cleaning-rod shot smartly over my right shoulder, missing my right eye by a whisker, ending up in the barn roof. A very lucky near miss. I'd learnt my lesson!

Chapter 3

Commissioned into the Suffolk Regiment – The Twelth of Foot

During my time with Henry Pott there were few opportunities of seeing Murna and to make it even more difficult, her mother took the girls off to Villars in Switzerland each Spring, where they stayed in a pension for several weeks. When I did get home for a few days, I generally managed to get over to Stoke to see her, but it wasn't easy as I had no transport. A memorable occasion was when Kathleen, Murna, myself and another chap went by taxi to the Colchester Garrison Tattoo. I was determined to sit next to Murna – and succeeded. The benches in the stand were narrow, a good excuse to squash up close to her, I even plucked up enough courage to hold her hand, she smelt wonderfully fresh and fragrant, it soon got dark – an added thrill.

On another visit to Hill House I met Murna's uncle, Major Ramsay Eley, of The Suffolk Regiment. Murna had told him about me, and I think had mentioned my prowess with a rifle. We got on well. He asked me if I'd had second thoughts about making the army my career. I said that as I was over the age limit to get into Sandhurst, I'd given up on the idea. He then explained the possibility of getting a regular commission through The Supplementary Reserve of Officers, via the 'back door' as it were, and promised to write to my father. As we were a very non-military family, neither my father nor I had heard about this method of entry.

Ramsay duly wrote, my father contacted the authorities, and before long I found myself being interviewed by Major D.R.A.

Eley, DSO. Officer Commanding The Depot, The Suffolk Regiment, at Gibraltar Barracks, Bury St. Edmunds, some seventeen miles from Hadleigh. I must have made a good impression as not long afterwards I was 'Gazetted' Second Lieutenant in the Supplementary Reserve, and instructed to report to Gibraltar Barracks to carry out three months training.

This method of getting a regular commission had some advantages over the normal entry through Sandhurst. Once commissioned as a Second Lieutenant in the SR, while undergoing training one got paid the princely sum of 'ten bob' a day, plus a uniform allowance of £40. Apart from doing one month's annual training with a regular army battalion, there were no further demands, other than having to report to the Colours immediately in the event of a National Emergency, even before the mobilization of the Territorial Army. The major disadvantage was that one couldn't get commissioned until reaching twenty-one, a serious handicap in later years. Other disadvantages were that one didn't get to know chaps of one's own age with whom one would serve in all sorts of circumstances, nor undergo the exceptionally demanding but essential drill and general military training all Gentlemen Cadets were put through at Sandhurst. I think I'd have held my own there, my chances of ending up one or two ranks higher than I did would certainly have been better.

Anyway, off I went to London to cram for the army entrance exam to be held in the autumn of 1934. My Crammer was Lieutenant Colonel MacGregor-Greer, late of the Royal Scots. A charming old boy, but I had my doubts about the effectiveness of his methods of preparing the half-dozen aspiring officers, who attended classes in his suburban house in Perivale, West London.

Where to live was the problem. It was inconvenient for me to stay with Uncle Charles in Sloane Street – I can't remember why – so I started off by sharing a room in a Young Men's Christian Association (YMCA) hostel near Gloucester Road Underground Station, with Tony Edwards, who'd been at Sherborne with me – he'd joined the Royal Naval Volunteer Reserve as a Able Seaman.

Tony and I got on well together, rather too well; we got up to all sorts of mischief, eventually being kicked out – very reprehensible! I moved to Cromwell Gardens for a few weeks, sharing a room with a strange chap, Jerrick Payne, the son of a Methodist Preacher, who was, of all things, a member of the British League of Fascists. He wore a black shirt with a stand-up collar the whole time, and hung a photo of Mussolini on the wall facing one of my father. He took me to a Fascist rally in Olympia which ended in a vicious fight between Communists and Fascists – the Commies put razor blades in the peaks of their caps – not funny. I kept a low profile and was glad to get away in one piece.

Realising I needed digs nearer Perivale, I was told by Geoffrey York, a friend of mine, who was also cramming with MacGregor-Greer (he was killed while serving with the York & Lancaster Regiment in WW2), of a Mrs. Lamb, of Shaa Road, Acton (where my niece Brita Morse now has a house, it might indeed be the same one), who took in lodgers. So round I went on my pedal-cycle to see what she could offer me.

Mrs. Lamb, a substantial woman in her fifties, the widow of a former Mayor of Acton, was someone with whom one didn't argue the toss. I took to her, and she seemed to like me, offering me a ground-floor room looking out onto a lovely garden full of flowers, with a loo and hand-basin in a cloak-room just across the corridor; I moved in straightaway. There were five other lodgers – three female clerks employed in a Government office in Acton Way, and two men, both in the meat trade in Smithfield Market. I got on alright with them all, but really only saw them when we all had supper together in the evening.

Mrs. Lamb had two sons, the elder a builder, the younger a Cambridge graduate working for His Master's Voice (HMV) gramophone company at Hayes; she must have been quite well off, as she played the stock market a bit. She owned a wonderful car, a six-cylinder three-litre Sunbeam tourer, usually parked in the drive, sometimes with a WC seat in the back – her builder son occasionally used it for business. She let me take it when it wasn't wanted on the condition that I drove her to visit gardens open to the public. Needless to say I made good use of this offer, but there was a snag, the engine was a petrol-guzzler so I could only use it when I was in funds – which wasn't often; it was terrific to drive, a very similar model had won the Le Mans twenty-four hour race in France a few years before.

Old MacGregor-Greer made us copy out whole sections of military manuals: Field Service Regulations: The Manual of Military Law: King's Regulations etc, it seemed pointless at the time, but it yielded results – in my case anyway. Doing out-door tactical exercises without troops (TEWTS) wasn't easy, but we managed to work out answers to the problems he set us on the Perivale Municipal Park and Golf Course. Realising my future depended on getting good marks in this highly competitive examination, and feeling guilty at still being a burden on my parents, I really buckled down to my books, only very occasionally going up to the West End for a boozy evening with old Sherborne friends working in London.

While I was cramming, my parents had moved again, this time to a semi-detached villa on the outskirts of Folkestone in Kent. I think the reason was that my father found Hadleigh offered little in the way of cultural entertainment and thought Folkestone, a seaside resort where plays, concerts and so on were produced at the Leas Cliff Hall, would make good these deficiencies.

Alas, this didn't prove the case. The semi-detached house in Radnor Park Avenue was real suburbia, far from shops and the sea front. Having no car, they had to rely on infrequent buses, not easy for my mother with an arthritic hip – she felt cut-off and lonely. Elizabeth was engaged to Doctor Otto Edholm, and too occupied with her own affairs to see much of her parents; my mother's sisters and Uncle Charles were too far away to visit easily – she hated it. It must have been rotten for her, poor dear. Even to have considered moving there was stupid, it showed my father's impracticability, indeed his unintentional lack of consideration for my mother.

I took the exam in December 1934 in the enormous gymnasium at Sandhurst; a hundred or so Supplementary Reserve officers on one side, and about the same number of Gentlemen Cadets facing them on the opposite side, each at a small desk. The exam lasted three days and included outdoor tactical tests. I revised each evening flat-out, many of the others took a more relaxed attitude. There was a good deal of rivalry between the GCs and the SR officers, ending in fights and people getting thrown into the lake. I kept a low profile, determined to allow nothing to affect my chances in the exam.

I think I was the least surprised of all my family when the following appeared in 'The Times' of 11th January 1935:

Commissions in the Regular Army

SUCCESSFUL CANDIDATES

The following is the list of successful candidates at the examination held in December 1934, of the Officers of the Supplementary List, Regular Army Reserve of Officers, Supplementary Reserve, and the Territorial Army for appointments to commissions in the Regular Army. The names of the officers are arranged in order of merit:-

Newsum. H.K. for appointment to Indian Army;

Bevan. W.S. The Suffolk Regiment (SR)

(followed by another fifty four names)

I'd been reasonably confident, but to come second was pretty surprising. It proved to my family that I wasn't quite the dunderhead they'd always considered me.

As a reward for my success, my parents arranged for me to stay in Paris for three weeks with the Scotts, old Cyprus friends, who had a flat in the suburb of Auteuil. Scotty worked for Lloyds Bank, his wife, born in Cyprus, had been a front-line nurse in France during WW1. Scotty was quite a one for the ladies. He and a colleague decided my experience of life should be broadened. So one evening they took me to an up-stage restaurant-cum-brothel, Le Sphinx, where Scotty seemed well known to the scantily clothed, giggling girls who clustered round him. However, I'm rather ashamed to say, that in spite of their enticements, I remained a pure young man when I left, nevertheless, my horizon had definitely been broadened!

In late February 1935 I reported to The Adjutant, 1st Battalion The Suffolk Regiment at Crownhill Barracks, Plymouth (my Commission was dated 25th February 1935 – my twenty-first birthday). The Adjutant was Captain Christopher Eley, Murna's cousin, a bachelor and an Old Etonian. His family lived in East Bergholt, a village on the Suffolk-Essex border, famous as the home of the great English landscape painter John Constable, who did many paintings of Stoke-by-Nayland church (one hangs in Chicago Art Institute), and also of Dedham church, where Murna was baptised.

I was posted to A Company, commanded by Major Phips Gardham, a pleasant chap who'd spent much of his service in staff appointments. A few weeks after my arrival all officers had to report to the Orderly Room (military jargon for battalion headquarters office) to sign the Officers' Memo Book. The memo in question was to the effect, that anyone wishing to volunteer to serve with the Second Battalion in India, should enter their name. Without a second's hesitation I wrote mine down – one of the most far-reaching actions of my life.

When I joined, the army was in poor shape. Recruiting was bad, the battalion was below strength, equipment and weapons were virtually the same as those used in the Great War of 1914–18; no motor transport or radios, training facilities were mediocre. As a 2nd Lieutenant my pay was ten shillings a day, despite very modest extras in the way of drinks and so on my Mess Bill took half. It was virtually impossible to manage on one's pay, I could hardly afford to run my car, an old square-nosed Morris Cowley (bought for £15) – taking a girl to a dance was quite out of the question. Life in barracks was tedious.

I did as much rifle shooting as possible. Officers were armed with a heavy six-chambered Webley .455 Revolver, a lethal weapon, only accurate in the hands of an expert like Captain 'Ossy' Watts, C Company Commander, the Army Revolver Champion, who could fire six shots in ten seconds, at ten yards each shot-hole being within a one inch group on the target, an amazing feat of strength and skill; he realised I was a keen shot and took me under his wing. An exceptionally nice man, he subsequently joined the Small Arms Experimental Unit carrying out tests on the Bren light-machine gun, before it became the standard army LMG. Two other Suffolk officers, Majors Ransford and Barnadiston were also involved in these tests, both were excellent shots.

In the summer I went on a Young Officers Course at the School of Musketry at Hythe, a few miles along the coast from Folkestone, my first opportunity of mixing with officers from other regiments. We dined in mess kit, the Scottish and Cavalry officers in particularly grand uniforms costing a fortune, lots of gold braid and gilt buttons – even The Suffolk Regiment's mess kit, scarlet monkey-jacket with yellow facings, set me back a packet. I qualified adequately, but didn't get an 'A', the top grading, as I'd hoped.

While I was on this course Murna happened to be staying with friends in Folkestone – we met briefly a few times. I spotted her once in an open two-seater car, being given a driving lesson by some chap I didn't recognise (before the days of driving tests). I was very envious, she saw me and waved.

Back again in Plymouth, I found great activity in progress preparing for the 250th Anniversary of the Regiment's formation in 1685. This was duly celebrated with the Battalion carrying out the old and demanding ceremony of Trooping the Colour. Being the most junior officer, and as my drill left much to be desired not having been to Sandhurst, I wasn't on the parade – I was rather bitter about this. However, I and several others, were given the job of escorting VIPs to their seats and generally making ourselves useful – rather a come-down for a keen young officer.

After the parade our guests were entertained in marquees, followed by lunch in the mess for the top-brass, a buffet lunch in the marquees for the rest. Plymouth had large naval establishments, an army garrison and Royal Air Force units; everyone who was anyone, plus all the local female talent, had been invited. A lovely August day, the sun shone, the band played, the young maidens looked exquisite, there was plenty to eat and drink, I began to enjoy myself.

Being unaccustomed to anything stronger than beer, I didn't realise the potency of the sherry the mess waiters kept plying me with, the result being that the Senior Subaltern, one Tiny' Heal, considering me the worse for wear, ordered me to make myself scarce – so I spent the afternoon on my bed!

I'd recovered in time to attend the Guest Night in the mess, a daunting ordeal. As Vice-President I sat at the bottom of the long table ablaze with Regimental silver, The President, (Major Louie Baker, I think) was at the other end, seemingly miles away. The Loyal Toast was always drunk after the meal, but before the coffee and cigars. To the President's "Mr. Vice, The King" I had to stand up and say "Gentlemen, The King", whereupon everyone would rise holding their glass of port in the right hand, the band would play the first few bars of the National Anthem, then everyone would toast "The King", down their port and sit down. Sounds simple enough, but looking down the long candle-lit table, through a haze of pink faces,' hard-boiled' shirts, scarlet jackets and medals at the President slightly out of focus, my head swimming, I felt sure I'd fluff my words – but I didn't!

Before departing for India I got Embarkation Leave which I spent with my parents who'd moved yet again, this time to a small house in the country near Newbury – Hatch Gate, Bucklebury, Berkshire. Its situation would have been perfect for younger folk but it was too cut-off for my parents, who by then were elderly and becoming infirm.

Bucklebury was only a hamlet, a pub, 'The Blade Bone', a butcher and a small post office-cum-general store, the nearest grocer was three miles away. Having no car my parents relied on the infrequent local bus service. My father was seventy-two and my mother sixty-six and very arthritic. The house was badly built, requiring an extension before they could move in, but I think it was probably the nicest home they ever owned. If they'd had a car, and could have spent a bit more on the house and garden, it'd have been delightful.

I'd sent my measurements to Fazaldin, the Indian Regimental tailor (darzi), who'd been with 2nd Suffolk for many years. In due course several large parcels arrived, sewn up in khaki cloth. I unpacked them while staying with Aunt Cis in the maisonette in 135 Sloane St. Everything fitted perfectly. Khaki shorts, slacks, shirts, thin scarlet mess jacket and white overalls (tight trousers with a strap under the instep originally designed for riding). The Suffolk and the Shropshire Light Infantry were, as far as I can remember, the only infantry regiments to wear scarlet tropical mess jackets, all the others wore white ones – why we were different I've no idea – we were rather proud of them.

I can't remember saying goodbye to Murna, perhaps she was in Switzerland with her mother and Kathleen. But I do remember going to Aldeburgh with her – a long drive from Stoke-by-Nayland. We sat on the shingle beach with our backs against an upturned boat – it was jolly cold and windy – and decided to consider ourselves unofficially engaged and dreamt of the time my pay would be enough for us to get married. Wishful thinking, officers didn't qualify for marriage allowance under thirty – but that didn't enter into our heads.

My parents arranged an afternoon farewell party for me in Uncle Charles's school, 134 Sloane Street. Family and friends turned up to wish me 'bon voyage'. My father, an accomplished speaker, said a few words, to which I replied. The old chap was clearly proud of his only son and upset at my leaving, realising he might perhaps not live to see me again – I felt quite emotional myself. My somewhat shaky start in life seemed at last to be coming right – a few glasses of sherry confirmed this, rounding off a happy occasion. I left in an aura of goodwill and affection.

Chapter 4

Soldiering with 2nd Suffolk Regiment, Mhow, Central India, 1936–37

At the time I was posted to India the Italians were invading Abyssinia in defiance of the League of Nations – international tension was building up. There was much head-scratching in the War Office, resulting in the up-dating of contingency plans and the rescheduling of trooping programmes. On arrival at Liverpool docks, instead of finding a British India Line troopship, with the distinctive livery of white hull with a broad blue band, I boarded the Anchor Line's fine ship *Tuscania*, partially chartered for trooping.

Troopships were comfortable enough for officers in First Class cabins with Indian Lascar stewards, excellent meals in the dining saloon and plenty of facilities, but pretty grim for the troops in over-crowded, stifling mess-decks where they fed, slept in hammocks swinging from side to side with the ship's motion, and spent much of their time.

Since about one third of the *Tuscania*'s First Class passengers were civilians, our route was unusual for a trooper. First call was Marseilles. I went ashore with a party of young officers one of whom was Arthur Denaro, a splendid chap in the Leicestershire Regiment (I'd met his parents, his father was from a well known Maltese family, his mother was English). Arthur, a devil-may-care fellow quickly took control, whisking us in a taxi to a 'Cinema Bleu' considered very risqué in those days – all sorts of rather improbable goings-on, filmed I imagine in about 1900, if not earlier – anyhow we thought it was terrific!

Inevitably we were late starting back, to make matters worse our taxi deposited us on the wrong side of a vast dock – we could see the *Tuscania* far away on the opposite side. Time was running out, we expected to hear the ship's siren blast-off at any moment signalling her imminent departure, I had visions of being Court Martialed for missing the ship. It was getting dark, the docks were deserted, but luck was with us – we found a rowing boat and with threats and bribery, persuaded the surly owner to row us over. Half way across the dock he tried the old trick of demanding twice the fare, Arthur quickly disillusioned him as to the wisdom of such a demand. We were the last aboard. (Arthur was mortally wounded in 1943. His nephew, named after him, commanded the Royal Irish Hussars, an armoured regiment, with great distinction in the Gulf War of 1991).

Leaving Marseilles we sailed south, past the Isle of Stromboli with its erupting volcano, through the Straits of Messina, then headed east. The next stop was Port Said at the entrance to the Suez Canal where most of the civilians disembarked. The thing to do was to visit Simon Artz's Emporium, close to the quayside, and buy a 'Bombay Bowler' – a solar topee covered in khaki cloth with a leather strap over the top and across the front brim – the hall-mark of a pukka sahib.

In those days ships were coal-fired, Port Said being a major coaling station. Coaling was done by an endless procession of chanting Egyptian coolies humping sacks of coal from barges alongside, up a rickety plank against the ship's side, pitching the coal down a shoot into the bunkers, then descending by another plank to repeat the process. This took the best part of a day, all port-holes and doors had to be shut to keep the dust out and stop the 'Gypos' from stealing anything they could lay their hands on. While this was going on most passengers went ashore – the troops went on a route-march for a bit of badly needed exercise.

As I wasn't with a draft, I didn't have to take part in the route-march, so I again joined up with Arthur and other kindred spirits. We set off in a hired Victoria, an open carriage drawn by a pair of horses, a form of transport common in Egypt and the Near East. The driver took us round the back streets of Port Said – a fly-blown town, notorious for every form of vice. We visited some pretty grotty 'joints', I had a small automatic pistol in my pocket, which gave me false confidence, especially when darkness suddenly fell as it does in the East.

As the *Tuscania* steamed slowly through the Suez Canal, we

passed Italian troopships crammed with scruffy soldiers en route to the war in Abyssinia. Much ribaldry passed between the British and 'Itie' soldiers; Mussolini's ears must have been burning.

Steaming down the Red Sea it was stifling in the cabin at night, so I slept on deck which meant getting up very early to avoid being hosed-down by the Lascar crew holystoning the decks.

A feature of any voyage to India and the Far East in a troopship was the Boxing Competition. A ring was rigged in the well-deck, spectators perched on every vantage point. The Ships's Captain and Officer Commanding Troops were in the best seats. There was a good deal of betting on each bout and much shouting and cheering. Boxing in those days was a far more popular sport than today, especially in the Armed Services – bouts often ended with bloody noses and the odd knock-out. If a young officer took part he came in for a lot of good-natured ribbing, and tremendous applause if he was knocked down, even more than if he'd won!

Sailing steadily through the Indian Ocean with its flying fish and dolphins, we passed close to a troopship returning home; the troops aboard her shouted "You're going the wrong way" – choice epithets were freely exchanged.

I first set foot on the Indian sub-continent at Karachi where a number of drafts disembarked. My first memory of India is of walking with a friend from the ship to find a tonga – a light horse-drawn trap – to take us into the town, and being puzzled by what I thought were splotches of blood on the ground. I later realised Indians chew betel-nut (pan leaves) which makes their mouths and teeth red, then spit out the unchewed bits leaving red splodges on the ground, an unpleasant habit. We sailed again that evening on the last leg of the voyage to Bombay.

As land hove in sight, despite hangovers from the previous night's farewell revels, everyone crowded on deck to catch the first glimpse on the horizon of the fabulous city of Bombay as it gradually materialised through the early morning haze. We docked at Ballard pier, hawsers were grasped by gangs of shouting, gesticulating, turbaned coolies, and made fast – we'd arrived in Hindustan. Little did I think that it would be twelve years before I'd finally leave the sub-continent.

A posse of officious Embarkation Staff came aboard, closely followed by friends of passengers hoping to get a free drink or two and some English cigarettes in the First Class bar. Leaning over the ship's rail watching the hubbub on the quayside, I spotted a Suffolk officer – three Indians in khaki jackets and trousers with coloured turbans seemed to be with him. Two other Suffolk officers had travelled out with me – Captain 'Sweat' Dean and 2nd Lieut. Alan Hinde, the latter had shared a cabin with me. 'Sweat' knew the Suffolk chap (I think he was Tony Turner) and told Alan and me to follow him. As soon as I'd set foot ashore, one of the three Indians I'd seen from the ship approached me, touching his turban in greeting he enquired "Bevan Sahib?" He was a round faced, thick set, smiling fellow of about twenty-seven, who told me, in remarkably good English, he was to be my bearer, showing me a letter from the Regiment to this effect – his name was Babu Krishna Mazde, to be my friend and loyal servant for the next four and a half years – I wish it could have been longer.

We three Suffolk officers dressed in khaki drill jacket and shorts, Sam Browne belt and a Wolsley pith helmet (which had to be worn till six o'clock in the evening) took a taxi to the Taj Hotel, the best in Bombay, close to the Gateway of India – an archway similar to Marble Arch in London, built as the landing place for King George V and Queen Mary at the start of their state visit to India in 1911 to attend the Great Durbar in New Delhi.

It was hot, I was grateful for an iced nimbo pani – fresh lime, sugar and soda water – very refreshing. We stayed till it was time to go to the pseudo-Gothic Victoria Station, to board the romantically named Frontier Mail for Mhow, Central India.

We shared a four-berth compartment – seats each side which doubled for beds, the two upper berths hooked back by day, a lavatory with a hand-basin and shower.. Our bistra (bedding rolls) had already been laid out by our bearers who occupied a small compartment at the end of the carriage. The train trundled off after dark, hauled by an enormous steam locomotive. We arrived early next morning at Rutlam Junction; after breakfast in the station restaurant we changed to a narrow-gauge line.

By the time we left Rutlam the temperature was stoking up. We were joined in our smallish compartment by Loïs (I forget her maiden name) the fiancee of 'Monty' Moriarty, one of our officers. Loïs had been on the *Tuscania*, but as she'd travelled 2nd Class we hardly ever saw her. She married 'Monty' soon after arriving in Mhow – we all went to their wedding. Many years later when she was a widow, I stayed with her in Suffolk quite frequently. There were two others in our compartment, Rex Barton a Gunner, and an officer's wife joining her husband in Mhow. We bought a large block of ice in a metal container, placed on the floor with the electric fans playing on it, the temperature fell quite appreciably. It was a slow, dusty journey, through what seemed to our inexperienced eyes sparsely inhabited, parched dun-coloured country.

We arrived at Mhow station late that afternoon, the Commanding Officer, Lieut. Col. Harry Gadd, The Adjutant, Captain Dick Goodwin, and other officers with their wives were waiting to greet us. I was taken to the junior subalterns' quarters in Krishna Building, close to the barracks, a monstrosity of a place, home to six 2nd Lieutenants. We each had a sitting room with small bedroom in an alcove, a ghusal khana (bath room) with tin bathtub, one tap, a wash-hand stand, and a commode – known as the 'thunder-box'.

The officers' mess and quarters were in bungalows in the immediate vicinity. The barracks were nearby, but a bicycle was essential – one had already been provided for me by the Regimental Contractor, the impressive Khan Sahib Haji S. Shaboondeen (reputed to be worth ten lacks of rupees, say £1 million). A venerable character, with a henna-dyed red beard, indicating he'd made the Haj to Mecca (hence the Haji) and an enormous turban of ivory coloured silk. Over the years I got to like the old fellow, he helped me when I got into financial straights, as I'm sure he did for many other officers.

Mhow had a garrison of brigade strength: one British and two Indian infantry battalions; a Field Regiment Royal Artillery (18-pounder WWI guns); a British Military Hospital (BMH), and the usual supporting services.

The British infantry barracks were on a slight rise, some distance from the predominently Hindu city. 2nd Suffolk was up to strength – about 750 all ranks, including an excellent band and Corps of Drums. On parade quite a number of men still wore Great War medals. The standard of drill was high; woe betide anyone who was slack, the Adjutant, Captain Dick Goodwin, never turned a blind-eye to any mistake or idleness (he rose to the rank of Lieut. General and was Knighted). Although we were behind the times in tactics, the battalion was highly efficient. The standard of musketry was outstanding, ammunition for range work was plentiful, so we had ample opportunity to fire our weapons. The soldiers were fit and hard, capable of marching twenty five miles a day in temperatures of up to and exceeding 100 degrees fahrenheit.

To my delight I was posted as a platoon commander to D (Machine Gun) Company, commanded by Major Jackie Lloyd, an un-predictable officer, considered a bit of a joke in the battalion, but quite harmless and pleasant when one got to know him – he was having matrimonial trouble at the time which no doubt accounted for his occasional eccentric behaviour. D Company had

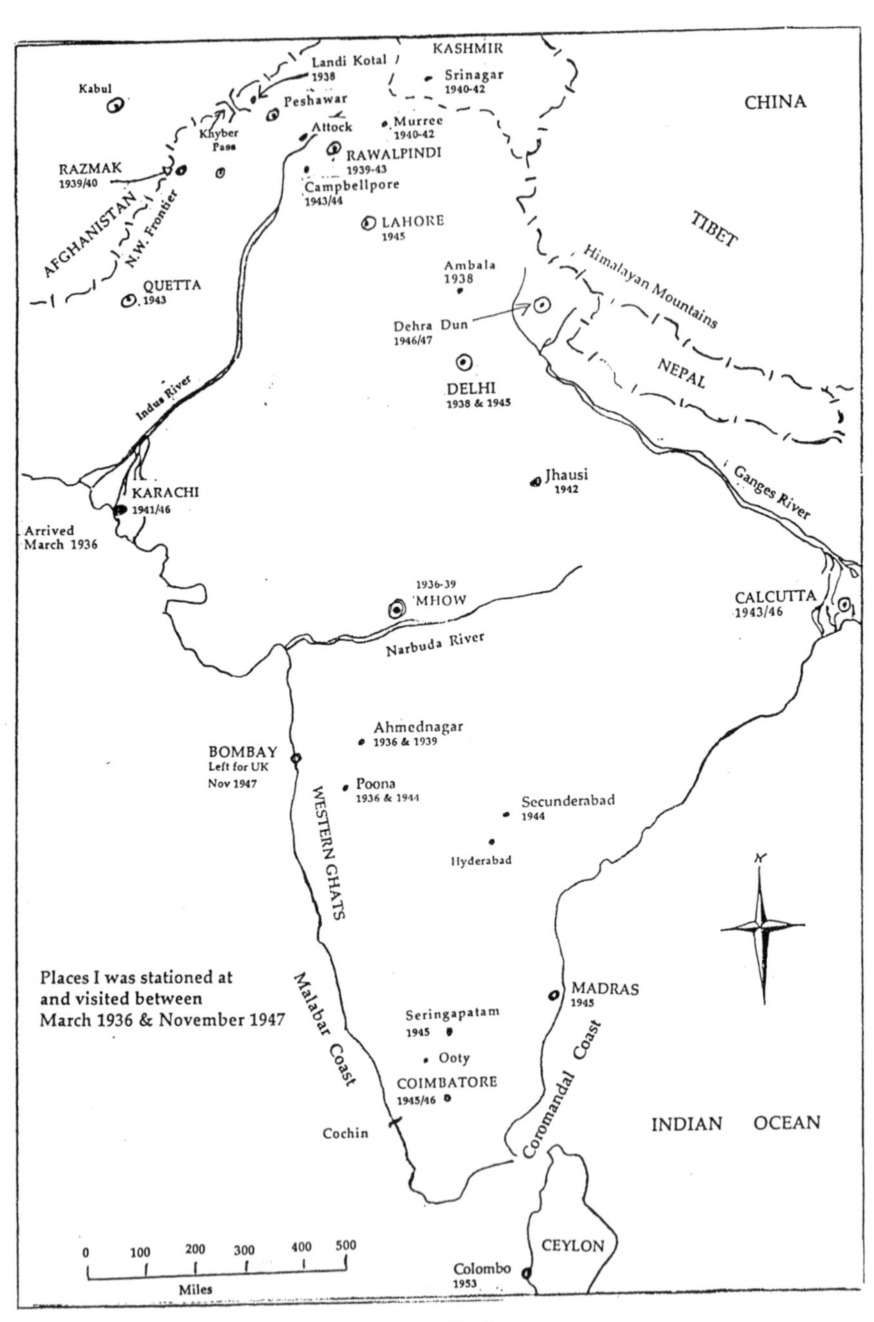
KASHMIR
Landi Kotal
1938
Srinagar
1940-42
Kabul
Peshawar
CHINA
Khyber Pass
Attock
Murree
1940-42
RAWALPINDI
1939-43
RAZMAK
1939/40
Campbellpore
1943/44
AFGHANISTAN
N.W. Frontier
LAHORE
1945
TIBET
Ambala
1938
Himalayan Mountains
QUETTA
1943
Dehra Dun
1946/47
DELHI
1938 & 1945
NEPAL
Indus River
Jhausi
1942
Ganges River
KARACHI
1941/46
Arrived
March 1936
1936-39
MHOW
CALCUTTA
1943/46
Narbuda River
Ahmednagar
1936 & 1939
BOMBAY
Left for UK
Nov 1947
Poona
1936 & 1944
WESTERN GHATS
Secunderabad
1944
Hyderabad
Places I was stationed at
and visited between
March 1936 & November 1947
Malabar Coast
MADRAS
1945
Seringapatam
1945
Ooty
COIMBATORE
1945/46
Coromandal Coast
INDIAN OCEAN
Cochin
CEYLON
0
100
200
300
400
500
Miles
Colombo
1953

Map of India

three platoons, each of four Vickers .303 water-cooled machine guns, providing the battalion's main supporting fire-power. This splendid, reliable, robust weapon, first came into service just before the Great War (1914–18), remaining the infantry's only heavy machine gun until well into WW2. As the twelve guns were carried on pack-mules, MG Company officers were mounted and wore spurs; a platoon of Indian Muleteers (Sepoys) formed an integral part of the Company.

Although still very impecunious, I wasn't as desperately hard-up as I'd been in England, pay in India being better than at home, at least it seemed to go further. I could even afford a few luxuries such as membership of the excellent officers' club which boasted a ball room, billiards, tennis and squash courts, a swimming pool and golf – of a sort. I enjoyed myself, everyone was friendly. Even though still very junior, I soon got to know most of the officers in the garrison and met their wives at club dances, gymkhanas, race meetings and so on. There was always a lot going on, social life centred round the club – it was fun.

Good Queen Victoria had decreed that Thursdays in India were to be half-holidays. Both the officers' and sergeants' messes had shikar clubs, so shooting parties were held most Thursdays and at weekends. Game was plentiful – painted partridge, quail, snipe, green pigeon, many varieties of duck and hares, to mention a few. Not many miles south of Mhow the country became broken, seamed by valleys and river gorges, dry for most of the year, but during the monsoon becoming torrents of brown muddy water. Good country for deer – shambur, nilgai, chetal, blackbuck, ckinkhara – and wild pig, also panther and tiger.

The garrison had shooting rights over blocks in this jungly country, allocated on the payment of a small fee, by The Station Staff Officer (SSO), Captain Harry Carrigan, who happened to be a Suffolk officer (his wife was born in Cyprus, she remembered meeting my parents). Harry was an exceptional officer, he spoke Hindustani like a native, and without doubt was the finest shot with a scatter-gun that I've ever known. In some uncanny way he was always at the right spot at the right time; if you were lucky enough to be near him you could count on good sport. He encouraged me to try for big game; it was in great part due to him that I bagged three panther, wild-boar and other game during my time in Mhow. He didn't quite fit into the Regiment, no doubt because of his lack of a Suffolk 'county' background – some of our senior officers were rather stuffy. I liked him, we hit it off wonderfully well – a splendid chap.

The garrison had a Tent Club – not what the name might imply. Over the Easter holiday horsey types forgathered for a 'pig-sticking' meet in a camp on the banks of the Narbudah river, some sixty miles south of Mhow, where a road and railway bridge spanned the river. I volunteered to help prepare the camp, setting off with a Gunner officer called 'Pechi' Byrne (pechi being the Hindustani for behind – he certainly had a large bottom), a florid fellow with an enormous blond moustache. We squeezed into his open Buick car, bedding rolls stuffed between the bonnet and front mudguards – normal procedure, our bearers were in the back, with assorted gear and crates of beer, which we cooled by pouring into thermos flasks of crushed ice, then quickly decanted it into mugs – it tasted like nectar. We needed copious draughts, the temperature was terrific, well over a hundred fahrenheit, and the clouds of dust churned up by the wheels on the un-metalled road increased our thirst.

The horses arrived that evening having been ridden down by their syces (grooms). The following afternoon everyone turned up – including several intrepid females – they all seemed pleased with the way 'Pechi' and I and our helpers had set-up the camp under shady mango trees. We all fed at a camp table – a wonderful curry, washed down with countless burra pegs – large whiskies and sodas.

At five o'clock the following morning, when still quite cool, about a hundred local wallahs (villagers) – the beaters – materialised from nowhere, squatted round a thorn bush fire until organised into teams.

It was time for us to mount. I'd been allotted a light- draft mare, a powerful animal, normally used to pull artillery ammunition limbers. She had a regulation saddle, apparently made of cast iron, and a mouth to match. We'd been split up into 'heats', groups of about half a dozen riders, each armed with a 'hog spear', a fearsome weapon some six foot long with a short steel blade at one end and a lump of lead as a counterbalance at the other. We wore thick topees to ward off the sun and protect our heads should we fall off – extremely likely in my case.

The first move was to trot to our assembly positions – my heat's was close to a tall neem tree on a track – our starting line – where we dismounted. I saw the jhanda wallah, a skinny old man in a dhoti (cotton loin cloth), clutching a white flag perched precariously in the branches of the tree, from where he could see the surrounding jungle. The signal to mount was when he raised his flag, we then had to wait until he lowered his arm and pointed the flag in the direction he'd seen the pig, only then could we set off in hot pursuit. The winner of each heat was the first to spear a pig.

The beaters were spread out in a line, half a mile or more long, a good distance behind us. When a bugle sounded they started moving forward, shouting and rattling their sticks on the stumpy teak trees and undergrowth, as much to give themselves courage, as to flush out the pig or anything else in front of them. Nearly always deer – nilgai, sambar and cheetal – came charging through, as well as peafowl – making a tremendous screeching and clattering of wings – hyena, large grey long-tailed langur monkeys and even the occasional panther.

It was incredibly hot, I could hardly see for the sweat pouring down my forehead into my eyes. Being an indifferent horseman and unaccustomed to handling a long, heavy, dangerous spear, I was a menace. The fact that my horse did exactly what it liked, irrespective of my strenuous efforts to control it, didn't make life easy for me or anyone nearby. I came in for plenty of curses, not least from the two ladies in my heat.

The big moment arrived – the jhanda wallah dropped his arm. Mounted and more or less under control, I set off at a tremendous pace – flat out – luckily my horse seemed to know precisely what to do. The ground was rocky and covered with thick prickly scrub, making it difficult to see far in any direction – I followed the others, who were charging ahead like fiends possessed along a dry nullah. Suddenly I saw a 'sounder' of pig, a family group, scuttling away through the dry yellow undergrowth. I spurred after them, made an ineffectual jab at the one I thought was the biggest (to spear an immature hog, or a sow, was a heinous crime – 'just not done, Sir!') my horse swerved, I almost came off. I'd had enough, so feebly decided to call it a day! Apart from anything else, my fingers were skinned raw through tugging on the reins, my throat was parched, an iced nimbo pani under the mango trees in camp was irresistible. In the afternoon I went off by myself and shot a few green pigeon, restoring my self-confidence and producing something for the pot.

The next day I was lent a more docile mount, a mare, belonging to Mrs. Fraser, the wife of the Commander-in-Chief of the Indore State Forces, an Indian Army officer holding the local rank of Major General, a charming man. The mare gave me a good ride; I took it gently, saw a lot of sport but didn't allow myself to get carried away again. The General suggested we might have a go at shooting mugger in the Narbudah in the evening, I jumped at the opportunity of having a crack at the elusive, carnivorous Indian crocodile.

The sun was dipping towards the horizon as we gingerly lowered ourselves into an unstable dug-out craft – a man with a pole in front and one behind – kishti wallahs. The river was about half a mile wide, being the dry season water flowed in only a few channels. We poled forward slowly and silently – I was in front with my BSA .375 rifle across my knees, searching the sandy spits between the channels, hoping to see a mugger resting on one, or in the shallow water, but saw nothing.

Darkness was falling – we decided to return to camp. As we were turning round, the man in front whispered "Sahib, Sahib" pointing ahead. At first I couldn't see anything, but as we edged forward, I gradually made out an indistinct object bobbing about in the water to our right. I raised my rifle to my shoulder peering along the sights.

Whatever it was, it was barely moving, in the dusk it was impossible to see clearly. I was still baffled when the General tapped me gently on the shoulder, indicating I should lower my rifle, by then we were close to the object. As it slide silently past I saw the face of a young woman, mouth open, teeth gleaming – a ghastly putrid stench wafted up at us as the corpse slid silently by into the darkness. We completed our turn and made for camp, both lighting our pipes in an attempt to dispel the nauseating sickly smell of death. Back in camp we downed several stiff burra pegs in quick succession.

Hindus burn their dead at burning ghats on river banks, corpses are often only partially consumed as peasants cannot afford enough wood – this no doubt accounted for the corpse we'd seen, which had subsequently been dragged into the river by a mugger.

I'd learnt a lot about India during this short interlude away from the battalion; it heightened my interest in the country, and made me determined to master the language. On return to Mhow I engaged a munshi (teacher), who came to my quarter three afternoons a week – all I could afford. While the others in Krishna Building were sleeping under their mosquito nets, Munshi Sharma taught me the rudiments of Urdu, the lingua franca of the Indian Army. I've still got the official text-book -'Our Sowars and Sepoys' (Our Cavalrymen and Infantrymen) – for the Lower Standard Examination in Urdu, price One Rupee and Fourteen Annas, or three shillings and three pence. I think I'd have passed this exam fairly easily if my studies hadn't been interrupted, as I'll explain in due course. Although perhaps I shouldn't say so myself, by the time left India I spoke Urdu as well as many Indian Army officers.

Colours 2nd Battalion, The Suffolk Regt. Mhow, Central India, 1938

Colours 1st Battalion, The Suffolk Regt. Colchester, 1952

The next step in my career was to complete my training as a machine gun specialist. With this end in view, I was sent to the Machine Gun School at Ahmednagar, about eighty miles east of Bombay. Some forty officers attended the six-weeks course, half Indian Army and half British Service, I think I was about the most junior. I enjoyed the course and got a satisfactory report. Three years later I was to return to Ahmednagar under very different circumstances. During a break in the course I motored with some friends to attend a race meeting at Poona, a pleasant station in the Western Ghats, the range of hills running down the western side of India. While there I met Doreen Jerram, my father's godchild and a close friend of my sister Elizabeth. Doreen had just got engaged to Hugo Du Pree of the Royal Warwickshire Regt., stationed in Poona.

The year was drawing to a close, back again in Mhow Christmas was upon us. The 'Fishing fleet' had arrived – young unmarried girls from England who travelled round the various cantonments in the cool season, staying with friends or relations for a couple of months or so, hoping to land a husband. More often than not they succeeded, there being a superfluity of eager bachelors to choose from. Regiments laid on parties in their messes; dances were held in the officers' club, the most popular being the Bachelors' Ball, funded by the bachelors to repay hospitality they'd received from the 'marrieds' – and a very good time was always had by all.

Traditionally Christmas Day started with an early morning church parade when it was still comparatively cool, the battalion marched to the garrison church, the families also attended – the service was always the occasion for lusty carol singing. On return to barracks, officers served Christmas Dinners to their men. The Commanding Officer visited each Company in turn, making a short speech and drinking their health in a drink produced by the Company Sergeant Major. The single officers were then invited to lunch by the marrieds in their bungalows.

In the late afternoon, when it was reasonably cool, having slept off the effects of too much food and drink, the annual Officers versus Sergeants football match took place on the muti (hard earth) football ground which, in Mhow, doubled as the parade ground – an occasion for much ribaldry by spectators at the players' expense. It had rained in the early afternoon of Christmas Day 1936, turning the heavy cotton soil into sticky red mud. I was right wing forward, the ball was passed to me, I shot off down the line in great style. But alas, a great clod of red earth had stuck to my boot. As I centred the ball my right foot twisted with the weight, there was a distinct click followed by a searing pain in my right knee – I just managed to hobble off the field. Next day I was admitted to the BMH, where I languished for ten days.

Captain Allison of the Indian Medical Services (IMS), the Surgical Specialist and a friend of mine, explained that I'd torn the cartilage, an operation would be necessary. He was against operating straightaway as I was suffering from a bad go of eczema, so I was relegated to 'Light Duties' – debarred from doing anything strenuous.

My knee got no better, even when riding it tended to grate. Allison decided that I ought to return to England for the operation. So wheels were set in motion; before long I found myself travelling to Bombay on six months 'Indulgence Leave' as a Class B Invalid! Quite how I wangled this I can't remember, Allison somehow fixed it. There was really no reason why I shouldn't have been operated on in a hill station, where I could have convalesced. Of course I was delighted to be getting a free passage – I couldn't have afforded the fare home for several years.

I sailed in the British India Line troopship *Neuralia*, 9,000 tons (sunk by a mine off Italy in 1945) very slow but comfortable. I

'Swedebashers' of 2nd Suffolk, brewing-up a cup of char. Central India, 1937

made a lot of friends, everyone was in great spirits – going in the right direction. Being a 'Class B Invalid', I was excused the more irksome duties such as Ship's Orderly Officer, which involved visiting the troops' mess decks, galleys and so on by day, and the lookout sentries by night. With gin at tuppence ha'penny a tot, we drank far too many pink-gin-sodas in the snug bar. I was about the youngest officer, most of the others were Indian Army with many years service, returning home for the third or fourth time. In spite of my short service in India I considered myself a real 'Koi-hai' (old India-hand), I could at least swing the bat, as the troops said, in other words – speak a bit of Hindustani.

Apart from fun-and-games with Egyptian girls in a Port Said night club, where my French, which they spoke, got steadily more muddled-up with Urdu as the night progressed, the passage was relatively uneventful. As we entered the Solent, passing close to The Needles (which I can now see from my bedroom window) the troops rushed to the port-side of the ship – making her list – to watch the pilot coming aboard from a launch, accompanied by a little man wearing a bowler hat, some sort of Port Official. The soldiers gave him a great cheer, they'd not seen a real English 'civvy' for many a long year.

I'd been granted sick leave on the understanding that I'd have the operation at my own expense, and present myself before an army Medical Board within six months. Providing the Board passed me fit, I'd be returned to 2nd Suffolk in Mhow – I hadn't any time to waste. After a day or two with my parents at Bucklebury, I set about finding a surgeon. I can't remember how I managed this, but I was soon admitted to the Charing Cross Hospital, off The Strand in London. Kathleen visited me, she was then working in London, but Marjorie Rolleston forbade Murna to do so. The operation was a success. I was discharged after ten days and told to take it easy for a month.

The next step was to get a car. My funds were limited, but for many years I'd had a small accident insurance policy, which now paid me the handsome sum of thirty shillings a week (about £35 in today's money) that, plus my army pay at Indian rates, meant I was well off! A friend in the second-hand car business sold me an Austin Ten saloon for £30, on a guaranteed buy-back agreement, providing I'd not bashed it up in the meantime. So I was all set for a wonderful three and a half months holiday, and determined not to waste a second of it!

Winter was approaching; I was keen to do some wildfowling. Duck, geese and other wildfowl would soon be arriving on their annual migration from Scandinavia. I'd read about a village pub, The Townshend Arms, Stifkey, near Wells-next-the-Sea on the north Norfolk coast, it sounded just what I was after. I booked a room for a week at seven shillings and six pence a day, full board, and set off from Bucklebury on the long drive to Norfolk. The pub was small, only one guest bedroom, but I had sole use of a private sitting room for my meals. I spent the evenings in the small public bar, chatting to the locals – mostly farm labourers in those days. One of the regulars was Henry Williamson, author of the much acclaimed book 'Tharka the Otter'. He'd been through the Great War and had never got over the horrors he'd witnessed; a difficult fellow to get on with, I didn't take to him.

I was advised to contact Percy Barrett, a professional wildfowler of Wells-next-the-Sea, who took chaps like myself out shooting on the marshes. Wells was then an unspoilt little town, originally on the coast, the sea had receded leaving a narrow channel navigable only to small trawlers and light craft. Percy was a 'sure shot' – he didn't fire unless he was sure he'd down a bird. He made his own cartridges, could call any bird with a whistle made from a round piece of tin bent in half with a hole pierced in the centre, which he put in his mouth; there was nothing he didn't know about the marshes, birds and country law. We became good friends; over the next three months I really got a 'feel' for wildfowling – I've never lost it. Percy Barrett was a splendid chap, it was a privilege to have shot with him.

Every morning and evening the sky was filled with endless skeins of geese, honking and making a tremendous clamour as they flighted from the marshes and estuaries around The Wash to their feeding grounds inland, and back again to the safety of the mud flats and open sea at night. I bagged a White Front goose – the occasion for much celebration in the bar that evening, and also shot various species of duck: mallard, wigeon, pochard, teal, garganey and pin-tail. Curlew with their long thin curved bills and distinctive 'Whee-O, Whee-O' call were our constant companions on the marshes; when we ventured into the open sea off Blakeney, we got close to colonies of grey seals resting on sandy spits.

Percy sometimes took me out in his long narrow gun-punt. We lay on our bellies, propelling it between the mud banks of the marshes with a small paddle in each hand over the gunwales. Hard work, especially when the tide was flowing fast down the channels and ditches, but I was young and fit, it was fun and exciting, the discomfort and frozen fingers didn't register. A muzzle-loading punt-gun, as used by professional wildfowlers, had a barrel up to five foot long, mounted in the punt to fire forward, loaded with a heavy charge of assorted shot; the punt's shallow draught and low profile made it difficult to spot, improving the chances of getting within range of duck swimming in the sea. When I was wildfowling with Percy, very few punt-guns were still in use, generally one used a twelve-bore shotgun, loaded with heavy-shot cartridges.

Once when out with Percy in his punt, a sea mist came down making it difficult to see far ahead. We'd spotted a bunch of wigeon in the open water, and 'set to'. I was the gunner and very conscious of the big gun's heavy recoil, but getting the punt into position as stealthily as possible absorbed all my concentration. I pulled the lanyard attached to the trigger, there was an almighty explosion and a cloud of black smoke. The bag was three wigeon and a mallard – could have been worse, luckily there were no 'cripples' to finish off with a shotgun, always distressing and time-consuming. A professional wildfowler wouldn't have fired unless he'd been certain of bagging ten or more birds.

Those were exhilarating carefree days. I would never have believed that war was only two years away and everything was soon to change. The marshes became an RAF bombing range, the wildfowl were scared away for a while, but soon disregarded the noise. I've never gone back, nor really wanted to – it wouldn't be the same without Percy Barrett.

* * * * *

There is now a gap in my memory – I just can't remember how often I saw Murna during the short time I was in England. I'd been granted six months sick leave. Sea journeys, time in hospital and convalescence accounted for at least three months; wildfowling occupied over a month, so I had barely two months in which to visit relations and friends. I did go to Suffolk, staying a night or two in Hadleigh with Doctor and Mrs. Everett – he'd been our doctor when we lived there. I'd always had a crush on their daughter, Jokie, a very pretty and rather naughty girl, who subsequently married a chap in a Highland Regiment. Years later we saw quite a bit of each other, I was very fond of her – she was a dear.

Without prior warning, I went over to Stoke-by-Nayland one evening from Hadleigh, full of expectation, only to arrive just as Murna was setting off in a taxi for a dance at the Colchester Garrison Officers' club, with Ian Freeland of the Norfolk Regiment (he rose to become Lieutenant General Sir Ian). Needless to say I was very put out at her going off with a chap senior to me – Ian was then a Captain. I was so narked that I pushed off back to Hadleigh, and didn't see her again before returning to India. Why I saw so little of her I can't remember, it was all so long ago. The difficulty I think was the long drive from Bucklebury to Suffolk, and the problem of where to stay when I got there – Mrs. Rolleston didn't consider it proper for me to stay at Hill House, but I must have done so on occasions.

I have to admit there were other female attractions. One was Elizabeth, who taught at Downe House, a well known girls school near Newbury. I got to know her through my cousin Mary (now Mrs. Dudbridge) who lived in Newbury with her parents, my Aunt Audrey and Uncle Dr. Willie Heywood. Elizabeth was an attractive, vivacious girl with shoulder length blond hair, blue eyes and a super figure. Her father was a clergyman, I think the vicar of a parish near Newbury; she had a brother, who for some reason seemed to take a dim view of me – I was to discover why!

Cousin Mary asked me to join a party going to a subscription dance in the Newbury Corn Exchange, about six miles from Bucklebury. Soon after getting there I spotted this ravishing girl, made a dead-set for her and proceeded to monopolise her for the rest of the evening. No doubt I shot an awful line about soldiering in India. Anyway, we hit it off in a big way, I was completely smitten. We agreed to meet a couple of days later on her afternoon off. She'd asked me not to drive up to the school's front entrance, I vaguely wondered why, so I waited in the road a little way off as bidden. She hurried out on time and bustled over – looking absolutely terrific, we set off for the Bear Inn in Marlborough.

Sitting at the bar with her I noticed she kept fiddling with a ring on the fourth finger of her left hand. I asked her why she kept doing this – she replied "Can't you see?" waving the ring in my face. I replied I thought it was very pretty, but why keep on twiddling it round? The penny-dropped – eventually. I wasn't at all non-plussed, suggesting when she was with me she should twist it round so the stone didn't show – and she did!

We saw a lot of each other over the next month or two. She came to Bucklebury for supper and met my parents, we even went to a dance with my sister and brother-in-law, Elizabeth and Otto Edholm. Once, getting her home in the early hours of the morning, we found she was locked out. Naturally anxious not to wake anyone, and being a girl of spirit, she slipped off her long white silk party dress and climbed up a drainpipe to an open window.

Sounds improbable, but it's true. She was engaged to a chap who had his collar turned halfway round, in other words was preparing for the Church, which accounted for the somewhat sour reception I'd got from her family. She married him, he became a parson; I hope they lived happily ever after. She was super – we never met again.

I went several times with a bunch of boozy characters to the famous Brooklands motor racing circuit at Weybridge, not far from London. It was great fun in those days; everyone congregated at the bar of the club house in the centre of the circuit, and downed enormous quantities of beer, while Bentleys, Lagondas, Fraser-Nashes, Sunbeams, Mercedes and other wonderful giants of the race track thundered round the circuit outside, tremendously exciting, more so I think than nowadays when everything is so commercialized, high-tech and organized. Young women were always hanging around, one in particular was most accommodating, I didn't need any encouragement to succumb to her advances – my first experience of the sex thing. I was twenty-three, unbelievable by today's standards when most lads seem to have done it all while still at school. Anyhow, in those days, before the advent of the pill, girls were jolly careful – thank heavens!

Christmas was approaching, I spent it quietly at home, anyway I had no choice as by then I was pretty broke, and, what's more, Murna had gone to Switzerland with her mother for a couple of months, staying at their usual pension in Villars. I've some snaps of her at a dance in the main hotel – looking ravishing in a black evening dress – surrounded by admirers.

Whilst I was on leave, my father exercised his right under the rules of Patrimony, to have me made a Freeman of the Worshipful Company of Ironmongers (the tenth senior Livery Company), thereby carrying on the tradition established by my grandfather in 1883. It was to be another ten years before I took out my Freedom of the City of London.

I wish I could remember more about that period but my memory fails me – just as well perhaps.

CHAPTER 5

The Last Years of Peacetime Soldiering in India, 1938–39

In the middle of December I was instructed to attend a Medical Board in London. I was fairly confident but a bit apprehensive. What I'd do if the Board found me unfit for service in the infantry didn't bare contemplating. After the usual questions, I was put through stiff tests, my luck was in, the old knee behaved magnificently – I was passed fit for duty. What a relief!

Soon afterwards I was instructed to return to India aboard the British India troopship *Nevassa* (9070 tons), sailing from Liverpool on 18th January 1938. Saying goodbye to my elderly parents was distressing, especially to my mother, who was frail and in constant pain from arthritis in her right hip, but they knew I was keen to get back to my Regiment, and happy that the operation on my knee had been successful.

The *Nevassa*, built in 1913, was slow – many years later I travelled to Cyprus in her successor. Two rather ghastly young subalterns in the South Staffordshire Regiment on first posting to India shared my cabin, no doubt I shot an awful line to them. One was pimply and fat, even so to my surprise and a touch of envy, he succeeded in getting-off with the nanny to children travelling out with their mother. I once caught him in our cabin with her and kicked them out – spoil sport! The journey was uneventful – we coaled at Aden – I'd not been there before. A British battalion served in this hot, arid, god-forsaken place for a year, then was moved to a more salubrious station. I thanked my lucky stars I was going back to Mhow.

On rejoining the battalion I found I was to share a bungalow with Jack Prescott and Peter Smitherman – a great improvement on Krishna Building. The front garden was tended by the mali (gardener), who spent most of his time watering the so-called lawn, the khanna lilies which thrived on the water from our bath tubs, zinnias and small button roses. We had a chowkidar (night watchman), who slept on the verandah, in theory he chased away badmashs and loose-wallahs – scallywags and thieves – actually he slept most of the night. We also had a chokra, a lad to do the odd jobs and run errands, a mehtar (sweeper) the lowest caste of Hindu known as 'Untouchables' or Harijans, who emptied our thunder-boxes, and generally swept up inside and outside the bungalow. We each had a bearer, mine being Babu.

Officers' bungalows in India were grouped together in cantonments near the barracks, generally a mile or so from the native part of the city. They were leased by the army from Indian contractors, and allocated to the various units in the garrison, who in turn allotted them to individual officers. Married Quarters in the barracks, occupied by Warrant Officers, Sergeants and Other Ranks, belonged to the army and were allotted by unit Quartermasters.

Our bungalow, No.30, was almost opposite the Officers' Mess where we had our meals. Although rather ramshackle, it had a certain charm, the verandah round the front was shaded by a climbing jasmin, giving off a wonderful scent in the evening. A communal sitting room, separate bedrooms and ghusal khanas with tin bath-tub and thunder-box; the furniture was sparse but adequate for bachelors.

Our servants lived in outbuildings in the rear compound where there were stables. Jack Prescott owned Birdlip, a mare named after a place near Cheltenham where his mother lived. I acquired a 'Fifteen Chipper', an artillery light-draught mare, called Swan. She cost me fifteen rupees a season – a rupee being colloquially known as a 'chip' – hence the name. I had full use of her except when she was required by the Gunners for training and manoeuvres which wasn't often. I provided a saddle, the artillery supplied the harness and fodder, I also paid the syce, her groom.

About this time Murna's uncle, Major Ramsay 'Pat' Eley, joined the Battalion with his wife Mary, and two young daughters whom I'd not met before – tragically they were both retarded – nowadays they'd have been described as handicapped. Ramsay was appointed Second-in-Command, shortly to take over from

Lieut. Col. Harry Gadd, who had almost completed his time in command.

On meeting Pat Eley in the mess, after a few inconsequential remarks, he said "Oh, by the way Silvanus, Murna asked me to give you her love". I'd not heard from her since leaving England; being back with the Battalion I'd been so occupied I'd had little time to think of her, although actually she was always there in my mind, just below the surface as it were. Hearing her name spoken came as a shock – my throat dried up, I was completely overcome. I visualised her smiling at me and heard her soft, slightly husky voice. A great yearning for her welled-up inside me – I downed two iced beers in quick succession!

I was back with D (MG) Company – not much had changed during my absence. The 25th February 1938 (my 24th birthday) was the third anniversary of my Regular Commission, having three years service I was promoted to Full Lieutenant, putting up my second 'pip' – a small but important advance in the military hierarchy. A Full Lieutenant was quite someone in those days, many officers remained in this rank for ten or even more years – promotion was by 'dead mens' boots' – very slow.

During 1938 I proved my skill with the rifle by winning the Officers' Shooting Bowl, my first success, it did much to boost my morale. The ranges were close to barracks, ammunition was plentiful so we were constantly banging away, not only with rifles but also with the Vickers Bethier, the Indian Army version of the Bren light machine-gun. 2nd Suffolk had a high reputation as a 'good shooting battalion'.

The 6th Field Regiment, Royal Artillery, still armed with obsolescent horse-drawn 18-pounder WWI guns, was an exceptionally fine unit – many of the officers distinguished themselves in the war that was about to engulf us. Philip Papillon (killed during the Normandy landings in 1944), Jack Prescott, Peter Smitherman and I – all in 2nd Suffolk – were detailed to attend an Equitation Course run by the RA in their lines not far from our barracks. There were about a dozen officers on the course, mostly keen horsemen, I was far and away the least experienced. We assembled in the early hours of the morning, did all sorts of frightening exercises in the riding school, jumped endless obstacles, and were generally chivvied by the Rough Rider Sergeants. Luckily I'd learnt to ride as a boy when we were living in Northiam, so in spite of finding it pretty terrifying, I quite enjoyed it. I've never again felt awkward when mounted, and can generally apply the correct aids effectively – having said that, I still maintain a horse is 'dangerous both ends and uncomfortable in the middle'.

The highlight of the year for D Company was the Annual Machine Gun Concentration. Each infantry battalion in Bombay District – geographically about the size of the UK – sent a unit to take part in this three-day event, held on the field-firing area a few miles from Mhow. The only other British Regiment represented was the Lincolnshire Regt. (I think) stationed at Nasirabad, near Ajmir, two hundred miles north of Mhow. The others were Indian Army – about seven units in all.

My platoon was selected to represent 2nd Suffolk, very gratifying – but a weighty responsibility. This event afforded an excuse for HQ Bombay District 'Staff-wallahs', from Major General to humble Captain, to get off their bottoms and see some real soldiering. Their well-ironed khaki drill uniforms, highly polished leather Sam Browne belts and red and black arm-bands, indicating their superior status, made them easily distinguishable.

The first two days were spent firing with complete disregard for ammunition expenditure. The belt-fed Vickers heavy MG fired 450 rounds a minute – very slow by modern standards – the optimum range was one thousand five hundred yards, if the gun was elevated, the range was increased. On the third day an inter-unit competition was held, consisting of an Indirect followed by a Direct shoot.

Indirect-fire meant the guns were fired from concealed positions behind a rise in the ground, the targets being out of sight from the gun positions, the platoon commander controlled the fire from the crest. Having first located the target and got the range from his Range-Finder, a soldier trained in the use of this quite complicated instrument, he then had to calculate the elevation required and shout it back to the four guns twenty yards behind. When each gun had been laid correctly, the Section Corporal raised his right arm, when all were ready the platoon commander shouted 'Fire'.

This all sounds straightforward enough – all I had to do, when our turn came, was to shout 'Action', double forward with the guns still on the mules – three mule-loads per gun – indicate where the guns were to come into action to the platoon sergeant, double to the crest and engage the targets. Speed into action was of the essence, there was no time to dawdle. I should mention that the top-brass and spectators had taken up positions on the crest of the ridge to the left of the line of fire from where they were keenly watching the targets through binoculars.

Our turn came – I shouted "Action" – we dashed forward across a hundred yards of dry grass in great style, sweating profusely, the Sepoy Muleteers shouting encouragement to their animals, harness gingling, ammunition boxes rattling, the troops swearing. I rushed up to the right of the crest – did my calculations, waited to see all the corporals' arms raised, then bellowed – **"FIRE"** – for all I was worth. There was a tremendous roar as the four guns opened fire simultaneously, a heartening sound to any machine gunner. But why were all the spectators throwing themselves flat on the ground?! Why the cloud of dust and pebbles on the crest?!

The awful truth dawned on me – I must have given a 'depression' instead of an 'elevation'. Bullets were still hitting the crest, I bellowed "Cease Fire", luckily heard above the pandemonium. No one was hit, no damage done except to my pride. But there were a lot of very shaken staff officers who'd not bargained for coming under fire. I eventually lived this down, but suffered a good bit of justifiable ribbing.

My friend Harry Carrigan, the Station Staff Officer, was keen that I should bag a panther, he'd shot several himself, and suggested I found a shikari, a villager wise in the ways of big game, who would report immediately a panther had been sighted in one of the game blocks we were permitted to shoot in. Word got around, and in due course an old chap turned up at my bungalow offering his services. It was agreed that for twelve rupees a month, he'd get word to me the moment he had good khabar – information. He looked about ninety, but was most probably only forty or so.

The only way an impecunious subaltern, like me, could afford to shoot panther was from a machan, a hide made with a charpoy (a wood framed string-bed) secured in the branches of a tree, near where panther were known to prowl – with a tethered goat as bait. As dusk fell one climbed a rickety ladder into the machan, settling as comfortably as the restricted space and the mossies (mosquitoes) permitted, invariably excruciatingly uncomfy and when the mossies really got to work, biting through one's drill shirt and slacks – absolute hell. Insect repellents were unheard of, I smothered myself in tincture of aloes, which helped slightly. To add to the discomfort, absolute immobility and complete silence were essential; smoking was out – the smell of tobacco would have given one's presence away. The heat was intense, sweat poured into one's eyes, clothing stuck to one's body, making it easier for the mossies to inflict damage – which they did with a vengeance.

Much of the jungle around Mhow consisted of stunted teak trees, the ground was covered with their large, light-brown, brittle dry leaves, making a loud crackling noise when trodden on. With the sudden descent of darkness the jungle was eerily silent, emphasising the incessant buzz of mossies and the almost audible thumping of one's heart. Being in a machan not high off the ground, waiting for a dangerous cunning beast to pounce on the wretched bleating goat, made me feel guilty – not a very courageous way to shoot big game. One could of course just sit on the ground, hidden, and hopefully protected, by a screen of prickly thorn bushes. This didn't appeal to me. Quite apart from being almost as vulnerable as the goat, there were all sorts of creepy-crawly things on the ground, including snakes and scorpions.

Harry Carrigan took me to a dance at the Railway Institute, he professed this was part of his job as SSO, actually he really went there to ogle the attractive Eurasian girls known as 'chilly-crackers' to the troops; I must admit this angle had occurred to me too. Following on from this, I became friendly with an Anglo-Indian (Eurasian) freight-train driver who was keen on shikar, he offered to take me on his footplate down the Choral gorge, and drop me off at a rendezvous with my shikari, whenever I wanted a lift.

In due course my shikari sent khabar; a panther had killed a goat near a village about ten miles down the Choral gorge – I should come that evening. I sent Babu to the freight sidlings; my Anglo-Indian friend said it would be okay for me to go down that afternoon. I told the chokra who'd brought the shikari's message, to return 'ek dam' – double quick – and say I'd be at the RV at five o'clock.

I went by tonga to the sidings, met my friend, climbed up onto the footplate, and with a couple of toots on the engine's whistle – off we chugged. There were three of us on the footplate: myself, the driver and his Indian stoker. I'd never been on a footplate before – steam and smoke chuff-chuff-chuffing out of the funnel, the rhythmic beat of the pistons, the clatter of the driving shafts, the engine's peculiar 'hunting' movement swaying from side to side between the rails as if it was alive, especially when passing through the numerous tunnels, the sound thundering back off the roof and walls, acrid smoke and sparks blasting out of the funnel covering us with soot – all adding to the fun and excitement. The driver let me take the controls; entirely different from driving a car, no clutch or gear-box as such, one had the impression of controlling great latent power, particularly on the return run up the steep gradient to Mhow, with the engine at full power straining under the load. Most exhilarating – at any rate for a short time.

My shikari met me as planned, we set off on foot down a road from the Halt where I'd been dropped. I thought this a bit odd, but was told a machan had been placed in a tree just off the road close to a small village, really only a huddle of mud huts with grass roofs. It was almost dark when I clambered into the machan, I tested the torch clamped to the barrel of my BSA. .375 rifle by training it on the goat tethered about five yards away, then settled down to await events. Quite a noise was coming from the huts, oil lamps flickered here and there; I thought the chance of a tendua (panther) showing up were pretty slim. Hardly anything other than bullock carts ever moved along the roads after dark, but I wouldn't have been surprised if a local bus had come along in a cloud of dust; however, except for the sounds from the huts behind me, all was silent. Sweat was pouring down my forehead into my eyes and along my nose; mossies were busy where my trousers were stretched tight against my thighs, I was horribly cramped, but prepared for a long wait.

What was that? I was instantly tense! I'd definitely heard a sort of sawing, grrr...ing sound, where was it coming from? I waited – my heart pounding, mossies forgotten. A scuffle below me – I switched on my torch – the goat was standing quite still, behind it I could clearly see two yellow-green eyes shining in the torchlight. I aimed and fired. I'd shot my first panther – all within ten minutes of getting into the machan!

With hindsight it was all rather tame – I'd been lucky. If I'd wounded the beast it would have made off, and I'd have been honour-bound to follow it up and finish it off, the really dangerous part of big-game shooting, calling for extreme caution. A wounded panther crouching in the undergrowth merges into the background, and is virtually impossible to pick out – when cornered it attacks. Mercifully I never wounded one.

That little episode took place fifty-six years ago, now panther, although protected, are almost extinct in parts of India due mainly to the depredations of poachers, not sportsmen. Why did I find hunting big game so exciting? I think the thrill came in the challenge to achieve something out of the ordinary, demanding planning, perseverance, skill, sweat and discomfort, sometimes a considerable degree of danger, and yes – even a touch of glamour. In the next eighteen months I shot two more panther. Altogether I probably sat up in a machan some twenty or more times in vain, and covered many miles on foot through the jungle, in intense heat, my water-bottle invariably empty – it wasn't all as easy as my first success.

The skins were cured by a firm in Madras; I couldn't afford to have the heads mounted. The last panther I shot in September 1939 I had to skin myself. Normally this would have been done by the shikari, but on that occasion I hadn't got one, so there was nothing for it but to do it myself by the light of a pressure lamp, with the help of my bearer, Babu. It had to be skinned straight away before rigor mortis set in – a gruesome, terribly tiring job. We worked away for most of the night in a temperature of 110 fahrenheit, sweat cascading off us – dawn had arrived before we'd finished.

A few years ago I presented two of the skins to the 1st Battalion The Royal Anglian Regiment, the successor to The Suffolk Regiment. I think they are kept in the Officers' Mess and displayed on special occasions. I'd hoped they would be worn by the drummers, but the Regiment decided otherwise. The third skin was eaten by white ants when my kit was stored in Delhi Fort during the war.

For most of 1938 the tenor of army life in India remained much as it had been for generations. It's difficult to appreciate that hardly anyone owned a wireless set; the Officers' Mess acquired one sometime that year, it was tucked away in a room reserved for ladies – they weren't allowed anywhere else in the mess! I clearly remember hearing the changes in army promotion, the Hore-Belisha reforms, being announced over All India Radio (the BBC was unobtainable). At a stroke the number of majors in a battalion was almost doubled, Captain 'Sweat' Dean, the Adjutant, who was listening with me exclaimed, "At long last I'm a Field Officer" (the rank of major and above) he'd been commissioned for almost twenty years; several Lieutenants automatically became Captains. I realised my chances of promotion within the foreseeable future, as opposed to some dim distant time, so remote that one never really believed it could ever happen – had suddenly become a possibility. These reforms gave the army a much needed shot-in-the-arm, affecting not only Officers but Warrant and Non-Commissioned Officers as well.

Gradually it came home to us that war against Germany was on the cards – but it was all such a long way away. However, these promotion reforms, more than anything else, made us realise that we too, hidden away in Central India, might indeed be required to fight some day, maybe not too far ahead, and perhaps be wounded or even killed. Like most of my brother officers I rather envied the chaps in the 1st Battalion serving in Malta; they'd undoubtedly be recalled to England and become involved in any fighting. We visualised our contemporaries covering themselves with glory on the battlefield, gaining decorations and promotion, while we languished in India on Internal Security duty – what a depressing outlook.

In April we marched to a camp site some fifteen miles away. Battalion kit was carried in Animal (mule) Transport Carts (A.T. Carts), officers kit in bullock carts – one per two junior officers, escorted by our bearers. We were likely to be in camp for a month; starting with battalion training then manoeuvres for the whole of Mhow garrison and local forces, including the Indore State Force and the Dhar Irregular Light Horse – very irregular and extremely light – fierce looking warriors clad in medieval chain mail jerkins and spiked steel helmets, mounted on what looked like tonga ponies.

We did a lot of marching, were constantly sweating, thirsty, and bitten to pieces by mossies on night schemes. Artillery batteries galloping past towing obsolete 18-pounder field guns made a fine sight, but were sworn at by us infantry for raising clouds of choking dust. In spite of the discomforts we enjoyed the training, we also drew 'Hard Lying' allowance when in camp, perhaps three rupees a day, speedily downed in Britannia Beer in the mess tent.

About twenty-five miles south of Mhow was a small hamlet, Chota Jam, near an old stone Mahratta fort, deserted except for snakes and scorpions. A well-preserved crenellated gateway commanded an ancient route up the escarpment from the Narbudah river valley, probably built in the eighteenth century, by the Mahratta warrior-king Shivaji the Great. Nearby was a small dak bungalow (rest house) looked after by an old man – the chowkidar. Jack Prescott, George Springfield, Peter Smitherman and I rode there, sending our baggage and bearers in an ancient Oldsmobile Whippet car, lent to us by a merchant named Murlidah – he'd sold some quite valuable Persian rugs to Jack and was always prepared to loan a hundred rupees or so, at not too extortionate a rate of interest, a facility which frequently saved my bacon when it came to paying my mess bill on time!

We hoped to bag a panther or two, and perhaps with luck see a tiger. Two whitewashed graves, within a low picket fence, of Artillery officers killed by tiger in the late nineteenth century, lay beside the track we had to take going to sit up in a machan – a bit spooky passing them in the gathering dusk. After a week spent covering many miles on foot by day and sitting up each night at different places – we'd had no luck. A disappointment, but for me partially compensated for by coveys of fat painted partridge near the dak bungalow – excellent shooting and tasty curried. We got on well together, the change from barrack routine was a relief. Our bearers cooked excellent hot curries, beer bottles kept remarkably cool if hung in a basket lined with damp grass in a shady place; we had a portable wind-up HMV gramophone and plenty of pipe tobacco – most enjoyable.

Soon after returning from Chota Jam, Jack Prescott began preparations for driving to England in his six-cylinder open Chevrolet car. Peter Smitherman, a brainy fellow, had been selected to attend a course in England on the use of Radar by artillery, still categorised as 'Secret', he got permission to accompany Jack. I was keen to go with them, but Colonel Eley said he couldn't spare me as I was the only trained machine gun officer. A disappointment at the time, but with hindsight perhaps just as well; if I'd joined them my subsequent life would undoubtedly have been very different.

Jack and Peter set off early in 1939. After many adventures, including getting snowed-up in the British Embassy in Khabul, Peter had to leave Jack, who'd gone down with malaria, in a tiny missionary hospital in south of Persia and complete the journey by air so as to arrive on time for his course. Jack reached England four months after leaving Mhow, quite an epic solo drive, typical of the man. (He was badly wounded while a Company Commander with 1st Suffolk in Holland in 1944 and awarded the Military Cross.) Peter was captured by the Japanese in Singapore but survived – he retired after the war and qualified as a doctor.

An important part of an officer's job was to take an active part in organised sport. During the hot weather hockey was played on hard-earth (muti) pitches. The standard was high, inter-company and inter-unit competitions were rough and fiercely contested – by no means unusual for a full-back to hit the ball shoulder high from one end of the pitch to the other; I sometimes played for D Company. We were no match for Indian Army units – Sikh regiments in particular always fielded marvellous players.

Any spare time I had I spent shooting. Through the bunia Murlidah, I hired an old motorbike, so was able to get around the neighbourhood. Koolen, large grey birds with a wing-span of at least five feet, a species of crane, migrated south from far away to the north, arriving in Central India in large numbers in September. Just before dusk, flying in endless undulating skeins several miles long, like ribbons in the sky, they settled on open dry grassy slopes at Hima, a few miles from Mhow. No one seemed interested in having a shot at them, so I went out on the ropy old motorbike and located where they rested at night.

W. S. B. on shikar near Mhow, 1938

Mahratta gateway near Chota Jam on track to the Narbuda River. Central India

Next day I set off in time to take up a concealed position before they arrived. I managed to shoot a couple – the problem was how to get them back? Tying their necks together I slung the birds on my back. It was getting dark, the bike had an inefficient silencer and a feeble head-lamp. I spluttered and banged through the small bazaar area on the outskirts of Mhow, the enormous wings flapping in the slipstream made me resemble a giant bird – I heard later my progress had struck terror into some of the more faint-hearted locals. After all the effort, the mess cook declared they were too large to go into his oven, and anyway they were inedible!

When the monsoon broke in late June, grass sprouted and everything suddenly turned green, making it possible to play rugger on a field near the ranges, liberally supplied with flint stones. I designed a scrum-practice machine based on one we'd had a Sherborne, the Regimental Pioneers quickly knocked one up and we got down to serious practice. Rugger is not played much in Suffolk, so few of the troops knew the rules. However, after the inter-company competitions we selected a team which included five officers – all good players. I was appointed Team Captain and leader of the Forwards. By dint of hard practice, keenness and enthusiasm, we succeeded in defeating all local teams, thereby qualifying for the finals of the Bombay District Black & White Cup, to be played in Bombay.

It was terrific getting an unexpected week's leave in Bombay – at The Queen's expense what's more! We were attached to the Royal Artillery at Colaba Point, then exclusive to the Services with a private swimming beach. I succeeded in getting the team to put in a good deal of training, which was put to naught by high-jinks in the evenings. Nevertheless, we returned to Mhow about ten days later with the Cup, having defeated a Royal Artillery team in the finals on the Cooperage Ground. This was a no mean feat for a non-rugger playing regiment.

Every year each station in India held its 'Week', during which all normal activities ceased. Officers for the most part being occupied in organizing and participating in garrison horse race meetings, gymkhanas, band concerts, dances in the various service clubs and messes, regimental concerts, All- Ranks dances, and so on. During these 'Weeks' the 'Fishing fleet' was much in evidence, migrating from one station to another, hoping to land a lonely bachelor, preferably a senior captain, but even a subaltern wasn't to be sniffed at.

Mhow Week activities in 1938 were noticeably muted. Officers and NCOs were beginning to leave for staff appointments and extra-regimental jobs in India, or posted to England. Change was in the air, the even tenor of our lives was under threat. Our bearers and the local merchants were becoming apprehensive – "Sahib, what is happening to the Raj?"

In spite of these portents, Minden Day was celebrated traditionally, as it had been since the decisive battle on 1st August 1759 at Minden, North Rhine Wesfalar in Germany, when six British Regiments withstood and routed the flower of the French cavalry during the Seven Years War against France. The Suffolk Regiment, then the 12th Foot, on the right of the front line suffered the heaviest casualties, and like all the other regiments, acquitted itself with glory. It was the first time for a hundred years that the French had been defeated. Church bells rang throughout England to signal this magnificent feat of arms, equal in impact then to the victory at El Alamein in 1942.

Minden Day 1938 began, as always, with Trooping the Colour ceremony – watched by guests from all other units in the station. The Battalion on parade, with the Colours, Band and Drums garlanded with yellow and red roses, and all ranks wearing red and yellow 'Minden Roses' in their topees, as their predecessors had done in 1759, when they plucked roses from gardens and stuck them in their headdresses as they marched into battle. Later in the day other activities followed; bare-back mule races – the rider who managed to hang on generally being the winner, side-shows, stalls and so on, ending with a regimental concert – the Band featuring prominently. Free beer was supplied to the troops by Shabo in the Wet Canteen.

Christmas was again upon us, few of us younger officers imagined it would be the last under peacetime conditions, although those who'd taken part in WWI, and there were quite a number of them, must have realised this was a distinct possibility. The PMC (President Mess Committee) Captain Alan Goodwin, a super chap recently back from shooting lions in Kenya, where he was bitten by tetse fly and almost died as a result, organized a bumper dance in the mess. Everyone had to come dressed as a pirate and 'walk the plank' up to the main entrance – electric fans having been strategically placed under the plank causing much embarrassment and hilarity when female guests 'came aboard' – an unforgettable party. Alan was soon posted to a staff job in Egypt; he took part in the early fighting in the Western Desert, was captured in late 1941, and spent the remainder of the war as a POW in Italy and Germany. After release he married, but sadly died soon after. He was a good friend – I felt his loss deeply.

A week after Christmas I was instructed to attend a six-week course at the School of Physical Training at Ambala in the Punjab, where there was a large garrison. There were about twenty-five on the course, five were officers. I enjoyed it and learnt about organizing and teaching athletics, boxing, gymnastics and physical training generally, which later stood me in good stead. This was my first experience of soldiering in what is now Pakistan; Babu, my Hindu bearer wasn't at all happy in the predominantly Muslim environment, I think he was rather scared.

The day after I'd arrived by the Frontier Mail was New Year's Day 1939. A fancy dress dance was to be held at the Sind Club, named after the Province, to which all five officers on the course were invited. I donned my pirate gear – yellow and red striped Regimental rugger shirt suitably embellished. Off we set in two tongas from the small rather ramshackle hotel where we were accommodated. I'd never met the others before, but we soon became good friends, all being much the same age and seniority (two were killed in WW2 – one by the Germans and one by the Japanese).

It was a splendid affair. Unlike Mhow where females were scarce, here there seemed to be hordes of 'girls' – mostly officers' wives of course – but that didn't cramp my style when I'd downed a few burra pegs. I found myself dancing almost continuously with one young woman – a good deal of kissing under the fake mistletoe – and generally taking mild liberties with her. She was older than me, but was jolly good fun and didn't seem to object to my behaviour. I had absolutely no idea who she was, but I reckoned I'd got off to a good start!

All five of us were invited to a cocktail party at the Chief Instructor's bungalow the following evening. The others seemed amused about something, sniggering and smirking, I couldn't make out why. Time to go arrived, we'd tarted ourselves up and set off in two tongas. The Chief Instructor, a major, met us; after shaking hands he turned to me and said "You know my wife, I think?" indicating a lady standing behind him, who I'd not noticed up to then. She was, I need scarcely say, the young woman I'd danced with so lustily. She showed not the slightest embarrassment, but I'm sure I did! My initiation into the ways of Indian cantonment society had begun, albeit rather belatedly.

Three Danish businessmen connected with cement works in the vicinity, all a lot older than me, were staying in our hotel; they asked me to join them for lunch to celebrate the New Year – I was surprised and flattered. I'd had little contact with businessmen –

dubbed 'box-wallahs' by Service people, their offices having postal box numbers, hence the sobriquet. After an excellent curry lunch, helped down with copious quantities of schnapps, the potent Scandinavian liquor, I was more than prepared to call it a day, but not so the Danes, they had other ideas.

Summoning a taxi, we set off for the back streets and bazaars of Ambala. I'd never before ventured much beyond the confines of cantonments, this was a new experience, especially in the company of three rather sloshed Danes. It soon dawned on me that they were looking for the red-light area, but as there were no such European or Eurasian establishments, they settled for a native brothel.

Watched by cheeky urchins and amused passers by, we rather self-consciously climbed an outside stairway to the first floor of a two-storied house, into what at first, after the brilliant sunlight outside, seemed a darkened room. Six heavily made-up girls were sitting on cushions around the room, all in native dress – long silk qamiz or shirt over satin pyjama trousers, a silk scarf over their shoulders half covering their shiny black oiled hair. Each girl had a small wooden box by her, containing her make-up kit – tiny brushes for outlining the eyes with kohl, scarlet cochineal for the lips, henna for tinting the hair, rice powder and a small mirror. It was all very decorous; we were offered refreshments and invited to sit down on good Persian rugs. The girls, who couldn't have been much out of their teens, held no temptation for me, nor did any of the Danes fall for their charms – anyway by then their ardour seemed to have cooled! It was a diverting experience, although perhaps rather tame, it certainly broadened my knowledge of the country.

Chapter 6

2nd Suffolk Warned for Duty on the North-West Frontier

Frustrated with peacetime soldiering in India and looking for promotion and more pay, in the hope that I might be able to ask Murna to marry me, I decided to apply for a Secondment to one of the many Colonial Forces throughout the British Empire, a way for impecunious, enterprising, young officers to broaden their experience and, more importantly, improve their finances.

The RAF was then accepting army officers. I had visions of sporting 'Wings' on my chest, but I knew I wouldn't be accepted as I'd failed the eyesight test when trying for the RAF before plumping for the army, so I applied for The Iraq Levies. If accepted, I'd have become a Temporary Captain, and my pay more than doubled. Disporting a somewhat glamorous turban, I'd have commanded a company of Iraqi soldiers and swanned about Iraq in an armoured car, quite exciting and not too dangerous, far better than marching in sweltering heat over India's arid plains in the thankless and unpleasant task of Internal Security.

However, it wasn't to be, we were suddenly told that in a few months the Battalion would move to Razmak in Waziristan, on India's fabled North-West Frontier. My application for a Secondment was consequently immediately quashed. I wasn't unduly upset, like all my colleagues I was thrilled at the prospect of some real soldiering against the fierce Pathan tribesmen – the dream of most young officers. I wouldn't have missed it for anything.

Shortly after this exciting news, I was detailed to run a P.T.

Course in Mhow for young officers and NCOs from other units in the District; this kept me busy for six weeks and gave me the chance to put into practice what I'd learnt at Ambala. Following that I was appointed Battalion Messing Officer, responsible for all the Regimental Cooks and the troops' meals, involving endless paperwork connected with rations and menus. Inevitably the Messing Officer and his staff were the butt for complaints, real and imaginary – the Cook Sergeant was traditionally dubbed 'swill-wallah'. I soon appreciated Napoleon's dictum that 'An army marches on its stomach'.

The pace began to quicken, training was taken more seriously, there was even talk of getting wireless sets (radios), but the Orderly Bugler still stood outside the Orderly Room to sound-off calls when ordered by the Adjutant. A significant indication of things to come was the constant stream of Gunner horses trotting past our barracks on their way to be put-down by Farrier Sergeants near the Parsi Towers of Silence at Baircha, three miles away. The 6th Field Regiment was being re-equipped with modern motor-drawn 25–pounders, so all the superb horses, previously used to draw the obsolete 18-pounders, were redundant. Rather than sell them to the locals, who it was feared might ill-treat them, it was decided they should be put-down. There were a good few hundred horses originally shipped from Australia, known as 'whalers'. It was tragic seeing them trotting past to their doom.

In spite of all the activity, I managed to get in a good deal of shikar – snipe, duck, partridge and big game too. My train driver pal kept in touch. With his help I managed to get to a 'kill' in the Choral gorge and bagged my second panther – again from a machan. I don't think many officers in the Regiment, other than Carrigan, had previously shot two panther, I went on to bag a third.

Training in mountain warfare began in earnest. The whole Battalion marched twenty-five miles to an area of scrubby jungle, stunted teak trees, long dry grass and low hills – difficult to have found anywhere less resembling the forbidding bare mountains of the Frontier. However, we learnt how to make sangars – circular breast-works to hold ten men constructed with boulders, lay ambushes, put down prophylactic fire and the all-important picketing the heights drill, second nature to the Indian Army but novel to British troops. Our instructor was Major Cummings, of the 12th Frontier Force Rifles, Indian Army, two years later he won the Victoria Cross fighting the Japanese in Malaya. I met him again several times, the last being in Cyprus in 1957, when he was Superintendent of Police in Kyrenia District .

Not long afterwards Majors Jimmy Yates and 'R.Q' March, Captains Alan Goodwin and 'Ossy' Leach, and myself – still a Lieutenant – were sent on a Familiarisation Visit to Landikotal, a large permanent camp at the northern end of the Khyber Pass. We had a hilarious two-day train journey on the Frontier Mail – the two majors shared a compartment, the rest of us were in a four-berther. Alan Goodwin was tremendous fun, always up to some nonsense, keeping us in fits of laughter – just as well since it was unbearably hot, even with the glass windows, louvered shutters and anti-fly wire-mesh window blinds firmly shut, dust seeped in coating everything. Constant iced nimbo pani, followed after six o'clock by burra pegs, eased the discomfort.

At Attock a bridge spans the mighty Indus river, the boundary between the Punjab and N.W. Frontier Province. Here the fast-flowing river sweeps through a gorge dominated on the south bank by a vast, lowering, purple-grey fort, its walls clinging to the vertical rocky sides almost to the water's edge (constructed in the sixteenth century by Shah Jehan, builder of the Taj Mahal in Agra in memory of his wife). Ranjit Singh, the last great Sikh warrior-king to oppose the British, occupied the fort in the early 1800s. Some years later, when stationed at Campbellpore not far away, I visited it and peered into the tiger pits where Ranjit was reputed to have thrown anyone foolish enough to incur his displeasure.

Just across the bridge, on a bend in the line, we passed a stone monument in the form of a huge bullet, commemorating the fallen of the Frontier Force Regiment. Set in this awe-inspiring rugged gorge it made a deep impression on me, emphasizing that we were entering a completely different part of the sub-continent. We'd left Hindustan, this was the land of the Muslims, seven years later to become Pakistan.

Peshawar lies in a vast valley, the Himalayas forming the backdrop to the north. From time immemorial it has been the main entrepot for merchants bringing their wares from Afghanistan through the Khyber Pass into India. Alexander the Great, the Greek king, came down this route in 327 B.C. with his elephants and conquering hordes. For the past hundred years Britain had been preoccupied in defending the Pass against invaders – Russia posing the chief threat.

Our arrival coincided with a farewell ball in the Peshawar Club, given by The King's (Liverpool) Regiment, before its departure for England. The ball was a terrific do which I thoroughly enjoyed as I had friends in the regiment. We spent the night in tents pitched on the club's tennis courts.

Early the following morning, with a No.1 hangover (Aspro hadn't arrived on the scene then), Ossy Leach and I set off for Landikotal in an open car hired by the army, the Pathan driver showing scant regard for our jaded nerves. The squat sinister mud-brick Jamrud Fort, the Union Jack flying proudly from its round central tower – garrisoned by a Company of soldiers – guarded the southern entrance to the pass. Here, in the 1880s, young Lieut. Winston Churchill nearly lost his life, defending it in hand-to-hand fighting against Afghans.

The road wound up for some thirty miles between towering barren granite hills rising to over seven thousand feet, riven by dry valleys and guarded by the strategically positioned Shagai and other forts. This was the territory of the hostile Afridi and Mohmand tribes, constantly engaged in bitter fighting against the British Raj for more than a century.

Strings of haughty, disdainful camels from far off Central Asia, north of the Hindu Kush mountains in Afghanistan, padded effortlessly along tracks running parallel to the road, laden with bundles of merchandise, a youth leading the first camel; magnificent aristocratic long-haired Afghan hounds loping alongside. The caravans were mostly Powindahs, nomadic Afghans, fierce hawk-eyed, hook-nosed men with daggers in their cummerbunds, a rifle and bandolier over their shoulders, wearing dirty, long grey chadar cloth shirts over baggy wide pyjama trousers, black loosely wound turbans round their oiled shoulder-length black hair and chaplis – the universal tribesmens' sandal. Old crones and infants perched among family possessions – chickens in wicker baskets and rolled-up black camel-hair tents piled high on the swaying beasts. Traffic on the road was scarce, mostly army vehicles, with the occasional local bus crammed to bursting with humanity, sheep and goats with their armed owners perched on the roof.

Landikotal, only a few miles from the Afghan frontier post, had a garrison of several thousand; our Suffolk party was accommodated by the Royal Engineers in their mess. As quarters were scarce, Oscar Leach and I were given camp beds in the billiards room. The Sappers were justly proud of the concrete billiards table they'd made, the only one in the camp, it played remarkably well. Being seven thousand feet up, it was warm by day but cold at night. Despite the rocky ground, gardens had been made where English flowers, not seen in the plains, thrived. The garrison consisted of one British and two Indian Army battalions, Mountain Artillery and supporting services. Next day we attended lectures on mountain warfare tactics given by officers with vast experience in this specialised form of warfare; I found them fascinating and exciting.

The Brigadier had decided to take the Brigade on a three-day column up to the Kabul river and along the frontier with Afghanistan to 'Show-the-Flag'. We set off at six thirty next morning. I was attached to a Mountain Battery of 3.7-inch howitzer 'screw guns' – so called as they took to pieces for carriage on pack mules. They were amazingly accurate; Indian Gunners could bring them into action at a fantastic speed, a hundred percent professional, the first round more often than not being 'spot on' the target, perhaps two thousand feet up a hill-side and a mile or more away. To become a Mountain Gunner was the ambition of most Royal Artillery officers in India.

To see a mountain battery of four guns crashing into action up a steep slippery ravine, the huge, sure-footed Argentinian mules straining under their heavy loads, leather harness creaking, bridles and bits jingling, tall bearded Sikhs urging their animals on, signallers frantically sending messages in Morse code with flags 'on the run', orders from the Forward Observation Officers being shouted back, while at the same time realising everything was under complete control – was a thrilling and unforgettable experience. Pukka soldiering by a highly experienced professional army – now alas – a thing of the past.

The column could only advance when pickets of up to a platoon of thirty men strong, had occupied the crests of all the hills commanding the route, a laborious, dangerous procedure. The troops sweating up the hill-side were at their most vulnerable to ambush by tribesmen lying hidden behind boulders – their grey clothing making it impossible to spot them. As each picket was being positioned, the 'screw guns' and Vickers machine guns were 'laid-on' areas from which an attack might be expected, ready to open fire at a second's notice. Every yard of a picket's ascent was followed anxiously through binoculars by the column and battalion commanders at the head of the main body. Only when the picket had displayed a small yellow cloth screen, indicating that it was in position, could everyone relax and the advance be resumed. As the column progressed, the procedure was reversed. Pickets were recalled by the Rearguard Commander located close to a large red flag at the tail of the main body. When ordered to withdraw the picket scrambled down flat-out, waving their yellow screen to indicate their progress to the watching Gunners. Pretty terrifying on a steep slippery scree slope, through spiky holly bushes, with the possibility of a Pathan suddenly rising out of the ground in front of you, his deadly dagger poised to rip open your belly!

Providing no opposition was encountered, as was the case on this occasion, a column could expect to cover at the most fourteen miles, before making camp at a predetermined site – not closely overlooked by hills, with water available, vital for the troops and the hundreds of pack animals. Having reached the selected site at least two hours before dusk, camp pickets were immediately established on prominent features within rifle range, where they remained until called in next morning. Meanwhile, in a flurry of organized activity, a four foot drystone perimeter wall was built around the camp with boulders ready to hand, each unit being responsible for its section of the perimeter as indicated by the Column HQ staff.

Before long cooks were preparing a meal – goat or sheep pilau for the Musalmans; chappatis, vegetable curry and rice with maybe chicken and spices for the Hindus; bully-beef stew for the British troops. A wonderful savory aroma soon wafted over the camp – I realised I was damned hungry!

Sentries were posted along the perimeter wall, interlocking arcs of fire fixed for the Vickers guns, the mules tethered in long lines in the middle of the camp. The Field Ambulance established for casualties – on this column there were only cuts, bruises and malarial fevers – endemic in Indian sepoys – for the doctors to cope with. A hundred and one other tasks not the least the digging of latrines, had to be completed before dusk when the whole camp 'stood-to', manning the perimeter wall until it was quite dark.

I had a meal with the Mountain Gunners in their mess; we sat in two shallow trenches, separated by a level bit of ground forming a table, impossible to dig deeper as the ground was too rocky. I then got into a shallow trench prepared for me by an orderly, unrolled my bistra and was soon asleep.

At dawn next morning the camp came to life with 'stand-to' until daylight. The weather had closed in, rain and a bitter icy wind swept down from the north – we were soon wet through and chilled to the bone. I felt rather bedraggled as we set off at about six thirty. However, I'd got my second-wind as it were, felt I knew it all, quite the old frontier-wallah – my spirits rose. The weather improved, although it remained bitingly cold; our clothing in those days was totally inadequate, none of the wonderful rain-proofed, quilted kit the army has today. I was young and fit, the weather didn't bother me much, but one of our party, Major Roy March, found it hard going, in his younger days he'd been a fine

The Khyber Pass – looking towards Afghanistan.

Razmak Camp, Wazinstan

sportsman, but he'd put on a lot of weight, at one stage I thought he might not last out. Jimmy Yates, on the other hand, the oldest in our party, made light of it, despite constantly cursing and blasting about the cold and discomfort.

The next two days followed the same pattern. On reaching the Kabul river, where it gushed spectacularly through a narrow gorge on its way to join the Indus at Attock, we headed back by another route for Landikotal. On the last evening local Afridi malikhs (headmen) arrived for a 'jirga' (gathering). After paying their respects to the Brigadier, they presented him with several fine goats in token of their good faith (?) – he thanked them in Pushtu. The unfortunate animals were speedily decapitated with a single blow of a Gurkha kukri and passed to the cooks.

* * * * *

Back again in Mhow I found things in a state of considerable flux. Preparations for our move to Razmak in Waziristan were under way, including the move of the families to the small hill station of Chuka Gali near Murree, north east of Rawalpindi. With all these changes, although still only a Lieutenant, I found myself becoming one of the more experienced officers in the Battalion. I acquired a dog for ten rupees from a Private Soldier about to be posted home – a black Labrador-Collie cross, I called him Rover. He was soon a well known character, even accompanying me sometimes on operations; he was my loyal companion until tragically killed by a car in the Mall in Rawalpindi.

In spite of the increased training activity, I managed to wangle ten days shooting leave in a block in the Choral ghats (hills) some twenty miles south of Mhow, taking my bearer Babu, my shikari and Rover with me. I pitched two small tents a couple of miles from a little railway station at the tiny village of Bavi. It was extremely hot, well over 110 fahrenheit at mid-day.

The Indore State Forest Reserve boundary abuted my block, so I got permission to visit one of the Maharaja's hides. I set off just before dawn with my shikari quite a distance into the jungle; the hide was like a machine gun emplacement, entered through a low door at the back. At first it was too dark to see anything through the rifle slits, but as it gradually grew lighter I could make out about five tiger not more than twenty yards away feeding on a dead boda. Young bullocks were regularly tethered there as bait, so the Maharaja, or a guest, could be sure of getting a shot at any time.

It was a wonderful sight. Speckled shafts of sunlight slanting through the trees onto the magnificent orange-yellow-black striped beasts, growling at each other as they tore at the boda's carcase; peacock strutted and scratched about in the teak leaves, displaying their iridescent vivid greeny-blue tail feathers. I was a bit concerned about leaving the hide, but as the sun rose the temperature rose – suddenly the tigers had vanished. Vultures hovering around waiting their turn then took over, flapping about pecking at the carcase – a disgusting sight. My shikari whispered it was alright to leave, which we did at a rather rapid rate.

Painted partridge and green pigeon were plentiful near my camp site, I shot a few for the pot. For the same reason I wanted to shoot a peafowl, but being sacred to Hindus they were protected – to have shot one would have caused a great furore.

One day when out after partridge, I came across a large family of big grey black-faced long-tailed langur monkeys – the biggest and most common monkey in India – feeding on berries in a big tree. They took exception to Rover, jumped to the ground and leapt towards him, making an angry chattering noise, baring their long sharp teeth, giving every indication of intending to tear him to pieces if they could catch him. Rover meanwhile was barking furiously, I had difficulty in restraining him from rushing at them; only after I'd fired a couple of shots in the air did they decide to return up the tree, still chattering. Rover and I beat a hasty retreat – without any hesitation on my part!

At dusk a few days later I sat up in a machan over a tethered goat – its bleating made me feel uncomfortable, however, this must have attracted the panther, which came soon after darkness fell. When I switched on the torch clamped to my rifle, I saw the panther directly in my sights, took the second pressure on the trigger and despatched it with a single shot through the head; it was the third and last panther I was to bag. As I've already explained, I had to spend most of the night skinning it by the light of a pressure-lamp, in a temperature well over 100 degrees Fahrenheit, helped by Babu. We rubbed powdered alum crystals – brought specially for the purpose – into the skin then put it in an empty ghee tin (cooking oil), making it as air-tight as possible. I sent it off by rail to taxidermists in Madras as soon as I'd got back to cantonments

The next day Babu went to Bavi station by bike, to collect a slab of ice I'd ordered to be sent down from Mhow. I saw him some distance away returning sooner than I'd expected, leaving a trail of dust as he pedalled furiously across the dry fields. I vaguely wondered why, normally he took his time.

Breathlessly he explained – the Indian Station Master had told him to tell me, that he'd just heard on the railway telegraph that war with Germany had been declared – it was 3rd September 1939.

Chapter 7

The Central Internment Camp, Ahmednagar, 1939

The day after I got back from shooting leave, I was told to report to 'Sweat' Dean, who had succeeded Dick Goodwin as Adjutant. 'Sweat' told me that I was to move in a day's time to Ahmednagar, where I was to take charge of one of the Wings of an internment camp for enemy civilians being set up there. I had little enough time to pack up all the bits and pieces I'd accumulated over almost four years in Mhow. Off I set with the faithful Babu and Rover on a thirty-six hour rail journey to Ahmednagar where I'd attended a six-week machine gun course three and a half years before.

As I expected to be at Ahmednagar for only a few weeks, I left most of my kit with our Quartermaster, Major Jackie Hill, to be looked after by the Rear Party when the Battalion moved to Razmak. Jackie made up for his lack of inches by being generally acknowledged as a giant in the elite ranks of Regular Army Quartermasters. Enlisting as a Drummer Boy in about 1900, he retired as a Full Colonel, a most exceptional achievement.

The Central Internment Camp was located in the empty British Infantry barracks. When I arrived it was in the process of being wired-in with a tall double barbed-wire fence by a squadron of Madras Sappers and Miners. The camp staff consisted of the Commandant (a major) and four Wing Commanders, all regular British service officers, also officers from the Auxiliary Forces India and about fifty British infantry NCOs and Other Ranks drawn from regiments throughout India. The day after my arrival the officer posted as Adjutant and Quartermaster became seriously ill – I was instructed to replace him. Straightaway I found myself working under tremendous pressure to get the place ready for the first batch of a hundred or so enemy civilian internees, due to arrive in two weeks time from all over India.

A major problem was the Commandant. Although a charming fellow, he was over-fond of the bottle. I can't remember exactly how it came about, but mercifully he was quickly replaced by Lieut. Colonel Quayle of the Rajputana Rifles, soon dubbed 'Killer Quayle'. Notwithstanding his quick temper, he and I got on alright – just as well since we shared an office. He smoked his height in cigars daily, and judging from his complexion, he'd downed his fair quota of burra pegs during his long service in India. The strange thing was that he resembled Mussolini in looks and stature; he often inspected the camp smoking a long Burmese cheroot, wearing highly polished black field boots, similar to a Fascist officer's uniform (The 'Raj Rif' like all Rifle Regiments, wore black buttons, belts and accoutrements). In spite of his somewhat forbidding appearance, I liked him; he let me to get on with my job and was frequently out of the office.

For the first six weeks the camp was guarded by the 1st/1st Punjabis, a fine Indian Army Regiment. The CO being on long leave, the second-in-command, Major Barker, was temporarily in command. (Major Barker retired to Milford-on-Sea, becoming a well known personality; he died the year before my arrival in the village). The Adjutant was Captain Johnny Worsley, later to be awarded the Military Cross whilst serving with Punjabs at the hard fought battle of Keren during the Abyssinian campaign. We became good friends; I think he was the only ex-Indian Army officer to reach the rank of Lieutenant General in the British Army and receive a Knighthood. When we were living in Camberley he was Commandant of the Staff College, my daughter Alice got to know his youngest girl, Thea, quite well. We went to his eldest daughter's wedding in the Staff College, a very grand affair.

During the following weeks the number of internees increased to over five hundred, later to exceed a thousand when Italy entered the war. Neither I, nor the other British Officers, had any idea of the scale of the horrors being perpetrated by the Nazis on the Jews. Of course we knew about Hilter's anti-Semitic pogrom, but being so far away we hadn't fully appreciated the deep, bitter hatred the Jews bore the Nazis – instant news via satellite TV and radio was still forty years away.

It was only after several ugly incidents that we realised the Jews would have to be segregated. There was also acrimony between Germans and Austrians, we learnt fast how to cope with these disorders. I employed an Austrian Jew as a book-keeper, a gentle elderly man who'd escaped, without his family, from Austria a year previously; he opened my eyes to Nazi atrocities, what he told me was almost impossible to credit. He'd been vetted by a team of German-speaking Eastern-European interrogators – a rum lot – under Sir Malcolm Darling, an eminent member of the Indian Civil Service (ICS), who arrived with his daughter, a pleasant young woman, more memorable for her intellect than her looks.

The Jewish Agency handled the interests of Jews in India, its representative Mr. Rosenbaum – affectionately known as 'Rosie' – a wealthy Bombay cotton-waste broker, made it his business to get to know the members of the camp staff. A jovial, corpulent, clever chap, always ready to help with the loan of a car, or to put one up for a night in his flat in Bombay. Through his good offices most of the German Jews in the camp were eventually released, but that was long after I'd left.

Many of the internees had held senior positions in German firms in India; they didn't take kindly to the British Other Ranks rations and requested permission to buy their own food, also that an Indian contractor should run a canteen in the camp – an arrogant lot, they were certain Germany would win the war. I approached the Commandant on the matter of a contractor, he told me to get on with it and find someone suitable. After interviewing several applicants anxious to secure this potentially lucrative contract, I selected a Parsee from Bombay, and arranged for him and the Commandant to sign the contract very shortly.

Returning to my office after lunch in the mess the day before the contract was to be signed, I noticed two Muslims squatting on the verandah – they rose and salaamed as I approached. From their appearance and dress I realised they were people of consequence. Large turbans of perfectly wound cream silk, three-quarter length tussore silk coats with stand-up collars, pristine white fine cotton pyjama trousers – most impressive.

On entering my office, my Jemedar Clerk of the Indian Army Corps of Clerks, equivalent to a Warrant Officer, hurried in and whispered, in tones of great awe, that Mr. Wazir Ali and his son wished to see me. "What about?" I enquired, "The contract, Sahib", he replied. "But, Jemedar Sahib, we've already fixed that up with the Parsee gentleman", I said. "Yes Sahib, but nothing is signed yet. Mr. Wazir Ali is a very important person, you must see him straightaway." I said "Okay, bring him in."

After the customary welcoming pleasantries, I enquired the purpose of this visit. The Jemedar Clerk had been right, Wazir Ali very tactfully raised the matter of the contract for the camp canteen and related services. I explained that I was sorry but I had already chosen a contractor, the contract was due to be signed by the Commandant the next day. With a slightly deprecatory smile, Wazir Ali asked me to be good enough to read a letter, which he drew from an inside pocket. It was typed on GHQ Delhi headed paper, dated a year or two previously. It stated, un-ambiguously, that in the event of war, and the establishment of a central internment camp for enemy civilians, Mr. Wazir Ali was to be granted the camp canteen contract. Signed – Edmond Ironside, Lieut: General, Quartermaster General.

General Sir Edmond 'Tiny' Ironside (later to become Field-Marshal Lord Ironside), an immensely tall, larger-than-life character of legendary exploits, became Chief of The Imperial General Staff at the outbreak of the war, the most senior officer in the British Army. (John Buchan, the well known author of the 1930s, writer of many classic novels including 'The Thirty-Nine Steps', took him as his role-model for Richard Hannay, the hero in several of his books). So that was that. There was obviously no point in arguing – it would have been like farting against thunder! How it came about that Wazir Ali had been awarded this lucrative contract I know not.

Years later, I heard an interesting footnote (for which I can't vouch the veracity) to the effect that when India was partitioned in 1947 and Pakistan became an independent nation, Wazir Ali shipped his gold bullion from Bombay to Karachi to finance the embryo National Bank of Pakistan. As an impecunious Lieutenant, on about five hundred rupees a month, I brushed close to serious money – perhaps I missed a trick – I wonder?

When the camp was running smoothly I managed to get the occasional day's shooting. My twelve-bore shotgun, given me by my uncle Charles, developed a fault in the ejection mechanism before I left Mhow. Since then I'd been using one belonging to Jack Prescott, which, when he sent off by car for England, he'd asked me to look after, and use if I liked – it had been his mother's, a 20–bore 'Lady's Gun', quite unusual.

I'd heard of jheels (small lakes) not far away reported to offer good duck shooting, so I set off in a borrowed car, with Babu and Rover to try my luck. I found a jheel covered in a mass of floating weed surrounded on three sides by tall reeds; a bunch of duck were swimming on the far side – the problem was how to get within range. I spied a reed-cutter, a very decrepit old man, thin as a rake, poling a raft made of bundles of reeds he'd just cut. I asked him to ferry me to within gunshot of the duck – the offer of eight annas was a sufficient inducement.

I stepped gingerly onto the centre of biggest bundle, which immediately partially submerged, but succeeded in keeping my gun and cartridges clear of water. The reed-wallah poled the flimsy sinking raft towards the duck, who took to the wing as we approached – I ineffectively banged away. Rover, swimming along beside me got excited and started barking and jumping on and off the raft which soon disintegrated.

Being a strong swimmer I hung on to my gear for some time by treading water, but soon realised I was being pulled down by the mass of weed tangled around the gun, my cartridge case and boots – I was gradually sinking. I tried swimming on my back, making as little movement as possible, but this didn't help, I just couldn't get rid of the weed. In a bit of a panic, I succeeded in slipping off my boots, making swimming easier, but still made no progress. I was weakening – in desperation I ditched my cartridge belt and bag, finally having to let go the gun!

Throughout all this Rover was swimming round barking, several times pushing me under. The old man floated off on a bundle of reeds, sufficient to bear his slender frame. I inched my way towards the bank, dragging myself through the reeds onto the bank – a shaken Babu was waiting to help me out.

I drove back covered in mud, minus boots, topee, and gun – ashamed of myself, feeling a fool. The loss of the gun was worrying, not only because it wasn't mine, but to lose a weapon was a serious matter. I reported the incident to the police, and offered a reward for the gun's retrieval. The villagers no doubt fished it up later, and sold it for far more than the reward. My insurance paid up, but only a fraction of the gun's worth. I sent this to Jack with a letter of apology – he took it very well. I did no more shooting while at Ahmednagar.

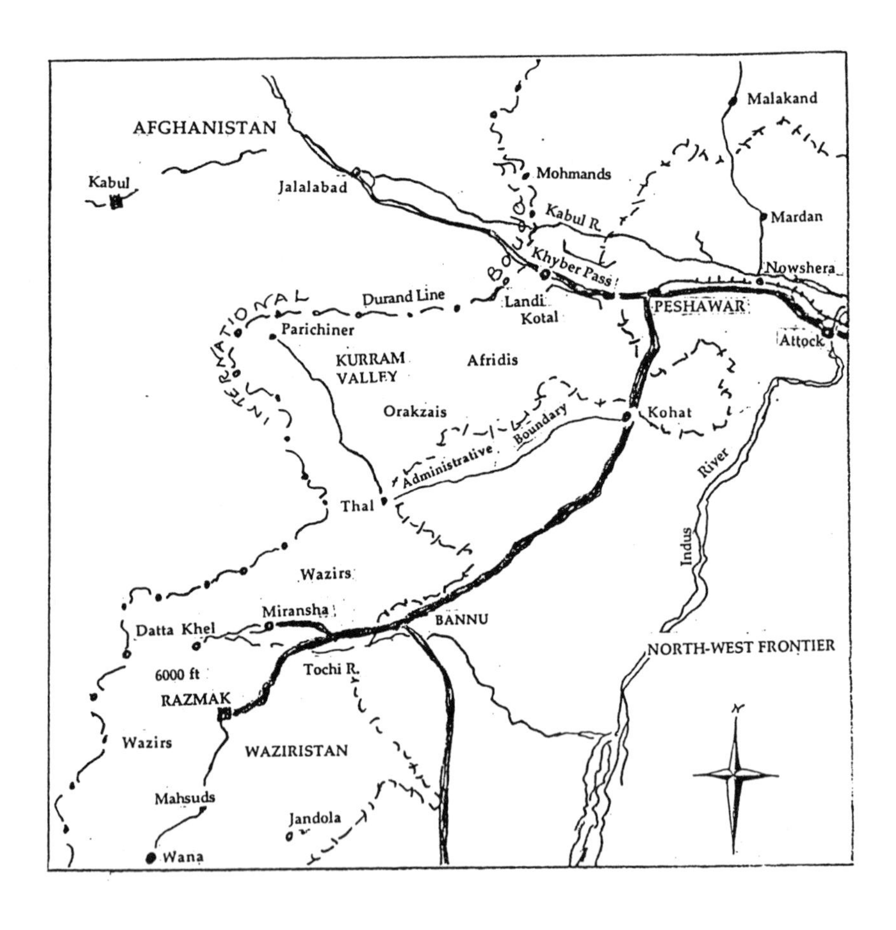
AFGHANISTAN
Kabul
Jalalabad
Mohmands
Malakand
Kabul R.
Mardan
Khyber Pass
Nowshera
Durand Line
Landi Kotal
PESHAWAR
INTERNATIONAL BOUNDARY
Parichiner
Attock
KURRAM VALLEY
Afridis
Orakzais
Kohat
Administrative Boundary
River
Thal
Indus
Wazirs
Miransha
BANNU
Datta Khel
NORTH-WEST FRONTIER
6000 ft
Tochi R.
RAZMAK
Wazirs
WAZIRISTAN
Mahsuds
Jandola
Wana

Chapter 8

The North-West Frontier, 1939–40

By the middle of December 1939 I was becoming anxious to return to my Regiment, which by then had been in Razmak for a couple of months. My Movement Order eventually came through. I bid goodbye to the friends I'd made in the past three and a half months, and set off with Babu and Rover on the long rail journey to Bannu, the railhead for Waziristan. First to Bombay, then by the Frontier Mail to Rawalpindi, thence to Mari Indus, where a long bridge spanned the Indus. From there one travelled on what was known as 'The heat-stroke Express', stopping briefly at Lakki, an isolated halt, one just had time for cup of char and bite to eat while the engine took on water. A wonderful rail journey in spite of the dust and slow progress, providing an opportunity to study the different races and castes of the sub-continent, ending in the hostile environment of The North-West Frontier Province.

The last lap of the journey was by army lorry from Bannu up the Tochi valley and on to Razmak, a distance of about eighty miles, where the road virtually ended. Vehicles could only move on days when the road was 'Open', generally twice a week, then only in convoy.

The procedure known as Road Protection (RP), involved picketing all the hills dominating the road from Bannu to Razmak, a major operation, which over the years had developed into a well practised drill – woe betide any unit which got it wrong. To do so could not only result in casualties being inflicted by the Mashud and Waziri tribesmen, ever ready to take advantage of any errors, but also resulted in the unit – its commander in particular – incurring the displeasure and censure of the Brigade Commander. A poor unit soon got a bad reputation, there was no room for anything other than top-line professional soldiering.

Mistakes couldn't be concealed, hundreds of eyes were watching every inch of a picket's progress as it climbed to the crest of an immense hill dominating the road, any sloppy action was immediately evident for all to see. Suddenly – men were seen falling on the hillside! Seconds later the crack of the tribesmen's rifles – 'tak dum, tak dum' – followed instantly by the 'whoomph' 'whoomph' 'whoomph' 'whoomph' of shells from the mountain guns and the accompanying 'chatter' of Vickers machine guns firing long bursts. Nothing unusual, the convoy of lorries keeps moving.

There was no trouble on the road the day I rejoined 2nd Suffolk in Razmak – it was tremendous being back amongst familiar faces and real friends. The CO – Murna's uncle, Colonel 'Pat' Eley – told me the battalion was shortly being issued with four Vickers machine guns (the ones we'd had before had been withdrawn before leaving Mhow), sufficient for one platoon, which I was to train and command. The guns duly arrived, I selected men who'd been with me in D Company, so it wasn't long before we were out on RP duties, charging along with our guns on pack mules, often coming into action, not that one could ever see tribesmen, they didn't advertise their whereabouts, all one could do was to plaster an area of hillside from where shots seemed to be coming.

Senior officers in the battalion were still being posted away, this helped us younger chaps. I was given command of B Company and promoted to Acting Captain, putting up my third 'pip' – a big day in my life, no longer a subaltern or plain 'Mr.'! I was just twenty-six.

I arrived in Razmak on the 22nd December, rather like joining one's family for Christmas – the date is significant. If I'd arrived nine days later, I wouldn't have qualified for the last Indian General Service medal to be struck. At the time we felt a bit self-conscious about wearing the ribbon, only someone with two frontier medals, as was often the case in the Indian Army, really counted for anything. However, I now treasure this silver medal with bar 'North West Frontier 1937–39', more than all the other eight I subsequently became entitled to. My name, rank, number and regiment are stamped around the edge (years later I qualified for the similarly stamped silver General Service Medal with bars

'Malaya' and 'Cyprus'. WW2 campaign medals (stars) were cupro-nickel and not stamped).

After four months, my bearer Babu went down with a severe bout of malaria. I realised he was unhappy and rather frightened, odd as there were many other Hindu bearers in Razmak. Regretfully, I decided it would be best if he returned to his family in Mhow. I replaced him with a useless Pathan lad, who didn't last long.

Razmak lies in a plateau 7000 feet above sea level – treeless, harsh, rugged, forbidding, inhospitable, dun-coloured terrain, formidable mountains to the north and west form the boundary with Afghanistan – the Durand Line. In the early months of the year the climate is superb, later on it becomes fiercely hot during the day – in winter the whole area is covered in snow; HQ Waziristan District, and a garrison of some seven thousand, lived in mud-brick buildings with corrugated-iron roofs.

There was a British Military Hospital (BMH), a cinema, an excellent officers' club, a small well-stocked bazaar and numerous hard-earth (muti) football and hockey grounds. The five foot drystone perimeter wall, with guard houses at frequent intervals, was manned for twenty minutes at dawn and dusk; outside the wall, beyond grenade throwing distance, was a thick barbed-wire entanglement. Permanent stone-built pickets were located on prominent features, manned by a section of men, providing security in depth. 2nd Suffolk was responsible for Rifleman's Picket, about three hundred yards outside our sector of the perimeter wall, guarding the rough landing strip. No females, not even army nurses, were allowed into the camp – it was in effect an enormous monastery.

Soon after my arrival, Jim Hildersley, a young Second Lieutenant straight from Sandhurst, who like me had been to Sherborne School, joined us and was posted to my Company as a platoon commander – George Springfield was my Second-in-command. Jimmy, a laid-back, good-looking chap, had somehow got to know Murna, too well for my liking from what he took pleasure in telling me – I was extremely put out. Not long after he'd joined us, as if to rub salt into the wound, he said "Oh, by the way Bertie (the nickname by which I was always known in the army) I got a letter from Murna today, she's engaged to an RAF fellow, Hugh Thomson – did you know?"

I didn't know and was devastated by the news, all the more so coming via 'Young Hildersley'. Pat Eley apparently didn't know either. Anyway, a few days later I got a letter from her (letters from

England took up to three weeks) telling me she'd known this chap Thomson for six months, he was stationed at RAF Wattisham in Suffolk, they'd just decided to get engaged, hoping to get married soon. She said how anxious she was that I should know, before I heard about it from anyone else (in which she failed), trying to soften the blow by saying how I'd always have a very special place in her heart. She hoped I'd understand and wish her happiness.

I was in no way mollified by the final sentence. Murna had meant so much to me for so long. I was terribly upset, what's more my pride had received a nasty jolt. If I'd thought about it rationally – which at the time I was incapable of doing – I'd have realised it was inevitable that an attractive young woman like her was bound to get engaged, particularly in wartime. I tried to forget her. No use feeling sorry for myself, I was many thousands of miles away, there'd only been a vague understanding that one day we might get married, unfair to blame her – but I couldn't completely write her off. Now, more than fifty-five years later, after many vicissitudes, I still haven't forgotten her, she's as clear in my mind as the first time I met her – and always will be.

We soon got into the swing of life on the Frontier. Twice a week we were on RP duty; the battalion quickly gained the respect of the other units. We were fit and prepared to give of our best, spurred on by the occasional casualty to keep us on our toes.

Serious incidents occurred on the road up from Bannu, including the ambushing of the Political Agent for Waziristan. Brigadier Denys, who commanded Razcol, the column based on Razmak, decided a 'Showing-the-flag' column was required. 2nd Suffolk set out on its first column in the early morning mist, dashing through the camp's main gate to avoid a bullet from 'Bakshi Bill', a notorious tribesman who regularly took ineffective pot-shots at the camp. The other formations were 10th Baluch and 1st/8th Gurkhas, plus Mountain Gunners, Sappers and Miners, Indian Army Service Corps sepoys leading endless strings of mules carrying water, rations, fodder, reserve ammunition, and a Field Ambulance – serious casualties were carried in kajawas (covered stretchers) either side of a camel – to mention but a few of the units forming Razcol.

The first day the column covered fourteen miles to Dam Dil, where the road descended an escarpment to Razani – a one battalion camp – without encountering any serious opposition, camping the night under the protection of Alexandra Picket, a permanent stone fort garrisoned by a Company of sepoys. Just as we'd finished digging shallow sleeping trenches, the heavens opened, and a torrent of muddy water gushed through the camp, filling our trenches and sweeping away a huge pile of chuppatis just prepared by the Gurkhas' cooks. We spent a pretty miserable night, but had no sniping from the hostiles, which was something to be thankful for.

Next day we moved on down to Razani. B Company 2nd Suffolk, the leading unit, had the task of picketing three tremendous hills quite a distance from the road, across a dryish nullah (river-bed) to our left. I remember George Springfield's look of horror, when I told him he'd got to establish a picket on the highest one.

Later on in the day, I was following the rear elements of the 10th Baluch, their Drum Major, a magnificent chap well over six foot tall, acting as Intelligence Section Havildar (sergeant), was a few yards in front of me. We'd almost reached the camp when tribesmen suddenly opened fire from across the nullah to our left. The Drum Major was hit in the back and crashed to the ground, the first time I'd seen anyone wounded in action close to.

We'd begun building the perimeter wall and doing all the things that had to be completed before dusk and stand-to, when 'Sweat' Dean, the Adjutant, told me I was to report to HQ Razani camp, adjoining our temporary camp site, apparently the Brigadier wanted to see me, I couldn't think what I'd done wrong – why should I be sent for?

I duly reported myself to the Brigade Major, who ushered me into the HQ mess tent. Who should I see but my old boss, from the Central Internment Camp, none other than 'Killer' Quayle himself, sporting a brigadier's badges of rank, with the inevitable cheroot sticking out of his mouth. He'd apparently heard that 2nd Suffolk were with Razcol and asked that I should be sent round. I was really very pleased to meet him again – we had quite a few burra pegs and some good laughs. Sad to relate, he didn't last long as a brigade commander; soon after he was retired, and emigrated to Australia.

George Springfield and I shared a shallow trench that night. We'd just settled down, hoping the mossies would let us get some sleep, when we heard the familiar 'tak-dam, tak-dam', apparently coming from across the nullah. We simultaneously said "Christ!" and tried desperately to burrow deeper into the ground – we'd no tools and were on rock, so we didn't achieve much! Having regained our composure, we lit our pipes and tried to appear unconcerned. Sniping continued for an hour or so, several mules in the centre of the camp were hit – their distressing braying continued until the farriers put them down.

Dossali Fort, the headquarters of The Tochi Scouts, was close to Razani camp. I managed to visit a friend based there before the column set off back to Razmak. I'd expected the fort, home to five officers and perhaps fifty or more Scouts, to be petty spartan. Actually the officers' quarters were jolly comfy, looking out on a well watered lawn in the centre – they certainly did themselves proud. If I'd been in the Indian Army I'd have tried for a Secondment to one of these irregular units: the Tochi, South Waziristan and Gilgit Scouts, and the Kurram Militia, controlled by Political Agents. Pay was good, there was plenty of scope for initiative and independent action, the job had an aura of adventure, excitement and glamour, missing in normal infantry soldiering. The Scouts were all Pathans, tall fierce-featured chaps; on a ghast (patrol), armed only with a rifle, uncluttered by transport, with perhaps a few chuppatis tied in their shirt tails, they could cover amazing distances across rugged terrain at terrific speed. The British officers, wearing the same uniform as their men – long grey chadar cloth shirts over baggy pyjama trousers and a khaki turban – had to be able to be in the lead on ghast. I envied them their obvious self-confidence and somewhat superior attitude towards run-of-the mill soldiering.

On return to Razmak, I was detailed to run a P.T. course for 120 Indian Other Ranks (IORs)] from units in Waziristan District, Indian NCO Instructors from the School of P.T. in Ambala were sent to help me. It was quite a task, lasting three weeks.

About the time I'd finished with the PT course, the powers that be, in this case the General Officer Commanding (GOC) Northern Army, Lieut. General Quinan, issued instructions that Razcol should proceed to Tappi, a large village in the Tochi river valley, to avenge the recent capture and murder of two Tochi Scouts officers, whose severed heads had subsequently been touted round the villages in sacks. Major Faulder, the acting CO of 1st/19th Hyderabad Regiment, being short of officers, and knowing my Urdu was reasonable, asked if I could be loaned to act as Adjutant to his battalion for the duration of the column; as 2nd Suffolk was not taking part in the operation, Colonel Pat Eley gave his consent. A few days later off I went with the 1st/19th Hyderabad, hoping my Urdu would be up to it. A British Service officer serving with an Indian Army unit on column – quite exceptional.

Razcol set off in the usual way, picketing the heights down the road to Razani. The second day we camped below Tal fort, much the same size as Alexandra Picket. That evening the Brigadier explained his plans for the next day to all the officers sitting in a semi-circle on the ground round him. His intention was to surround the village, blow-up the mud brick towers, set fire to the houses and return to Tal the same evening – the usual procedure. He expected the inhabitants would have fled by the time the village was surrounded, and ended by saying that the Army Commander had set up a forward HQ not far from Miram Sha, the RAF base in Waziristan, some six miles from Tappi, and would be following Razcol's progress – with interest!

The Brigadier was followed by the Political Agent, who anticipated that the Lower Daurs, who lived in Tappi and were responsible for the murders, would offer resistance as Razcol advanced through the surrounding vineyards, each enclosed by a ditch and a mud wall topped with thorns, with a squat mud-brick look-out tower hidden in the middle, forming formidable obstacles. He said that the Fakir of Ipi, for many years a thorn in the Government's side, known to be financed by he Axis Powers through Afghanistan, was stirring up the Wazir and Masud tribes and had declared a jehad (holy war). He finished by saying there were reports of sizable tribal lashkars (formations) moving towards the area round Tappi, some already displaying their flags and pennants on the hill-tops on the far side of the Tochi river.

I must say, when I got into my bedding-roll laid out in a shallow trench by my orderly, I was pretty apprehensive about what was in store for us next day. There was a bit of sniping during the night, one sepoy was hit, but I managed to sleep.

At five in the morning, when still dark, several thousand troops and hundreds of pack animals were astir. There was little noise and no confusion, everyone in Razcol knew from long experience exactly what to do. It was exciting – a small army of professional soldiers getting on the move, setting off on what would most probably end in a fight against a crafty, cruel and dangerous enemy. I felt a bit queasy in the tummy!

After a mug of chae (tea), I took up my position next to the Commanding Officer, Major Faulder. The Jemadar Adjutant, a British Corporal and a Signaller from the Royal Signals with a No. 19 wireless set on a pack mule – our rear-link to Razcol HQ – were immediately behind me. My job was to keep the CO au fait with the overall situation, anticipate and pass on his orders to the Company Commanders, keep HQ Razcol posted as to our progress and generally act as his assistant.

About a mile from camp we forded the icy waters of the Tochi river flowing in shallow channels down a wide valley. Tappi village was about two miles further on, difficult to pick out at ground level and set back from the river on cultivated alluvial ground. Fields of young corn and vineyards were directly ahead of us. The river, about a quarter of a mile wide, overlooked by low hills, was on our right; a couple of miles or so away a range of hills curled round to the left behind us. We advanced on a two-company front, making slow progress due not only to the vineyards and ditches, but because we soon came under fire from snipers in the mud brick towers hidden in the vinyards.

The 10th Baluch were on our left, HQ Razcol was some distance behind, the vineyards reduced visibility to a few hundred yards, keeping contact by flag – the normal means of communication – was virtually impossible. Our only wireless link was the No. 19 pack-set working to HQ Razcol, keeping contact within the battalion was only possible by Runner. John Bassett, a splendid chap and a friend of mine, was the Forward Observation Officer (FOO) from the Mountain Battery supporting us. As always with Gunners, he managed to keep in touch with his guns a mile or so away in some mysterious manner – by field telephone most probably.

About mid-day it became evident that the tribesmen were prepared to put up a fight in the open, not their usual tactics. We could see that the crests of the hills to our front and on our right flank across the river were swarming with hostiles, I could make out their standards fluttering in the breeze. Groups of tribesmen were bounding across the river, presumably to reinforce those confronting us, presenting a target no machine gunner could resist. With Major Faulder's permission, I called up the MG platoon 'at the double' and got it into action at the optimum range of fifteen hundred yards, firing long bursts at the tribesmen crossing the channels, the strike of the bullets on the water was clearly visible, the four guns must have inflicted considerable casualties – my training had at last been put to good effect.

At this rather critical moment there was a heavy burst of firing and a lot of shouting from the direction of our forward company. Sepoys carrying casualties streamed back in some panic through battalion HQ to the Regimental Aid Post (RAP) in the rear, yelling that 'Ghazis' (religious fanatics dressed in white clothing, believing they were immune to bullets) were attacking our advanced positions. The CO told me to organise a lay-back position a hundred yards to the rear. While running back I took the rifle from a casualty on a stretcher – I was determined, if things became dicy, to have a crack at the enemy with a weapon I was

Officers 1st/19th Hyderabad Regt. during the Tappi operation. Waziristan, 1940.

Front Row: Capt. Robert Gowing; Major Rudolf Muller; Major Faulder C.O.; Capt Bevan; Capt. Dutt M.O..

expert with, rather than with my .38 revolver, in which I had little confidence.

The situation seemed precarious, but John Bassett brought fire down just ahead of our positions and onto the tower to our left, from where snipers were being particularly troublesome. The Sappers and Miners, awaiting just such an opportunity, rushed forward encircling the tower with a necklace of prepared charges, and blew it up. This spirited action restored our sepoys' confidence, a counter-attack was put in, lead by Subadar Major Umrao Singh, a Viceroy's Commissioned Officer (VCO) – equivalent to a British Warrant Officer – which forced the Ghazis to withdraw (six months later Umrao Singh distinguished himself again, was awarded the Military Cross and Commissioned in the field).

Doubling after the CO I tripped over the half-concealed body of a young Pathan, still grasping his rifle, just outside a vineyard wall, he'd been hiding in a hole under a charpoy – a common ruse. Our forward companies held, we resumed our advance, so, perhaps a trifle thankfully, I didn't get a chance to put my marksmanship to the test.

There was still a fair amount of small arms fire coming from our front and left flank, but the Ghazis seemed to have taken to their heels. I was beginning to think the worst was over, when the mule carrying the No. 19 set was hit and crashed to the ground, breaking the aerial in the process. The two Royal Signals Operators transferred the set to a spare mule, rigged-up an aerial and restored contact with Razcol HQ. Shortly afterwards a message came through, ordering us to abandon any further advance and prepare to withdraw to camp, only to be quickly followed by another message, instructing us to start falling back forthwith, keeping level with the 10th Baluch on our left. As we couldn't see the Baluch, nor had radio contact with them, it was impossible to make out their exact position, which made things tricky as a considerable racket was coming from their direction. Anyway, Major Faulder decided to fall back, leap-frogging one company at a time. I'd just got these instructions out to all company commanders, when a further message came through from HQ Razcol, cancelling the withdrawal, and ordering us to move up into the hills on our left, where we were to remain over night. The tribesmen had clearly got their tails up.

Controlled confusion ensued. It was getting late, only an hour of daylight remained, we'd had no respite since about five in the morning, had nothing to eat and suffered quite a few casualties, indeed I'd been hit in the left elbow by a stray bullet, quite a bit of blood, but it looked far worse than it actually was, luckily only a graze.

The Service Corps pack-mules with rations, ammunition, medical supplies etc: had been sent back to camp several hours previously. Razcol now issued orders for them to return 'at the double'. Strings of these long suffering beasts, some with their loads swinging about under their bellies as they'd been too hastily loaded, came trotting back across the Tochi river, urged on by their muleteers, up into the hills where Razcol was establishing a defensive position.

As soon as all units were in, the Brigadier held an 'Orders Group' which the CO and I attended. He said the GOC had issued instructions that Razcol was to remain over-night where it was, and complete the job of surrounding and destroying Tappi village next morning. Intelligence sources reported that the Faqir of Ipi was influencing the tribes; if Razcol withdrew to Tal camp for the night, this would be taken as a sign of weakness, opposition would be stiffened, making Razcol's task next day far harder.

Mountain Batteries would put down prophylactic fire during darkness to prevent more tribesmen from reaching the area of the village, supplemented by two 6-inch guns firing from Razani at almost extreme range, and 4.5 – inch 'Post Guns' firing from Dossali. Additionally, at first light, Wapiti aircraft from Miram Sha would systematically bomb the vineyards with 20–pound bombs. Razcol would resume the offensive immediately the aerial bombardment ceased. The GOC would be watching progress and required rapid results.

Before returning to my unit, I stopped off at the Field Ambulance, which I found with some difficulty in the dark, and got my elbow dressed. The senior Indian Medical Service Officer (IMS), an Irishman, as so many of them were, whom I knew slightly, reckoned I looked as if I could do with a drop of medicinal brandy – "begorrah!" – and poured a generous tot into a tin mug, which I knocked back gratefully, I had the distinct impression that he'd already sampled his stock.

We spent a wretched night on the hill-side; it was cold, my right knee was terribly stiff and aching, we had no grub, and constant gunfire made sleep impossible.

The next day was something of an anti-climax. Although the tribesmen continued to put up resistance, they had clearly been put off by the bombing and shelling, and no doubt realised the Sirkar (The Government) wasn't going to give in. We had no further casualties; the village was destroyed and burnt by about mid-day, then the column withdrew in good order across the Tochi river to the camp at Tal for the night, reaching Razmak late the following afternoon. 2nd Suffolk were on RP duty that day – I felt quite the old 'frontier-wallah' as I passed through Bn. HQ position.

It subsequently transpired that a large number of tribesmen had been killed and wounded, I can't remember how many, certainly a large number for a frontier operation, perhaps sixty killed. The Political Agent, following normal procedure, had given prior warning to the village malik (headman) of the impending attack, so all women and children had left Tappi before it was destroyed.

Major Faulder, who had been re-called to the Active List from retirement at the outbreak of the war (he'd been a Conservative Party Agent), was awarded the Distinguished Service Order (DSO) for his conduct on this operation.

Sepoys 1st/19th Hyderabad Regt. in action – Tappi Operation – 1940 – (photo by author)

Chapter 9

On leave in Kashmir 1940

For some time Arthur Campbell and I had been hoping to take leave in Kashmir. George Springfield, just back from three weeks leave in Srinagar, whetted out appetites with stories of the wonderful time he'd had with the numerous young – and not so young – unattached girls, assuring us they'd be only too anxious to give us an equally good time. To prove the point he casually mentioned that he'd got engaged to Joan Raynor, the daughter of a Punjab Police Officer in Lahore, who he'd met in Kashmir,

Arthur and I duly set off for Bannu in a local bus, a somewhat un-orthodox but cheap method of transport, squashed between Khassadars (armed Pathans in Government pay, theoretically employed to prevent trouble, in practice bribed not to misbehave themselves), goats, chickens, the lot. I don't think we told anyone, if we had we might not have been given permission as it was perhaps a bit risky – but all went well. From Bannu we went by train to Rawalpindi, where we hired a taxi to take us to Srinagar the capital of Jammu and Kashmir, a Hindu State, although ninety percent of the population were Muslims, hence the constant internal strife, still persisting today. The ruler, Maharaja Hari Singh, a Dogra – high caste Hindu – was advised, supervised would perhaps have been a more appropriate word, by a British Resident. As a young man he'd been involved in a much publicised scandal in England, he was always referred to in Court as 'Mr. A'.

The two hundred and fifty mile journey from Rawalpindi to Srinagar began with a climb of seven thousand feet to Murree, a large hill station, where the pungent smell of pine trees reminded me of my childhood days in the Troodos mountains in Cyprus, bliss after the heat and dust of the plains. The road, hacked out of the hillside, followed the course of the mighty Jumna river below as it tore twisting and turning between vast hills, dotted here and there with apparently inaccessible hamlets – so high up they were almost out of sight from the road – on its way to join the Indus river hundreds of miles away, surging through narrow gorges carrying floating timber down-stream at a tremendous rate. We stopped at the frontier Customs Post at Baramula, prior to entering the Vale of Kashmir. A memorable drive, stupendous scenery, the whole journey an adventure – we were in great spirits as we neared the fabled city of Srinagar.

The manjhi, the owner of our houseboat, met us as arranged. We settled into our small floating home on Nagin Bagh, a breathtakingly beautiful lake, surrounded by magnificent tall red and purple leafed chenar trees, a species of maple, casting long reflections on the still water, with a backdrop of hills constantly changing colour throughout the day. Houseboats were moored all round the lake; they had originally been built for Government Officials and Service Officers in the days when home leave could only be taken once in seven years, often at much longer intervals, before the advent of liners made the passage home quicker and cheaper. The boats were – and still are – flat-bottomed with a superstructure of unpainted carved deodar wood, all constructed to a similar design, adequately furnished and equipped. A sitting room facing the lake with steps down to the water, a corridor with bedrooms off it, a bathroom with tub and thunder-box. An outside staircase led to the flat roof where one could sit under a canopy and watch the world go by. Behind was the cook-boat where the manjhi and his family lived and meals were prepared.

The following morning we joined the little informal club, the centre of activity on the lake. It had a dance floor, a bar, and served simple meals. That evening we met several friends there and danced to a five-piece Indian band, jolly good they were too – until the early hours. The girls were pretty, the drink reasonably cheap – we enjoyed ourselves.

As there were hardly any roads and few cars, we hired shikaras, small flat-bottomed skiffs with a canopy, embroidered curtains round the back and sides and a long reclining cushioned seat for two. They had strange names – ours was 'Suffering Moses'! The crew, generally two Kashmiris squatting in the stern, could move them along the endless canals and backwaters at a good lick with their heart-shaped walnut paddles. Ideal for taking a girl back to her house-boat after a dance – as I soon discovered.

Most people on leave were army or in Government service, but there were also a few box-wallahs from Calcutta, Bombay and even from far away Madras. Families of officers stationed in the plains spent several months in Kashmir, so there was a lot of choice for lusty young bachelors, I didn't miss many opportunities, but I wasn't in the same league as Arthur, who quickly fixed himself up with a very obliging 'grass widow'.

Before leaving Razmak I'd been unofficially deputed to vet Joan Raynor, George Springfield's fiancee, who was then staying in Gulmarg, ten miles south of Srinagar and several thousand feet higher up (9,000 feet); the only way to get there was by riding a small local pony – a tat – up a steep winding track, there were no vehicles. It was a lovely peaceful place – with wooden chalets, known as huts, amongst the fir trees around two quite good golf courses; in winter it was the skiing centre for India.

I located Joan who was staying with friends, and asked her to go to the golf club with me for a meal. When I arrived to pick her up, she was already mounted on her tat, wearing a short fur coat over a long evening dress. Before riding to the club we stopped off at a hut where some friends were having a drinks party – then on to the club for a meal, followed by dancing. I'm ashamed to say that over indulgence, coupled with the rarefied atmosphere, was too much for me, I felt distinctly squiffy. I liked Joan and was able to report favourably on her on my return to the Battalion – more than she could do for me I imagine!

After a week on Nagin Bagh, Arthur and I thought we ought to give a party. Arrangements were duly made by the manjhi and our bearers. A lot of folk turned up, it must have been a success judging from the many return invitations we got. The impact of so many young women and 'grass widows', after years of celibacy, was pretty traumatic – they were all so attractive, desirable and sometimes accommodating! I had a close shave with a 'deserted wife', then fell for an extremely pretty girl, the daughter of a Sapper Colonel – I proposed to her in the Shalimar gardens where we'd gone by shikara for a picnic – what more romantic a place could one find to propose? – she was too sensible to take me seriously. Many, many years later we met again in Camberley – she was a super girl.

The *in* place to go for a dance in Srinagar was Nedou's Hotel.

Officers 2nd Bn. The Suffolk Regt. Raznak – Waziristan 1940

Standing: Lieuts: Ingle, Newton, attached Sikh Officer, Henderson, Swannell, Capt. Springfield,
Lieuts: Hildersley, Richards, Rasul Singh, Forrest, Mathieson.
Sitting: Capts: Ferrier, Bevan, Majors: Yates, Dean (Adjt), Lt.Col Eley (CO), Major (QM) Hill, Major March, Capts: Freeland and Copinger Hill

One went after dark by shikara along the canals, a longish distance from Nagin Bagh, so one had plenty of time to get acquainted with one's partner, conducive to intimacy – especially on the return journey. The excellent Kashmir State Police Band, under a British Bandmaster, played there during the summer season. In those days everyone danced pretty well, the marvellous music of Cole Porter and Gershwin helped, we all knew each other – great fun.

After three weeks poodle-faking, it was time to take some exercise, I was keener than Arthur. So, following a shopping spree on the Bhund (bank), a footpath beside the Jumna river, choosing numdas (embroidered felted wool rugs), walnut cigarette boxes and pipe-racks with the regimental badge carved on them, raw silk bedspreads beautifully embroidered with silk thread in the chenar leaf motif, papier-marche lamp holders, exquisitely painted with kingfishers and flowers, we decided to visit a firm of Kashmiri contractors to hire camping equipment for a short trek.

Following the customary flowery welcome, the two contractors sat us down on fine Persian rugs, gave us sweet green tea in tiny cups, then, speaking in Persian through an interpreter, gradually got round to business. We left an hour later well satisfied, having agreed to hire tents, porters, ponies, food etc: at half the figure they'd first mentioned – even so I'm sure they made a handsome profit.

Our three-day trek through pine forests, up to and above the snow-line, was a great experience. On the track we passed colourfully dressed Kashmiri women on tats, hiding their faces as they went by, otherwise, except for woodcutters sawing the magnificent deodar cedar trees into planks with a double-handed saw – one man standing on the propped up log the other in a pit below – we hardly met a soul. The second day we climbed Mount Aphawat, 11,500 feet, to a frozen lake. I was very short of breath. Even at that altitude it was hot – we still wore our topees! I wished we'd had time to do a longer trek.

When we got back to the houseboat our leave was almost up, time to make arrangements for our journey down to Rawalpindi. We cadged a lift in a friend's car into Srinagar. Also getting a lift was a chubby, bubbly, young married woman of about thirty, brown eyes, snub nose, shortish dark brown hair, sexy, terribly attractive and full of character – quite a one. Four of us squashed into the back seat, Peggy (as I'll call her) sat on my lap. I told her I hoped I'd meet her again in about three months time in Rawalpindi, where her husband, a major in the Indian Army, was stationed – apparently her marriage was a bit dodgy.

While in Kashmir we'd been out of touch with world events, so knew little about the progress of the war in Europe. On rejoining the Battalion I noticed a distinct air of foreboding in the mess, the older officers with WWI experience were deeply concerned about the fate of the 1st Battalion, serving with the British Expeditionary Force (BEF). Maps of Europe were pinned to the walls – the delights of Kashmir faded rapidly – the war suddenly became personal and sinister.

By then I'd been an Acting Captain for six months, so qualified for Temporary Captain, which meant that I'd keep Captain's rank for the duration of hostilities unless I gained further promotion. Such speedy advancement had never entered my head in peacetime, it gave me quite a kick getting letters from my parents addressed to 'Captain Bevan' – but none came from Murna.

I was still OC B Company. RP duties continued as before, but the tribesmen seemed to have decided to lie low after the Tappi operation. Emergency Commissioned Officers started to join us. Two of the first to arrive were Peter Forrest, and David Ingle. Peter served with great distinction with 2nd Suffolk in Imphal, during the Burma campaign, winning the Military Cross and Bar – he now lives in Canberra.

Great effort was devoted to keeping the soldiers fit and entertained. George Springfield, Arthur Campbell, an attached officer named Maurice Newsom and I put on a 'Minstrel' turn at a Regimental concert – rather racist by today's standards – banjo, ukueles, and singing by Arthur, who fancied himself as a tenor and actually sang extremely well. I don't remember much about it, we'd fortified ourselves with copious doses of dutch courage, it went down well with the troops.

Before leaving Razmak we carried out the 'Shield Hanging' ritual in the Officers' Club, an occasion for a mammoth party thrown by a departing unit for all officers in the garrison. The shield, displaying the regimental crest, was hung on a wall in the bar, the chap chosen to do this had to climb round the room hanging onto the picture rail without touching the floor with his feet, rather puerile, but good fun.

Before departing, all British units fixed a brass plaque – engraved with the regiment's badge and dates of service in Razmak – on the Guard Room wall close to the camp's main entrance – perhaps 2nd Suffolk's plaque is still there?

Late November 1940 the Battalion clambered into Bagai open

trucks, the Government approved Pathan transport firm, and to the stirring strains of the pipe-band of The Patiala State Infantry, set off down the road we'd all got to know so well – closing yet another chapter in The Twelth of Foot's long history.

Chapter 10

Last Days with 2nd Suffolk

Shortly before 2nd Suffolk moved down to Rawalpindi ('Pindi), the CO's Orderly came to my room one evening and told me the Colonel (Pat Eley – Murna's uncle) would like a word with me. Crossing the small lawn to his room I tried to think of any horrors I'd committed, or things I should have done but hadn't, I couldn't think of any – why should he want to see me so late in the evening?

Pat was as affable as usual; we chatted for a while about Murna and this and that. I was still wondering why he'd sent for me when he said "Silvanus – can you keep a secret?" I said he could rely on me. He then said Colonel Bill Gough, CO of the 1st/2nd Gurkhas, who I'd met on a few occasions, wanted a word with me – I was to go to his billet in the Gurkha lines straightaway. I asked Pat Eley to give me some idea what it was all about, he said he couldn't, Bill Gough would tell me. As I was leaving he emphasised that I wasn't to mention a word about this to anyone. I was mystified – what was up?

Arriving at the Gurkha mess several chaps I knew pressed me to have a drink, wanting to know the reason for my unexpected late visit – I gave a guarded reply and was taken up to Bill Gough's rooms. He was a thickset chap of about forty three, he'd lost his right eye in WW1 and been awarded the Military Cross; a very popular CO, beloved by his Gurkha riflemen. He soon came to the point – GHQ Delhi had decided to raise a parachute battalion of four companies, one British, two Indian and one Gurkha, he was to be the CO. He would shortly be going to the UK for a course at the Parachute Training School at Ringway near Manchester. He'd heard about my stint with 1st/19th Hyderabad during the Tappi operation, and thought I'd be useful in a composite unit – would I like to be the battalion Intelligence Officer?

This came as a complete surprise. I'd been dreading the prospect of more regimental soldiering. Here was a golden opportunity of getting away from dreary Internal Security duties, perhaps even a chance of seeing some action. No one at that time had much idea what parachuting involved – there was something special about it, even a touch of glamour, and maybe extra pay! Without hesitation I gave my answer – a very definite "Yes." Bill said he'd keep me posted.

With hindsight, this was undoubtedly one of the turning points in my life. The whole direction of my army career changed. Had I not volunteered my war would have been very different – it's pointless to speculate on what might have happened to me. At the time I realised I might well not come through the war unscathed – not that I gave it much thought – but I did, to tell this tale.

On arrival in 'Pindi the Battalion marched from the station round Queen Victoria's statue to the barracks we were to share with The East Yorkshires (I think). Our Mess was near the barracks, I was allotted one of three single officer's quarters close to the Mall, the main thoroughfare in the large cantonment.

At about this time Pat Eley handed over command of 2nd Suffolk to Lieut. Colonel Hugh Monier-Williams, and left for the UK with his wife Mary and their two small daughters. I was sorry to see him go, I liked him and he was a link with Murna.

I didn't relish the prospect of a Christmas in 'Pindi, so decided to try for sandgrouse and duck on a jheel I'd heard about forty miles away in the Salt Range, where there was a small dak bungalow. Our Bandmaster, Mr. Longstaff, lent me his collapsible rubber-skinned canoe, and off I set on the 23rd December 1940, with my bearer Babu, my dog Rover and several bottles of rum – whiskey being unobtainable – in an old open two-seater car provided by our contractor, Shaboodeen.

Babu and I settled comfortably into the tiny isolated dak bungalow. A small stream flowed through the little garden where jonquils grew giving a wonderful scent, unusual in otherwise almost desert conditions. I'd finished my curried chicken and rice supper, and was looking forward to a rum-lime-and-soda and a read by the light of an oil-pressure lamp, when I heard a great beating of wings and a lot of 'cawing' – I didn't recognise the sound. Rushing outside, I was just in time to see a large bunch of flamingoes wheeling over the jheel, the last shafts of sunlight catching their dazzling scarlet under-wing plumage – a fantastic sight.

I had three blissfully peaceful days and some excellent sport. At sunrise, flocks of sandgrouse, twittering to themselves on the wing, arrived from all directions at tremendous speed, to drink at the jheel. I got two brace the first morning, which was lucky as I was depending on them for food. Even with the canoe the duck were difficult to reach; I bagged a white-eyed pochard and several common teal – one of the prettiest of duck. When I got back to 'Pindi, I felt a bit guilty at having skipped the Christmas festivities, but I'd had an inexpensive and satisfying leave – the flamingoes had made it well worth while.

Late one afternoon not long after, two companies, one being mine, were ordered at short notice to parade in full marching order with rifles – no LMGs – and fifty rounds SAA per man. By the time we'd assembled, the parade ground had been invaded by a motley collection of garishly painted 'desi' (local) buses with civilian drivers.

The CO held an O Group (Orders Group) and explained that we were to move straightaway in the buses by a back route to Kohat, a frontier station ninety-five miles away, crossing the Indus at Khushalargh. Knowing the road was mostly unsealed and very indifferent, I thought we'd be lucky to make it in the ropey vehicles – the battalion still had no motor transport of its own.

Colonel 'Monier-Bill', as he was affectionately called by the soldiers, told us two company commanders, in confidence, that our task was to disarm a Nepalese battalion which had mutinied (not part of the Indian Army, the officers were mostly relatives of the ruling dynasty and of indifferent quality). A plan of action would be agreed with Kohat Garrison Commander on our arrival, only then could we tell our men what was afoot.

We set off as it was getting dark, strict orders were issued to keep quite and not advertise our departure. The troops took it in their stride, a welcome change from barrack routine. The road, as I'd expected, was atrocious. We stopped en route for a mug of char, surprisingly we had little trouble with the buses, only one failed to make it; as the windows were unglazed we were cold and stiff when we arrived at sunrise, another brew-up of char soon restored our spirits.

The Kohat Garrison Commander, Colonel 'Monier-Bill', a Gunner Major, the British Adviser to the Nepalese battalion, myself and the other Company Commander worked out a plan to tackle this rather tricky situation. The Nepalese Commander-in-Chief was due to arrive at seven, in about an hour's time, to address the battalion which by then would be formed up on the parade ground. We were relieved to hear that their weapons – other than their fearsome kukris knives, traditionally carried by Nepalese – had cleverly been collected the day before by Indian Army Ordance Corps armourers under the pretext of checking their serviceability, and were held in the Arms Kot (armoury) guarded by British troops.

Over night the Royal Artillery had positioned guns on low hills commanding the parade ground. The two companies of 2nd Suffolk, out of sight behind buildings, were to march on in column and take up a position in line, either side of a central flight of steps leading down to the parade ground. Magazines would be charged beforehand, when in position facing the Nepalese battalion, the order 'Load' would be given.

All went to plan. We marched on in column, wheeling to the right and left when we reached to top of the steps. Below us the Nepalese battalion, about five hundred strong, was drawn up in open order. Colonel Monier gave the order 'Load', followed by 'Port Arms' – rifles held across the chest with 'one-up-the-spout'. The mutineers were then told to remove their kukris, place them on the ground beside their right foot, then take a step forward. This was the critical moment – would they obey? Mercifully, after a few seconds of touch-and-go one or two obeyed the order, then, to our great relief, they all followed suit. The kukris were collected in sacks by BORs (British Other Ranks) and taken off to the arms kot.

No sooner than this had been accomplished than the Nepalese C-in-C, a relative of the King of Nepal, a stocky man with an enormous walrus moustache, dressed in an imposing uniform, accompanied by his entourage, appeared from the rear and passed through the centre of our ranks. Positioning himself at the top of the steps he proceeded to harangue the troops on parade in Gurkhali, which I found difficult to follow. After delivering a tirade on their despicable behaviour, how they had disgraced Nepal and so forth, an ADC read out the names of the ring-leaders. As each name was called out the wretched fellow left the ranks, climbed the steps almost on his knees, grovelled before the General begging for mercy. They were smartly shackled with handcuffs and leg-irons, then whisked away – presumably to their death in Nepal. The remainder were ordered to their barracks. We marched off, had meal, then returned to 'Pindi in the buses. It later transpired that the Nepalese officers had been watering their men's milk and pocketing the proceeds, which caused great resentment and lead to the mutiny.

Training was becoming more arduous. A large scale exercise was laid-on by HQ Northern Command, perhaps to establish the feasibility of defending the line of the Indus river against a Russian invasion, or just manoeuvres to test the efficiency of formations, I'm not sure which. In any case it was hard going for 2nd Suffolk, and the last time I was to be on training with the battalion.

I don't remember how the exercise began, perhaps we marched down the Grand Trunk Road, but I clearly recall getting into cattle trucks at Lala Musa, a railway junction seventy- five miles south of Rawalpindi. After a ghastly journey in stifling heat, we de-trained not far from Chilianwallah, the site of a particularly bloody battle in 1849, during the Second Sikh Wars. (It is commemorated by an impressive obelisk in the grounds of the Royal Hospital, Chelsea, in London, slap in the centre of the annual Chelsea Flower Show, though I doubt if anyone ever notices or knows anything about it). On de-training, a soldier became violently sick and unable to control his bowels. The MO pumped saline solution into him, but he was completely dehydrated – I don't think he recovered. The first time I'd seen such a severe case of heat exhaustion, rather frightening.

We marched along the bank of a wide canal for some thirty-five miles until dusk, when we took up a defensive position south of the Jhelum river, not far from a canal headworks at Rasul. We were completely exhausted – my knee was giving me hell. There was little water to drink, no food, the mossies made sleep impossible – agony! Colonel Monier-Williams, who'd won the Military Cross and Bar during WW1, said to me while we were trying to rest, that it had been the hardest march he'd ever experienced, I fully endorsed his remarks. A never to be forgotten ending to my service with 2nd Suffolk.

Instructions came through for me to attend a course at the School of Military Intelligence at Karachi – fixed by Bill Gough before he left for the UK – so the cat was out of the bag as it were. At the same time Lieut. Col. Martin Lindsay and Major George Lea, his Adjutant, arrived in 'Pindi to select volunteers for a parachute battalion he was to command. Interviews were held in the cricket pavilion behind 'Pindi Club. When my turn came I explained that I'd already been selected by Bill Gough – they didn't know this. However, I gathered that instead of one composite parachute battalion, a parachute brigade of three battalions was to be raised in New Delhi, consisting of a British, an Indian and a Gurkha battalion, under Bill Gough's command. This was a rather worrying change; I wouldn't know until Bill Gough returned from the UK how I would be affected. From then on I became a 'spare-file', still on 2nd Suffolk's strength, but liable to depart at any moment.

Anticipating leave would be difficult in future, I applied for and was granted two weeks, and set off for Kashmir, hiring a small houseboat moored in a backwater of Srinagar. It was cold, snow covered the ground, good duck shooting weather. There were few English people, however, the daughter of a Calcutta box-wallah (businessman), an attractive Russian girl of nineteen whom I'd met before in Kashmir, was living by herself on a houseboat nearby, we had great fun. I never found out why she was there – a spy perhaps!

She tagged along with me when I was invited to take part in big shoots on several jheels in the area organised for the Maharaja's benefit. We were taken in a punt to a hide; the Maharaja started the shooting on an adjoining jheel, the signal for everyone to blaze away, the idea being to keep the birds moving between jheels. On the second occasion I got my largest bag ever, 104 birds, mostly duck, a few snipe – the barrels of my gun got too hot to hold. I certainly wouldn't enjoy it now, but then there were vast numbers of wildfowl and whatever one may think – it was tremendous sport.

The totally unexpected alliance between Germany and Russia caused a scare – Russian parachute troops might perhaps be dropped into Northern India (now Pakistan). HQ Rawalpindi District decided to form an ad hoc Anti-Parachute Column, consisting of one platoon of the East Yorkshire Regiment (I think) and a company of Indian troops, commanded by a Jemadar, under the overall command of Captain Bevan of 2nd Suffolk; somewhat ironic in view of my future service with paratroops.

I was authorised to hire a car (previously Pat Eley's) and got a liberal petrol allowance; my second-in-command, the East Yorks platoon commander, hired an old motor bike. I also hired four clapped-out desi buses with civilian drivers to move the troops. No one had any idea as to how we should go about our nebulous role of repelling enemy parachutists. It was left to me to recce likely dropping areas – an almost impossible task in such a vast area. Major General Freeland, the GOC, gave me a pep talk. A charming chap in the Frontier Force Rifles, related to both Dick Freeland of my Regiment, and Ian Freeland of the Norfolk Regt.

(I've already mentioned that Ian knew Murna).

It was good fun, no one had a clue what we were up to. I could go more or less anywhere I liked with my little army. I reconnoitred the oil fields at Attock, and the area around Abbottabad, a cantonment the headquarters of several Gurkha Regiments with a good club, both possible VPs (Vulnerable Points). A large anti-parachute exercise was laid on by District HQ, my Column acted as 'enemy'. I don't think many lessons were learnt, however, I ensured that my outfit qualified for 'hard lying allowance' – very handy at several rupees a night.

As a result of Russia's alliance with the Axis Powers, and having heard about the black-out regulations in England, HQ Northern Command decided it was time something similar ought to be done in the Punjab; accordingly a black-out was instituted in Rawalpindi. In due course, the RAF was instructed to fly a Vickers Valentia transport aircraft over 'Pindi, to find out the effectiveness of these precautions. I was instructed to accompany three District HQ staff officers travelling the hundred miles up the Grand Trunk Road to RAF station at Peshawar, from where we would carry out this vital mission.

We duly arrived, clambered aboard the early 1920s Troop Transport/Bomber twin-engined aircraft – the pilot and observer sitting in the open cockpit wearing leather helmets and goggles – and took off into the dusk heading south for 'Pindi, one of the most uncomfortable and tedious flights I have ever endured. Top speed with a tail wind was 120 mph, cruising speed 80 mph. When climbing the exhaust manifolds around the two radial engines glowed bright red, levelling out at about 2000 feet there was a faint glow, descending all went black, it was possible to follow our stately progress by watching the exhaust manifolds. No sound-proofing, the engine noise was deafening and the hinged webbing seats on either side of the fuselage weren't exactly the height of comfort – it was perishingly cold.

As expected, apart from the cantonments, the black-out was virtually non-existent. Our pilot circled round a few times, then thankfully we headed back to Peshawar where we spent the night in the RAF mess. This was my first flight in a Vickers Valentia, it didn't occur to me that within a few months I'd be jumping out of one!

Apart from these diverting interludes life in 'Pindi began to pall – but there were compensations. In those days the 'Pindi Club, the social centre of the large military station, had a high reputation. As well as providing tennis, squash, cricket, a swimming pool and other sporting facilities, it boasted a restaurant and an excellent ballroom, where dances were held on Wednesdays and Saturdays.

Our Mess joined the Club en block. As it wasn't far down the Mall I went there the first saturday after our arrival. The ballroom and bar were crammed with officers, some in mess kit, some with wives. Members of the Queen Alexandra's Royal Army Nursing Corps from the British Military Hospital in their attractive uniforms – short scarlet capes over long grey silk dresses and white caps, a sprinkling of unmarried young girls and lots of 'grass widows' whose husbands were either serving overseas or out of station for various reasons.

I gravitated to the crowded bar, managing to squash in next to two young women sitting on high bar-stools and ordered a Murree beer – whiskey being unobtainable. There was such a crush that the two 'girls' at first didn't register. Then it dawned on me – I'd met them in Kashmir, the one next to me in a long black taffeta dress – rather low cut – was Peggy. "Hello there! Fancy meeting you again". I can't remember whether she said this first or I did. Holding her close we danced to 'Begin the Begine'. The feel of her soft warm body pressing against mine, the scent of her hair, the rustle of her dress, the look in her eyes as she smiled up at me humming the tune, was altogether too much, I was in a whirl – completely bowled over! We got on famously, dancing together for the rest of the evening – and I took her home!

Her husband was away on a course, she was living in quarters with her two children. Her father had been in the Indian Army, she'd been in India a long time and knew lots of the high-ups. Four years older than me, I must have seemed a very insignificant young officer to her, but she appeared to like me. I'd never before met anyone so sophisticated, sensuous, vivacious, outspoken and full of character – she dazzled me. I thought she was terrific, being with her flattered my ego. Years later my brother-in-law, Otto Edholm, put it rather neatly: "I approve of a young man having an affair with a married woman, always providing she's not my wife."

Instructions for me to attend the course at the School of Military Intelligence at Karachi came through. As I was to be accommodated in The Excelsior Hotel, I decided to leave Babu and Rover in 'Pindi. The six-week course was interesting, rather than stimulating. It was extremely hot, I found keeping awake during afternoon sessions difficult. I made tentative plans for a cheeta shoot, in the desert north of Karachi, during the mid-course three-day break, but there wasn't enough time as it involved a lengthy trek by camel, so I abandoned the idea. Instead, I went with two chaps on the course by car to see the Sukkur Barrage across the great Indus river. This enormous barrage, one of the finest British engineering achievements and a magnificent legacy to what is now Pakistan, controls the flow of five great rivers: the Chenab, the Jhelum, the Ravi, the Sutlej and the Beas, flowing through the Punjab to join the mighty Indus on its way to the Indian Ocean south of Karachi.

Back again in 'Pindi, I was terribly upset to find that my dog Rover had been killed by a car in the Mall during my absence. A great loss, poor old chap, we'd had many happy times together. I was daily hoping to hear about joining the parachute outfit, but nothing came through and no one appeared interested, try as hard as I could, I got no joy out of HQ 'Pindi District. So, thoroughly fed up, I went up to the flesh-pots of Murree, the hill station nearest 'Pindi, where most of the headquarters staff, and all those families able to find accommodation in married quarters or hotels, moved to during the hot season. The attraction for me was that Peggy was staying in a hotel there. The climate was marvellous, flowers in profusion, gladioli in particular, pine trees, a golf course not far away at Burban, and a friendly club which saw a good deal of us both.

All good things have to end, in my case the ending was abrupt and almost final. Leaving Murree in the early hours after a boosey party the night before, I'd negotiated the worst of the hair-pin bends down to 'Pindi and had about ten miles to go, when I must have fallen asleep at the wheel of my old MG Magnette and crashed into a culvert. All I can remember is finding myself on my back in a ditch, unable to move as my right arm was pinned under the overturned car above me. With great difficulty I summoned enough strength to prize the car up with my left foot just enough to extricate my arm. I made a tourniquet with my braces round my right wrist, which was spurting blood at an alarming rate, and lay down on the ground. Mercifully fairly soon some locals came along in a tonga; they got out and helped me up beside the driver who set off at a smart trot for 'Pindi. Although no one was about at that hour of the morning, and there were no villages in sight, word had somehow spread. After half an hour an army ambulance appeared, I gave the tonga-wallah what loose change I had and was whisked off to the BMH in 'Pindi.

I'd not been there long when Colonel Hugh Monier-Williams came to see me, typically nice of him. My injured right hand was examined – as it was the height of the hot season the doctors decided it would be best if I was operated on in the BMH in Murree where it was cooler. So off I was taken in an ambulance back up to Murree. I was operated on straightaway by an Indian Major in the IMS who did an wonderful job – I've very good reason to be grateful for his skill. I stayed in hospital for two weeks, then convalesced in Murree for a fortnight. Needless to say, with Peggy there, I didn't waste any of my unexpected leave.

I persuaded a young officer, fresh from a Motor Transport Course, that the wrecked car was what he needed for instructing his drivers. If a hose-pipe was substituted for the missing radiator the engine worked okay, the chassis was more or less intact, perfect for 'demonstration purposes', what was more – it was an MG. I got five hundred rupees – his CO was furious.

Captain W. S. Bevan – Rawalpindi, 1941

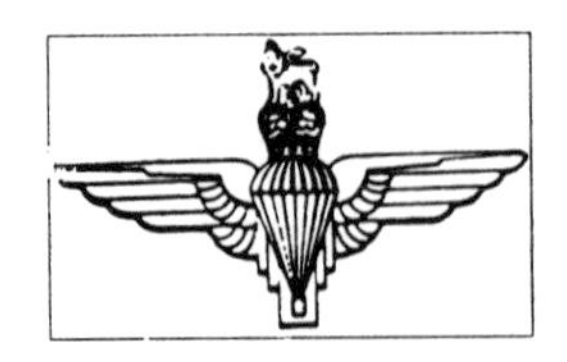

Chapter 11

The Early Days of 50 Indian Parachute Brigade 1941–1942.

Orders eventually came through that I was to take up the appointment of General Staff Officer Third Class (GSO 3) at the RAF Air Landing School (ALS) in New Delhi. I had no idea what it involved – presumably to do with parachuting. It was something of a comedown on arrival to find that the ALS had taken over the Willingdon Flying Club, a modest establishment with one hangar and a short grass runway. I was to share a sort of dormitory in the club with five RAF officers – not at all what I'd been accustomed to, but hopefully the precursor of better things.

The first few weeks in October 1941 at the ALS were pretty chaotic. The Station Commander, a Temporary Wing Commander, pleasant enough but rather ineffective, having neither the breadth of vision nor sufficiently high contacts at Air HQ India to overcome intrenched scepticism, in some quarters of the RAF down-right opposition, to the concept of a parachute formation in India.

No worthwhile job could be found for me at the ALS, so I became involved with the nucleus of 50 Indian Parachute Brigade forming under Bill Gough, by then a Brigadier. Bill, Bernard Abbott ('Abbo') CO designate of 152 Indian Para Battalion, and Paul Hopkinson ('Hoppy') the Brigade Major, had all just returned from a parachuting course in England. Bill with a leg in plaster, Hoppy in plaster from the waist to the neck – results of heavy landings in strong winds – not exactly an encouraging advertisement for potential volunteers! The others were the Brigade Staff Captain, Reggie Steward a regular Indian Army Officer and myself.

While Bill was still on crutches we held meetings in a prestigious government bungalow in Hastings Road, New Delhi, where he was living, it belonged to a friend of his in the Indian Civil Service (ICS). Afterwards we forgathered in a small bar at the Imperial Hotel for pre-lunch drinks, where we often met Bernard Fergusson of the Black Watch, then awaiting a posting. (He subsequently gained fame as a Chindit commander; on retirement was appointed Governor-General of New Zealand).

A number of parachuting instructors had been posted to the ALS from Ringway – Captain Peter Law of the Royal Ulster Rifles, and several senior NCOs. The Chief Parachuting Instructor was Flight Lieutenant Bill Brereton, then in his late forties, of imposing presence and many years service in the RAF. A tented camp for ALS officers was set up beside a dusty road close to the airfield, I was told to organise an Officers' Mess, and authorised to spend a specific amount setting it up from scratch. After much haggling, I bought everything we needed from a bunia in a back street of Old Delhi.

As PMC I was responsible for stocking the bar, so visited a firm of wine merchants in Connaught Circus, New Delhi. Ushered into the manager's office, I was surprised to be confronted by an English woman, most unusual, especially in India. She enquired how she could help me. After settling my business, I asked if I might look at the prints of wildfowl on the walls of her office, she said "Go ahead", explaining that she too was keen on shikar.

The upshot was that she invited me to go out shooting with her the following Saturday – she'd produce a picnic lunch and had a good shikari. Being in business she got a generous petrol allowance for her car – how could I resist such an offer? Over the next few months we went out most saturdays together, on one occasion I shot a bar-headed goose, the only goose I ever shot in India in spite of many fruitless attempts in Kashmir. We had a lot of fun. This sort of thing happens in wartime.

The ALS had three Vickers Valentia bi-plane troop transport aircraft, converted for dropping parachutists by the simple means of cutting a hole in the floor of the fuselage. They were very ancient machines, and as events proved, totally unsuitable for their new role.

151 Parachute Bn., the British unit under Martin Lindsay, recruited from the twenty-three British battalions serving in India, was in the process of forming in the cantonments about five miles

away. At first jumps were made onto the polo ground adjoining the ALS, but after several fatalities, due in part to the restricted size of the Dropping Zone (DZ), a new area further away at Palam was selected (now Delhi International Airport, then merely scrubby waste ground). John Waddy (Murna's cousin) a Lieutenant in 151 Bn., had a lucky escape when he had a 'Roman Candle', i.e. his parachute failed to develop fully, but lived to take part in several parachute operations including 'Market Garden' – the battle at Arnhem where he was wounded and taken prisoner.

Without any prior training, I got myself included in a 'stick' of ten the day that the Viceroy and Vicereine, Lord and Lady Linlithgow, visited the DZ. I was delighted to have made an easy landing, but surprised, to say the least, to be introduced to this immensely tall, august personage and his equally daunting wife. I'd managed to avoid landing with a bleeding nose, the tendency being to push off too violently when the Green Light went on and the RAF Despatcher shouted 'Jump!', resulting in hitting the cowling on the opposite side of the hole with a thud – and a nose soon spurting blood.

When Winston Churchill replaced General Sir Archibald (Archie) Wavell with General Sir Claude Auchinleck ('The Auk') in the Middle East, Archie Wavell became Commander-in-Chief of all forces in India and the Far East. Not long after we'd started parachute training, he came out to the DZ at Palam to see how we were getting on – I was detailed to accompany him.

Peering at my shoulder flashes with his one eye, he saw 'Suffolk', and said "A jolly good regiment, they were under me in Blackdown". I replied "Yes Sir, you interviewed me for a Regular Commission there." As he'd lost his left eye and Bill Gough his right eye, it was a bit tricky when they met, but they got on well together.

The General and his family lived in the C-in-C's House in New Delhi. Their son, also Archie, a Captain in the Black Watch, the General's old regiment, had been to my uncle Charles's school in Sloane Street. My cousin, Tommy Bird, the General's ADC, who also had been to Gibbs's school, invited me to lunch at the C-in-C's House on two occasions; I talked about my uncle with Lady Wavell, who said how fond she was of "Dear Mr. Gibbs". Young Archie was killed in 1954 during the Mau Mau campaign in Kenya.

While the Brigade was training in Delhi cantonments, the C-in-C often rode out in the early morning to see how we were getting on. We had a very dark-skinned Anglo-Indian (Eurasian),

Officers 151 Parachute Battalion – Delhi Cantonments, 1942

Back row: Lieuts Twidle PW(A), Taylor, Gibbs PW(A), Young, Adams, (A) escaped, Montgomery WPW(A)
Centre Row: Lieut. Wenner; Capts. Blundell, K(A), Buck (RMO) PW(A), Page, K(A), Waddy, WPW(A), Fowles (joined SAS), Clegg PW(A), Lees (Force 136), Lieut Willcock WPW(A), Capts Wainwright (A) escaped, Suter, PW(A), Gilchrist PW(A) 11 Para Bn.
Seated; Capt. Satterthwaite, 1 Para Bn., Sicily, Majs. Bevan, 50 Indian Para Bde, Webber PWW(A) 11 Para Bn., Thomas 2 i/c K with 2 Wilts, Lieut. Col. Hose (CO), General Wavell C-in-C India, Brig. Hope Thomson 50 Indian Para Bde, Capt Patterson – K with SBS, Majs Lea WPW(A), Lonsdale W(A), Powell (A).
Key; K – Killed, PW – Prisoner of War, W – Wounded, (A) – Arnhem.

Sergeant Macdonald, on Brigade HQ staff, who'd enlisted in India into the Black Watch, prior to being transferred to the Indian Army Corps of Clerks. I knew the General liked to have a word with the men, so I had the HQ clerks, who were in PT kit without any distinguishing badges, drawn up in line. Coming to Sgt. Macdonald I said "And here is a sergeant in your regiment, Sir". If he was surprised, he didn't show it – he wasn't someone you could try to be clever with.

Events in the Far East were moving swiftly to a climax. Japan, after joining the Axis Powers invaded the whole of the South East Asia, overrunning the Dutch East Indies, Malaya, Singapore and threatening Burma. Every aircraft that could be spared was hastily despatched from Europe and the Middle East to India, for onward routing to Rangoon. Despite the fact that the ALS's short runway was enveloped in a cloud of dust as hundreds of coolies, mostly women, were hurriedly lengthening it with the help of a few steam rollers, an assortment of fighter aircraft, including American radial-engined Buffaloes (?) touched down to refuel – I doubt if many of the pilots survived. This forcefully brought home to us the fact that the war was real, indeed on our doorstep.

Parachute training in Delhi from a Vickers Valentia, 1942

In mid-1942 prewar habits hadn't changed much in India, especially in New Delhi, the Imperial Delhi Gymkhana Club was still as formal as ever. Mr. Irvine, whose eponymous company was the leading producer of statichutes and parachutes in the USA, was invited to visit India with a view to setting up a factory in Kashmir, using local silk. I was detailed to look after him when he came to Delhi. I'd decided to take him to the IDGC for a drink and a meal the day after his arrival, which happened to be a saturday, a dance evening. I was in khaki drill uniform, Irvine was in a tropical suit. While having a pre-prandial drink in the bar, the Club Secretary came up to me and said that as my guest wasn't in a dinner jacket, he was afraid he'd have to ask him to leave. I was horrified, taking the Secretary to one side I explained the situation, but he was adamant. I enlisted the assistance of a senior officer who happened to be around, only then did the Secretary relent – "As a special case, mind you!" I felt extremely embarrassed.

My cousin, Major General Clarence Bird, Master General of the Ordnance at GHQ (later to become Lieut. General Sir Clarence Bird and to live to the great age of a hundred) and his wife Dorothy, asked me to dinner in their bungalow one evening, afterwards we went on to the IDGC. It was just about the time the battleships the *Prince of Wales* and *Repulse* were attacked and sunk by Japanese aircraft in the Bay of Bengal, a severe blow to British prestige in India. Not even this appeared to change the tempo of life at the IDGC.

The army presence at the ALS had been increased by the appointment of Major John Martin of the Dogras, Indian Army, as GSO 2. He'd come straight from the Staff College, Camberley, and had taken part in the disastrous campaign in Norway before returning to India – in theory he was my immediate superior. We got on well, but as there hadn't been enough for me to do when I was on my own, with two of us there was even less, I became very frustrated.

Brigadier Tim Hope Thomson had recently taken over as Brigade Commander – Bill Gough being considered too old for the job. Tim, only a few years older than me, one of the early army parachutists in the UK, had been selected to take over 50 Indian Parachute Brigade – he was then the youngest brigadier in both the British and Indian armies. His parent regiment being the Royal Scots Fusiliers, he insisted, against all Dress Regulations, in wearing his regimental Glengarry (head-dress), the standard dress being a pith helmet (topee).

Fortunately there was a switch round of jobs at HQ 50 Parachute

Brigade in Delhi cantonments – the job of Staff Captain became temporarily vacant. Tim fixed with the ALS for me to fill this post until a permanent replacement arrived; this suited me famously, at last I'd got a worthwhile job. I moved out to cantonments and soon got to know 151 British and 152 Indian Para Bns., both then almost up to strength.

Being at Brigade Headquarters Army Council Instructions found their way into my 'In-tray', one relating to applications for the Staff College at Quetta, the Indian Army equivalent of the Staff College at Camberley, particularly interested me.

Prewar, to qualify at either Camberley or Quetta Staff College, and get the vital letters psc (passed staff college) after one's name in The Army List, had been an absolute sine qua non for higher promotion. As a regular officer I felt now was the time to apply. Wartime courses lasted under six months, instead of two years, and the peacetime competitive entrance exam had been abolished 'for the duration'; if I survived the war, it would pay off handsomely later on. I approached the Brigade Major, Hoppy Hopkinson, who said "Go on and apply". The Brigadier recommended my application, which was duly forwarded to GHQ Delhi – and that was that. In the rush of events that followed I forgot all about it.

The political situation in India was anything but stable. Mahatma Ghandi, the venerated pacifist leader, initiated his Civil Disobedience Campaign of non-cooperation with the Government – adopting the slogan of 'Quit India' for his policy of forcing the British Raj to hand over power to Indians.

Sir Stafford Cripps, a member of the British War Cabinet, during a visit to India in March 1942, promised India Dominion Status and equality with the UK and the other Dominions – Canada, Australia, New Zealand and South Africa after the war. The 'Cripps offer', as it came to be known (I listened to him explaining it on All India Radio) was rejected by both the powerful Indian Congress Party, and the Muslim League representing the majority of Muslims in India – roughly those now in Pakistan.

Gandhi was arrested and detained until May 1944. The Indian National Congress was declared an illegal organization and Nehru was imprisoned. Subhas Chandra Bose, a pro-Axis Bengali agitator, escaped to Germany via Afghanistan. (He subsequently travelled by German submarine to Singapore, where he raised the Indian National Liberation Army (INLA), recruited from renegade Indian Army POWs captured by the Japanese). Such was the background to the widespread sabotage and violence which broke out all over

India, resulting in many deaths and thousands of arrests.

The situation in Delhi became critical. 50 Para Brigade, still in the cantonments, was called out to assist the police in maintaining order. We established our HQ in the Police station in Chandni Chowk, the main bazaar in Old Delhi. 151 Bn positioned Vickers machine guns at either end of this famous street leading to the historic Red Fort built by the Moguls – the Union Jack flying proudly over the entrance.

Travelling in a light truck with a Gurkha escort, I sped through New Delhi, and on to the Kashmir Gate in Old Delhi. (During Siege of Delhi in the Indian Mutiny of 1857, this famous gateway was stormed by Major General John Nicholson, commanding the relieving force who was mortally wounded in the assault). I joined Brigadier Tim Hope Thomson and the Commissioner for Delhi outside the Kotwal (Magistrate's Office), the latter had just been issued with a .38 revolver and appeared to be having difficulty loading it, I withdrew discretely to a safe distance.

We remained on duty in the Old City for about a fortnight, extremely hot and uncomfortable. The only occasion I personally got involved in any serious trouble was when word came through that the railway station was on fire. No troops being immediately available, the Brigadier told me to organise a patrol, which he would lead. Arriving at the station we saw no sign of a fire, but the excited Station Master, emerging from the fastness of his office, pointed up the line to where there was indeed smoke and flames. We raced up the line, lead by our gallant Brigadier – three British officers, three BORs and ten Gurkhas – without any idea what we were going to do.

Two buses were on fire on a bridge over the line, the arsonists made off as we approached. As there was nothing we could do about it we carried on, running down narrow alleyways jammed with people who dispersed up side streets. There was some stone throwing and an all-pervading rumbling, vibrating sort of noise – thousands of people bawling and shouting – one could almost feel the pent-up antipathy. I found this most upsetting; only a few months before I'd been walking around unarmed, everyone all smiles. Why the sudden change? I didn't believe there was any deep-rooted anti-British resentment.

Shortly after the riots had subsided, I was posted to 151 Para Battalion as a Company Commander, and promoted to Major – a big step to put up a Crown (major's badge of rank) on my shoulder straps. I'd achieved the rank of Field Officer after seven years service, unheard of in peacetime. The move was comparatively easy as I already knew most of the officers in the Battalion, some being good friends, notably Majors Dicky Lonsdale, who gained fame at Arnhem, and George Lea who was captured there (later to become Lieut. General Sir George).

When I joined, 151 Para Battalion had just been through a traumatic period. The original CO, Lieut. Col. Martin Lindsay, had quite unexpectedly been removed from command. As a young officer he'd been on an Antarctic Expedition and had the rare distinction of being awarded the Polar Medal. After the war he retired from the army becoming and MP. Subsequently he was created a Baronet. When acting as Staff Captain, I'd arranged the passage home for him and his family; prior to embarking at Bombay, he found time to write a letter of thanks for my help, a gesture I much appreciated. A controversial character, he slipped-up badly with 151 Bn., but later commanded a battalion of the Royal Scots Fusiliers with distinction in N.W. Europe, being awarded the DSO. His replacement, Lieut. Colonel 'Socks' Hose, of the Bedfordshire and Hertfordshire Regiment, awarded the DSO in the North African Desert campaign, was a very different type; he likewise didn't last long. I got on well with them both.

Just before I joined 151 Bn., Peggy arrived in New Delhi from 'Pindi to work in a high-grade cypher unit, part of Lord Louis Mountbatten's South East Asia Command (SEAC). We saw quite a lot of each other but it wasn't easy; I'd no transport and cantonments were five miles from where she was living. However, we went to dances at the Cecil Hotel in Old Delhi, and met when I could get away and she was off duty. I was still very smitten by her.

Rumour was rife that the Battalion would soon be leaving India. General Wavell paid us a visit and addressed all Officers, Warrant Officers and Senior NCOs. He said he knew how fed-up we were at not yet having been given an active role, but assured us our turn would come; meanwhile it was our duty to remain steadfast and not bellyache. He was a man of few words, what he said had a profound effect on all of us. Before we eventually left for the Middle East he inspected the Battalion, took the salute as we marched past, sat for an officers' group photo, I've still got a copy – many in it were later killed at Arnhem and elsewhere – I was one of the lucky few to survive.

Chapter 12.

With 156 Parachute Battalion in the Middle East. The Quetta Staff College

We embarked at Ballard Pier, Bombay, on 20th November 1942. On leaving Delhi, hoping to deceive enemy intelligence, we had changed our designation to 156 Para Bn. Our ship was fast, so we didn't have to sail in convoy, although Japanese submarines were still active off the Horn of Africa. I shared a cabin with Dicky Lonsdale, he taught me to play bridge during the voyage. An uneventful passage through the Indian Ocean, up the Red Sea to Port Tewfik at the southern end of the Suez Canal where we disembarked, then by rail to Gineifa on the Canal, a vast base area for Middle East forces. We marched from the station through tented camps, occupied for the most part by wartime soldiers who came down to watch us as we passed; they had never before seen a battalion of prewar regulars, real 'Old Sweats', many with years of overseas service – much banter and ribaldry was exchanged.

Our camp at Gineifa Point on the Suez Canal, between the Great and the Little Bitter Lakes, was non-existent. After a scratch meal knocked-up somehow by the cooks, we kipped-down exhausted on the sand – it was jolly cold. The camp was beside the Canal, a Greek Army battalion of scruffy brigands on one side, and the recently formed Special Air Service (SAS), who we got to know quite well, on the other. Tents eventually materialised – I shared one with Dicky Lonsdale.

We trained hard in the desert, up the escarpment to the west of the Canal as far as milestone 90 on the Cairo road. No aircraft were available, so we could only do ground training which I hated as it involved jumping from far too high a platform for my liking onto none too soft sand – agony for my gammy knee. A short course in tank driving was far more to my liking.

Soon after Christmas 1942, I was holding after-breakfast 'Petty Sessions' in the open-fronted officers' latrines, when the Adjutant, Captain Ian Patterson, who'd just rejoined us from India, spotted me ensconced reading the *Egyptian Times*. He called out: "Oh Bertie, I meant to tell you before, when I was in GHQ Delhi I heard that you'd got a nomination to Quetta, the course starts early in February". I thanked him for letting me know, thought about it, decided I didn't want to leave the Battalion at this juncture, and continued reading my newspaper.

Realising the prospect of 156 Bn. being employed in a parachute role in the near future was slim – transport aircraft was fully stretched supplying the Eighth Army in its advance under General Montgomery against the German and Italian forces under Rommel – I reconsidered this unexpected chance of attending the Quetta Staff College course. My friends told me I'd be a fool to chuck up the chance, so I approached the CO, 'Socks' Hose, who hadn't done a staff course himself and tended to play it down, especially as all I'd got was a verbal message through Ian Patterson. 'Socks' wasn't prepared to help, but said he'd no objection to my taking it up with the with Brigadier Shan Hackett, the recently appointed Commander of 4 Parachute Brigade. Time was of the essence – I fixed with the Brigade Major to see the Brigadier next day.

Shan Hackett was a cavalryman and very gallant officer. He subsequently commanded 4 Para Brigade at the battle of Arnhem, was seriously wounded – hidden by the Dutch partisans until fit enough to be secretly flown back to England. He rose to be a Full General. After retirement becoming, inter alia, quite a TV personality. I'm glad to say he's still going strong.

I explained the situation. Shan was prepared to let me go to India for the course, but said he couldn't fix transport without written authority, which wasn't forthcoming. Realising time was short, he asked whether I could get to Delhi under my own steam. I assured him I could. He then asked me what I'd do, if on reaching Delhi I hadn't got a nomination after all – did I know anyone who would help me? I told him a cousin, Major General Clarence Bird, was Master General of the Ordnance, I thought he would be prepared to help. Shan asked how was it that with such an exalted relative I hadn't already been to the Staff College? "Good luck, off you go" – or words to that effect.

The following day I set off on an army BSA motor bike for Middle East HQ in Cario, ninety miles each way, a terrible pot-holed road jammed with military traffic. After holding the accelerator twist-grip for sixty miles, my right wrist, which had been weakened by the car accident in Murree, started to ache horribly, the only way I could keep going was to stretch over with my left hand to steady my right hand – a somewhat dangerous manoeuvre but there was no alternative. I located my cousin Tommy Bird, then employed in HQ Middle East, and with his help succeeded in getting authority to go to India. Armed with this vital bit of paper, I returned to Gineifa Point, arriving late at night, very played-out, my wrist pretty well useless.

A few days later, having handed D Company over to Bill Satterwaite, I travelled in the back of an open lorry full of troops, to the transit depot in Kasir el Nil barracks in Cairo, where I shared a room with a wartime officer in Lovat Scouts, a solicitor in civil life. I'd arranged to meet my cousin, Tommy Bird, at Shepeards Hotel one afternoon – we'd only just met when General (later Field Marshal) Maitland-Wilson, spotting Tommy, came over and had a word with him; I was considerably impressed (Tommy had been awarded the DSO while serving with 2nd Rifle Brigade, he also won the MC and Bar and was severely wounded several times).

Realising that there was little chance of cadging a lift off the RAF, I decided to try my luck with the United States Air Force (USAF) based on the Heliopolis airport. Chatting to American officers in the bar, I succeeded in persuading the pilot (a Captain) of a large transport plane – very advanced at the time – to give me a lift to India. He wasn't sure when he'd be leaving, certainly not for two days, I assured him I'd come at a moment's notice, and would keep in touch. We left it like that.

My solicitor friend, a keen racing man, took me to the Heliopolis races next day. He knew the form, so we had a profitable and most enjoyable afternoon at this beautiful course – very sophisticated and civilized after Gineifa Point. He insisted that I take out a life insurance policy (I now realise he must have got a rake off). My life was duly insured for a thousand pounds with the Prudential Assurance Company, I'd become a man of substance! With no flight scheduled for the next day, we went off to Giza to see the pyramids and the Sphinx. There were no tourists, hardly anyone other than ourselves and the local guides, so riding on camels we had an unhindered look around.

Word came through 'We take-off tomorrow 0500 hours'. I got to the airfield by taxi with my baggage – a steel ammunition box and a kit bag – just in time. Clambered aboard an enormous plane, settled down as best I could amongst assorted cargo in the hold – a terrific vibrating and a deafening roar from the four engines – no sound-proofing – and we were off. An imposing Master-Sergeant informed me "Cartoooum next stop – Major, only a thousand miles – Okay?"

We landed on a grass strip south of Khartoum, where the Americans had set up an airfield. After dumping our kit, six to a room, the US Captain asked if I'd like to join a party going to Khartoum by taxi, I said "Thanks, I would". Following a meal in the all-ranks canteen, mainly American 'K' rations and coffee, nevertheless most welcome, five of us set off the fifteen miles to Khartoum. I was dropped off at the very British Khartoum Club, the others were anxious to visit the bazaar to buy mementoes, and generally enjoy themselves, not quite my line. I settled down to whiskies and sodas on the terrace overlooking the Nile, bliss after the shattering noise of the aircraft.

We took off again very early next morning. Flew over Eritrea sufficiently low to be able to see the country which I found fascinating, especially the areas the Italian colonists had successfully cultivated. After a flight of over fourteen hundred miles, we touched down at Salalah, a god-forsaken spot on the coast just inside the State of Oman, where we spent the night sleeping under the aircraft's wings, 'guarded' (?) by a local militiaman sporting a handsome curved dagger stuck in his belt, a bandolier and an ancient Lee Enfield rifle. The Yanks were fascinated, offered vast sums of 'rooopeees' for his dagger, but, strange to relate, he rejected their blandishments. The following day we flew on to Delhi, where I bade farewell to the American crew; they'd looked after me quite excellently – as nice a bunch of guys as one could ever hope to meet.

On reporting to the Military Training (MT) Branch at GHQ New Delhi I had a bit of good luck, the staff officer handling staff college postings was a contemporary of mine at Sherborne. Plunging straight in, I asked him: "Am I on the next course?" He thumbed through long lists of names. I was getting worried; turning back to the first page again he paused – then read out "Bevan. Yes, here you are, you're to report in two days time; leave here tomorrow, not much room on the line, so we're sending chaps up in alphabetical order; you're one of the early ones. I'll give you a rail warrant – Okay?"

My relief at finding my journey hadn't been in vain was tempered by the fact that I'd have to leave the next day, not at all what I'd had in mind. However, I'd heard that the course didn't actually start for a week, so I felt pretty confident I could delay my departure for a few days – I'd chance it anyway. I phoned Peggy, she was sharing a flat off Connaught Circus with another girl, conveniently away, so she offered to put me up. The time flew, we had fun, but the situation was becoming difficult and really rather hopeless. Being more worldly-wise than me, she wouldn't let either of us get hurt by becoming too involved. She meant so much to me that I found this difficult to accept, but I knew she was right.

When 151 Bn. left India, all heavy baggage including mine, had been stored in a large disused cast-iron water tank on tall brick piers in the Red Fort in Delhi. I needed some thick clothing as Quetta was about five thousand feet up. After a struggle, I found my boxes, got out the things I needed, but was horrified to find, that despite a liberal distribution of moth balls, white ants and moth had got in. There was nothing I could do about it except hope for the best.

Quetta lies four hundred miles north of Karachi in Baluchistan, at the western end of the Himalayas, now the boundary between Afghanistan and Pakistan. When I was there it was a large military base, guarding the Bolan and the Chaman passes into Afghanistan and Persia. In 1935 there was a tremendous earthquake, the bazaar area being the epicentre, thirty thousand people were killed instantly.

The original college buildings were inadequate for the increased number of wartime students, so hutted accommodation had been built. My neighbour was George Gilbart-Smith of The Buffs, a most exceptional character, we'd been at Prep school together. In 1941 he was on the troopship *Lancastria*, crammed with troops in a French harbour, when she was attacked by the Luftwaffe, a bomb passing straight down her funnel. George spent the next twenty four hours in a ship's rowing boat, frequently under fire, hauling men and bodies out of the water; a fine effort for which he was awarded the Military Cross. He arrived at Quetta straight from a Commando operation in China, his tin-trunk full of assorted weaponry including a 'Tommy gun', the sub-machine gun favoured by American gangsters. In civilian life he ran a night-club in London.

The Commandant, Major General Geoffrey Evans, was a short fiery officer, with a distinguished record in the Western Desert campaign. The Directing Staff (DS) were mostly Lieutenant Colonels with battle experience. We worked in syndicates of eight under a Tutor, mine was 'Mouchu' Chaudhri, a fine Indian Army

Cavalry Officer (after Independence he played a leading role in the absorbtion of Hyderabad State into the Republic of India).

We were worked hard, always against the clock, frequently until late at night, producing solutions to complicated exercises covering all forms of warfare. Syndicate solutions were discussed in the main hall; sixty students sitting on tiered seats on three sides of an enormous sand-model on the floor, the DS at the other end. It required strong nerves when the DS called out your name to get up and explain your syndicate's plan – especially if Geoff Evans was there.

At the end of the course we were all interviewed by the Commandant. When my turn came he told me I'd done quite well, I'd be returning to 50 Indian Para Brigade at Campbellpore as Deputy Assistant Adjutant & Quartermaster General (DAA & QMG), a Second Grade (major's) staff appointment. I saluted, about-turned, was just leaving his office, when he called out: "Just a moment Bevan" – I wondered what was coming next! "Bevan, you're inclined to be intolerant, watch it." I replied "Yes Sir" and marched out. As a matter of fact I think he was quite right – I expect 'Mouchu' Chaudhri had primed him.

I enjoyed the course, it broadened my military knowledge, previously limited to regimental soldiering. I was more confident and effective, what's more, I'd got those vital three letters, psc, after my name in the Army List.

Visit by Gen. Sir Claude Auchinleck. C-in-C, India and Major General 'Boy' Browing to 50 Indian Parachute Brigade, Campbellpore. Punjab, 1943. Brigade H.Q. Officers.

Standing, (from left): *Major Bevan DAA & QMG; (Capt.) Buckle Staff Capt.; Capt Allen Bde I.O.; three visiting officers; Major Beale BM; Capt. Sylvester Bde S&T Officer; Col. Ridgeway GHQ Delhi; two USAF pilots.*

Sitting, (from left); *Gp. Capt. Donaldson, OC 177 Wing RAF; Brigadier Tim Hope Thomson, Bde Comd.; General Sir Claude Auchinlech C-in-C India; Major General Sir Fredrick 'Boy' Browning; Colonel Abbott, Deputy Bde Comd.*

Chapter 13

With 50 Indian Parachute Brigade During the Burma Campaign

Campbellpore was a dusty, arid, little town in an extremely hot part of the Punjab, just over a hundred miles north west of 'Pindi, off the Grand Trunk Road to Attock and Peshawar, with few, if any, redeeming features. Garrisoned since Victorian times, the Elephant Lines were still standing, but no elephants. It is named after General Sir Colin Campbell, famous for his relief of the Residency in Lucknow during the Indian Mutiny of 1857, when the garrison, with their families, were besieged for many months under appalling conditions.

50 Indian Para Brigade consisted of 152 Indian, 153 and 154 Gurkha Para battalions; 44 (Royal Bombay) Para Squadron, Indian Engineers; a Signal Section; a Medium Machine Gun Company (Vickers guns) and 80 Indian Para Field Ambulance. The officers were almost entirely British, with Indian and Gurkha troops – all volunteers. I shared a bungalow with Gerry Beale, the Brigade Major, responsible for operations and training, I looked after what is was now termed logistics. The airfields were far away, but over the months we built up a happy relationship with the pilots and crews. The Wellington bomber aircraft, unsuitable for parachuting, were replaced in September 1943 by three squadrons of Dakotas of 177 Wing Transport Command, a great improvement and morale booster.

The war in the East was going badly – the Japs had driven the British out of Malaya and Burma. Apart from a small reconnaissance operation in late 1942, when a party of 153 Gurkha Para Bn. and Brigade Signals personnel, commanded by Captain Jimmy Roberts, was dropped into north Burma, there had been virtually no contact with the enemy (in the early planning I was to have taken part in this operation, in the event there was no room for me in the Hudson aircraft.) Jimmy was awarded the Military Cross (post-war he became a distinguished mountaineer – he now lives in Kathmandu). Tim Hope Thomson had to cope with endless hair-brained plans dreamt up by GHQ planners. One, I well remember, was to drop us onto Akyab, an island off the coast of Burma. The fact that it was stiff with Japs and a drop there would undoubtedly have resulted in the annihilation of India's only parachute formation, took a lot of explaining to the know-alls in GHQ.

There was a lot to do, but with no relaxation or social life we became stale and frustrated; we got the occasional evening at the 'Pindi club, but it was a long drive, and without Peggy it held little attraction for me. I shot partridge and green pigeon nearby, but there was little else.

We attracted an endless procession of visiting top-brass including the 'Auk' – General Sir Claude Auchinleck – who had by then taken over as C-in-C India from General Wavell. A splendid imposing man for whom I had the greatest respect, as did all the Indian and Gurkha troops. Major General 'Boy' Browning, Director of Airborne Forces at the War Office in the UK, stayed with us for a few days and lived up to his reputation as 'Number 1 Beat-up-king' (his wife Daphne Du Maurier, the novelist, chose maroon as the colour for paratroops' berets) – we were all pretty whacked by the time he left! There were many others all anxious to see 'the dare-devil parachutists', not really an appropriate description, I for one was only in it for the extra pay!

Just before Christmas 1943 we did a Brigade HQ drop – Tim Hope Thomson was in the aircraft in front of mine. Just as well neither of us knew that one of his 'stick' (section of parachutists) was to have a 'Roman Candle' (the parachute failed to develop properly) and was killed. This was the last jump I did in India – I can't honestly say I was disappointed.

I went at short notice on a liaison visit to HQ 14th Army at Comilla in East Bengal, close to the Indo-Burma border. I flew in an RAF Dakota to Dum Dum, the airfield north of Calcutta, where we spent the night under the aircraft's wing, mossies made sleep impossible; on to Comilla next morning, then to Chittagong to liaise with the staff there. This was my first glimpse of Bengal from the air, it looked flat, a network of lakes and ponds and predominantly green – a complete contrast to the Punjab.

14th Army, under General Slim, was engaged in heavy fighting in the hilly Arakan peninsular on Burma's west coast. Although the Japanese advance in this area had been stemmed, the situation was extremely critical. Further inland the Japanese had advanced north as far as the mighty Chindwin river. Although as yet there was no serious fighting on this front, V and Z Forces, small intelligence-gathering groups under British officers operating close behind the enemy lines with local Naga and Kuki tribesmen acting as scouts, were reporting a big Japanese build-up.

HQ IV Corps, commanded by Lieut. General Scoones, was in Imphal the capital of the remote State of Manipur, only accessible from Kohima to the north down ninety miles of tortuous road with many hairpin bends – still being improved to take heavy vehicles. In peacetime the only Europeans had been the Resident and a few Government Officials. The town lies at the north end of a large plain, forty miles long by twenty wide, swampy in the south, surrounded by high mountains covered by rain forests and thick bamboo jungle.

The local hill tribes were the head-hunting Nagas, a custom which, in theory, they'd given up. They wore little other than a red blanket and a profusion of beads; the men carried spears decorated with feathers, a long blow-pipe for poisoned arrows and a dah – a sort of machette – mainly for cutting bamboo – dangling over their bottoms; primitive and engaging folk, normally loyal to the British Raj.

On my return from Comilla, Gerry Beale straightaway told me that the Brigade was shortly going to Imphal for a limited period 'for jungle warfare training under active service conditions' including patrolling down to the Chindwin river, with the firm proviso that it was to avoid becoming involved in any serious fighting. I found this somewhat ambiguous.

During my visit to 14th Army HQ I'd sensed a feeling of uncertainty, perhaps even apprehension, in the air. Pondering what Gerry had just told me, I wondered whether the Brigadier fully appreciated what this training role might lead to. If the Brigade showed up well, surely IV Corps would be loathe to let us go. More likely we'd end up in a ground role, thus saying good-bye to any parachute operation for which we'd trained so long. 177 Wing RAF had been switched to transporting and supporting Major General Orde Wingate's Chindit Columns, operating behind the enemy lines in Burma, indicating to me that we were unlikely to be used in a parachute role in the foreseeable future. This, coupled with our lack of combat experience, accounted for an increasing sense of frustration amongst officers and troops alike. I felt Tim Hope Thomson was snatching at any opportunity to get us involved in operations in the hope of rebuilding our morale. I expressed my reservations to Gerry – he said the decision had been taken, it was up to me to get the 'Q' side (logistics) buttoned-up.

The Main Party consisting of 152 and 153 Bns., the MG Company, Sappers and Miners, Signals and the Field Ambulance would move by rail and river steamer to Dimapur, then by road up to Kohima (154 Bn. was not yet operational). I was to fly with the Advance Party and make arrangements for the brigade to camp in the vicinity of Kohima. Major Harry Butchard a friend in 153 Bn. and some others accompanied me. Flying low over Kohima to avoid Jap Zero fighter aircraft, we could only see a carpet of tree tops below and high mountains in the hazy distance. We landed on a bitumised hessian runway just north of Imphal and reported to HQ 23 Indian Infantry Division under which the Brigade was to operate.

That evening IV Corps Commander addressed his Staff outside his HQ. From what he said it was evident the situation was deteriorating rapidly – an involuntary shudder of apprehension ran through me – I didn't sleep much under my mossie net in my basha (attap hut) that night.

The few days before the Brigade arrived were hectic. I had a talk with the Officer in Charge of Administration, Major General Alf Snelling, a highly esteemed and charming staff officer, terribly overworked, but still able to make time to help a mere major in some newfangled formation. Having obtained a jeep, I motored the ninety odd miles of twisting road to Kohima, 5000 feet up in misty, blue-grey hills, where the Brigade was to be temporarily based. Kohima, a large hill-top Naga village, was the administrative centre of the Commissioner, Charles Pawsey, (later Sir Charles) a most excellent official with a fine WW1 record. Being in the cool of the hills, Kohima had developed into a Convalescent and Rest Area, with a large base installation nearby.

A camp site had been selected for us at Chakabama, ten miles east of Kohima, down a steep jungle track hewn out of the hill-side just wide enough for a jeep. There were no dwellings, merely a clearing in the jungle with a small stream. Thirty or more miles further east, at 6000 feet, the Assam Rifles had an outpost at Phokekeduzmi, the track then turned south west to Jessami and on to the larger village of Ukhrul, forty or so miles north east of Imphal.

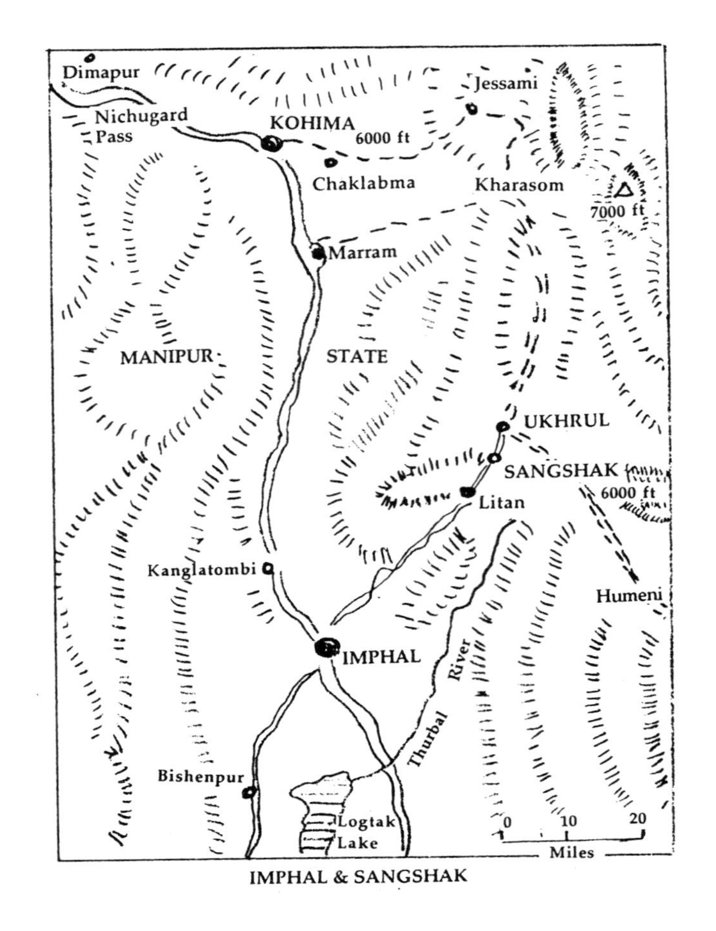

IMPHAL & SANGSHAK

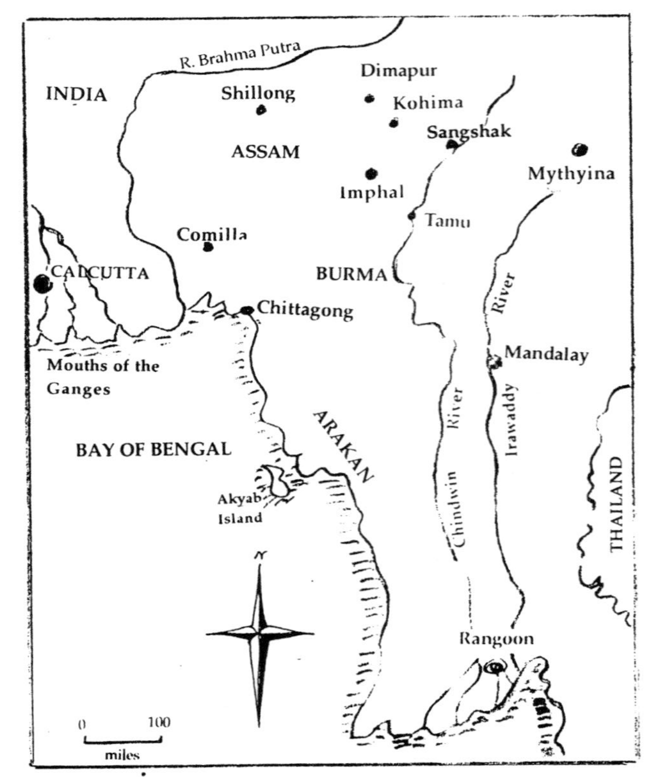

BURMA & ASSAM

Punjabi Musalman Paratrooper, 50 Indian Para Brigade, 1943

Gurkha Paratrooper. 50 Indian Para Brigade, 1943

While waiting for the Brigade to arrive, I was summoned by the Kohima Garrison Commander and told to assist Lieut. Col. Borrowman, Adviser to a Nepalese State battalion, who was carrying out a reconnaissance of the immediate area, with a view to producing a plan for the defence of Kohima. Borrowman was not only a delightful companion, but also a talented artist – his watercolours of Indian Army soldiers are well known, some hang in the Royal Military Academy, Sandhurst. We bumped about in a jeep over the surrounding hills deciding where we'd site company and platoon defensive positions, all rather academic. Little did we imagine that within ten days or less the whole area would be swarming with Japanese, Kohima itself besieged and under constant intense attack for the best part of two weeks.

After the tedious journey across India, the Brigade arrived and quickly sorted itself out at Chakabama. There was no tentage to speak of, but the rains hadn't started, so we made ourselves as comfortable as possible in our fox holes. A gang of civilian mochis (cobblers) arrived to adjust harness for pack mules for the machine guns, but the arrival of the animals was overtaken by events. We had no transport apart from a few jeeps. There was nothing to do but wait for instructions from HQ 23 Division – an awful anti-climax.

Chatting to Gerry Beale a day or two later we suddenly heard the sound of an aeroplane approaching. Looking up we saw the distinctive red circle on its wings – a Jap Zero! Gerry said "This is it", or words to that effect.

The next day (17 March I think) we received a radio message, instructing the Brigade to move immediately to Imphal and start training under the command of 23 Indian Division. The Brigadier told me to get up to Kohima and organize transport on the football pitch, the only suitable bit of level ground in the area. I shot off up the narrow track in my jeep, arrived at the football pitch to find the Inter-Convalescent Depot Football Championship finals in progress. Ordering play to stop – much to the spectators' annoyance – I marshalled the Royal Indian Army Service Corps (RIASC) vehicles on the pitch. After marching up the steep ten mile track, a rather puffed 152 Bn piled into the vehicles in great heart. Action at last! Everyone was excited and keen to get cracking, morale was high. Off they went – I was never to see many of them again. 153 Bn. followed a day later.

I then looked in on the Commissioner, Charles Pawsey, several other officers were in his bungalow planning the defence of Kohima – Borrowman's and my efforts seemed to have been overlooked. Pawsey gave me a welcome drink and a bite to eat, I gave him what information I had, then left in the darkness – feeling apprehensive and lonely. With hindsight this was quite an historic meeting. Within a few days Charles Pawsey's bungalow and tennis court became the centre of a very bloody and heroic resistance against ferocious Japanese attacks lasting ten days or more. 'Kohima' is now a proud Battle Honour of the Royal West Kent Regiment.

Events moved rapidly. The next day, 21st March, a radio message from Brigade instructed me to move immediately with everyone still in Chakabama, to Litan, on the track from Imphal to Ukhrul, where Rear Brigade HQ was to be established. Late that evening I set off to Imphal in my jeep with Major Mike Rolt, commander of the Sappers & Miners Para Squadron; unknown to me 2nd Suffolk (123 Brigade 5th Indian Division just flown in from the Arakan front two hundred miles away) moved up from Imphal to Kohima the same night, we must have passed in the darkness. Not until we reported to HQ 23 Division on our way through Imphal, did we hear that the Brigade had already been in action beyond Litan and had suffered casualties.

Litan was a small abandoned Naga village twenty miles north-east of Imphal and 3000 feet higher, at the end of a narrow winding metalled road, which from then on became a dirt track. It lay at the junction of two valleys, one with a stream, surrounded by dominating hills – totally indefensible. 49 Brigade of 23 Division had previously been based on Ukhrul, a large village further up the track, and had established a rear administrative area at Litan elements of which were still there when we arrived, including a motley collection of sepoys from several regiments, a Field Ambulance, a Mobile Surgical Team, an ammunition dump, three Mule Companies with hundreds of mules and stacks of bhoosa (bailed straw) a Ration Issuing Section, an LAD (light vehicle repair workshop) and canteen stores.

Everything was above ground, no defence had been planned, indeed, when we turned up the doctors of the Field Ambulance were enjoying cold beers in their mess tents with table-cloths spread ready for a meal – they were quite stroppy when we insisted they took urgent action to prepare to move – "Why all the fuss, old chap? There aren't any Japs within forty miles" was their attitude – they were soon to be disillusioned. We evacuated most of these units to Imphal during the next two days.

Jack Newland, second-in-command of 153 Bn, was appointed Litan Box Commander. He'd arrived with two hundred of his

Gurkhas, just too late to get through to Sangshak, where the Brigade was already heavily engaged. Although the senior by service, I carried on as Brigade DAA & QMG. Jack and I reconnoitred the position, decided on a defensive perimeter, allocated units to sectors and exhorted everyone to start digging-in whilst some daylight remained. We established a Rear Brigade HQ in a central and reasonably protected position, and made radio contact with Brigade. A stand-to was held at dusk; the small parties of sepoys from 49 Brigade were a bit jumpy but no attack was made on the Box (the name used for an all round defensive position) that night. The next day a Stuart light tank (also known as a 'Honey') was sent up, the young cavalry officer was unhappy – it was against all armoured teaching to use a tank singly.

The following four nights we were shot-up regularly after dusk, the Sappers & Miners Para Squadron took the brunt of the action, holding off repeated determined attacks and inflicting considerable casualties on the enemy. A dead Jap was recovered and displayed outside our HQ – the first soldier of the up to then Invincible Japanese Imperial Army we had seen. He didn't look quite the bogeyman we'd visualised, considering the gruelling time the poor chap must have been through he appeared remarkably fit. The Japs didn't bother us much during daylight, nor had they blocked the road, so we evacuated many of the remnants of 49 Brigade to Imphal.

On the 26th March, Brigadier Geoffrey Evans, Commander of 123 Brigade of 5 Indian Division (I'd last seen him when he was Commandant at Quetta Staff College), came up to Litan to assess the situation, he didn't like what he saw and ordered the Box to be evacuated forthwith. (5 Indian Division had just arrived in Imphal after being hurriedly flown in from the Arakan front to reinforce IV Corps – the first time a whole Division had been transported by air).

It was a rush to get all the units, vehicles and animals away from Litan before dusk, the last to leave were the Sappers and Miners. Anything which couldn't be moved was to be destroyed by delayed action incendiary charges – they didn't prove very effective. We got away before the Japs started their nightly 'jitter' tactics of sniping, mortaring, shouting, throwing grenades and generally making mayhem. It had been pretty unpleasant – it could have been a lot worse.

Meanwhile, ten miles up the track from Litan, the main body of the Brigade was in serious trouble. We followed the battle raging at Sangshak on our radio equipped with a loud-speaker powered by a contraption something like a bicycle. The Brigade was clearly in desperate straights – it was unnerving listening to the radio traffic and being unable to help.

After crossing the Chindwin, the Japs had advanced up the hill tracks with artillery carried on elephants, heading for Kohima via Ukhrul, thence, onward into India. 152 Bn. the leading formation in the Brigade, reconnoitring the tracks in hilly country to the south east of Ukhrul was slap in the way of the Jap advance and soon became heavily engaged. However, it inflicted such heavy casualties on the enemy that the Japs had to re-group and make new plans.

The Brigade, still theoretically on training, consisting of 152 Bn. and three-quarters of 153 Bn., most of the 4/5 Mahratta Light Infantry (left behind by 49 Brigade), two artillery heavy mortar batteries, the Brigade Vickers machine gun company – in all about two thousand men, had been surrounded and forced to take up a tactically unsound defensive position, centred on the little Naga hill-top village of Sangshak – boasting a Mission Church and not much else. There was no water supply to speak of, rations and ammunition were scarce, no defensive barbed-wire – a parlous situation.

All attacks on the perimeter were fiercely contested and repulsed. After six days of bitter fighting, casualties mounting, food, water and ammunition exhausted, re-supply drops by parachute mostly landing amongst the Japs and apparently no hope of help, a message was received over the radio from 23 Division saying 'Fight your way out. Good luck.' When dusk had fallen the Brigade withdrew in small parties through the steep jungle-covered hills and valleys the forty miles down to Imphal. Wounded who couldn't walk had to be left behind. Casualties amounted to about 900, including about 100 who were captured; the rest were either killed, wounded or died subsequently. The Japs lost about twice as many.

General Sir Geoffrey Evans in his book 'Imphal, A Flower on Lofty Heights', describes the action by 50 Indian Parachute Brigade at Sangshak as 'A Very Bloody Battle'.

General Slim, 14th Army Commander, ended a Special Order of the Day with these words:

> 'There is not a division or brigade in the Fourteenth Army which has not proved its superiority over the enemy and knows it. Your Parachute Brigade bore the first brunt of the enemy's powerful flanking attack, and by their staunchness gave the garrison of Imphal the vital time required to adjust their defences.

> To the officers and men of the 50th Parachute Brigade I send my congratulations. The Fourteenth Army has inflicted on the Japanese the greatest defeat his Army has yet suffered.
> He is busily trying to build up again and reinforce his broken divisions. He will fight again viciously, but we have paid him something of what we owe. There still remains the interest. He will get it.'

Whatever historians may say about this action, there can be no denying the fact that 50 Indian Parachute Brigade, by disrupting the Japanese timetable, significantly assisted in putting paid to their vaunted 'March on Delhi'.

* * * * *

After withdrawing from Litan I reached the forward positions of Geoffrey Evans's 123 Brigade at five in the morning, just as it was getting light, flopped down all-in on the ground and was instantly asleep – I'd not had much rest for the past four days.

The next thing I remember is waking up with a start – someone was shaking me by the shoulder. Coming to my senses, I realised whoever it was was wearing the brass numerals XII on the turned up brim of his bush hat. He asked if I was alright, I replied "Yes, but who are you, why the XII on your hat?" (The Suffolk Regiment, being the 'Old Twelfth of Foot', still used the Roman numeral XII). To my surprise he said he was second-in-command of the 2nd Suffolk. I explained I was a 'Suffolk' and knew everyone in the Regiment – I couldn't think who the hell he was! He said he was a Suffolk Territorial Army Officer – which accounted for my not knowing him – his name was Ken Meneer (he took over command of 2 Suffolk temporarily not long after). I had a lot to do, so was unable to visit 2nd Suffolk.

I found my Mahratta Driver and Orderly with my jeep, they'd become separated from me during the withdrawal from Litan. At HQ 23 Division I was told that elements of 50 Para Brigade were expected to arrive from Sangshak during the day; meanwhile what there was of us, was to take up a defensive position in Catfish Box, the name given to an open grassy area just outside the town of Imphal.

When I'd arranged the positioning of units, feeling hungry I cast around for my Orderly and Driver, but not a sign of them anywhere, nor of my jeep, they'd completely vanished – a major calamity. All my kit had been in the jeep, now I had nothing other than what I stood up in – jungle green jacket and trousers – a kukri and revolver. My bedding roll, binoculars, compass, camera, the lot – disappeared. I heard later that the vehicle had been shot-up about a mile south of Kohima, both my Driver and Orderly being killed. I never found out what really happened, presumably they misunderstood my instructions and drove the ninety miles up to Kohima. A ghastly tragedy. They were two pleasant young men. I still feel badly about it.

The whole Imphal Plain was soon surrounded and cut off by road, the airstrip remained in use to a limited extent in spite of straffing by Japanese Zeros. Food was strictly rationed – we got pretty hungry. I was re-kitted-out, and spent the next ten weeks with HQ 50 Brigade in a large, reasonably sanitary Manipuri house, constructed mostly of bamboo.

Understandably our morale was low, not only because we had suffered a defeat in our first engagement, losing many close friends and comrades which was bad enough, but also because our Brigadier, Tim Hope Thomson, who'd been in the thick of the fighting at Sangshak, to our amazement had been relieved of his command and evacuated 'on medical grounds' to India. This was unsettling for everyone, especially for his staff officers, like myself, who'd worked closely with him for so long. Not having been at Sangshak I wasn't fully in the picture, nevertheless, I felt he'd been harshly treated – made a scape-goat for IV Corps's lack of anticipation of the Jap attack through Ukhrul was the general feeling within the Brigade; I briefly met him in Delhi on my way home. (Tim returned to the UK in his substantive rank of Major, more or less under a cloud. He subsequently regained the rank of Brigadier, having been awarded a DSO and a CBE to add to his prewar MC and appointed ADC to the Queen.)

Soon after our withdrawal to Imphal, when many officers and other ranks had successfully made the difficult and dangerous trek down from Sangshak through the Japanese positions, Major General Ouvry Roberts, Commander 23 Indian Division, came round after dusk and talked to us candidly and informally. I can't remember exactly what he said, but he certainly didn't blame Tim Hope Thomson for the withdrawal.

We were now without a Brigadier; a large number of officers and men killed, wounded and missing, all our equipment lost with little prospect of a parachute operation in sight – not an exactly stimulating outlook.

As the Mediterranean was again safe for convoys GHQ decided all those with long overseas service should be sent home. I'd been overseas for eight and a half years, consequently was high on the list for repatriation. The Imphal road was reopened on 22nd June 1944, from then on the Japanese were driven back across the Chindwin and were in retreat throughout Burma – the siege of Imphal was over. There was a feeling of optimism about, but I didn't relish the idea of working for a new brigadier. Anyway, I was British Service, I'd been with the Indian Army long enough, it was time to serve with British troops again, perhaps with my Regiment – 1st Suffolk had just taken part in the invasion of Europe.

So, in mid-June 1944, I left 50 Indian Para Brigade. I'd been associated with it since it's formation in October 1941, and was sorry to go, but the thought of getting back to England was exciting, in some ways it was a relief to be making a break. I got a seat in the cab of a RIASC three-ton lorry; at the Kohima cross-roads, only a short time previously the scene of such fierce fighting, I spotted the Maharaja of Jiapur, resplendent in the uniform of the Life Guards, and waved to him, he'd been at Quetta with me – he was visiting Indian State forces. The road then dropped down through heavy bamboo jungle to railhead at Dimapur. I spent a few days in a Holding Unit, sharing a basha with a doctor from 80 Para Field Ambulance, Captain Bill Thompson, who'd been in Kohima throughout the siege (he was awarded the Military Cross) and had some staggering stories to tell.

The next stage in my journey home was in an RAF Dakota to Dum Dum, the airfield for Calcutta. The only other passengers were Major General Savory, a fine fighting soldier then Director of Infantry at GHQ Delhi, and his ADC. The aircraft was full of empty forty-gallon drums, smoking being strictly forbidden I presumed they'd previously contained aviation fuel. From Calcutta I went by rail down the centre of India to Secunderabad, just north of Hyderabad city the capital of Hyderabad State, ruled by the Nizam, a Muslim, reputedly the richest and most miserly man in India. 2nd Suffolk had been stationed in Secunderabad before moving to Mhow in 1936, so I'd heard a lot about the Nizam from the officers and their wives who'd been with the Battalion at the time.

I stayed in Trimulgherry cantonments an extension of Secunderabad, with 154 Gurkha Parachute Bn. the third battalion in the Brigade still under strength. Also there was the embryo 44 Indian Airborne Division under Major General Eric Down whom I knew slightly. After kicking my heels about for a week getting thoroughly frustrated, my Movement Order at last came through, so I set off by rail across the Deccan to Poona where officers awaiting repatriation were being assembled. I felt I was at last making headway and began to get quite excited at the prospect of seeing my parents and family again – and even perhaps a glimpse of Murna, now a widow with a small boy; her husband Sqn Ldr Hugh Thomson RAF, had been shot down and killed while flying his Blenhiem bomber over Holland in 1941, before his son's birth.

While in Poona I made friends with three splendid characters all 'Rankers' (commissioned from the ranks) we were all to share a cabin – they were older than me, two were majors, the third a captain. One was Major Hilton of the South Staffordshire Regiment, awarded the DSO while serving in Burma with Wingate's Chindits, he was quite yellow from taking mepaccrin anti-malarial pills over several months – I was also a bit yellow for the same reason. We heard that the ship was 'dry' – no alcohol allowed – so we each bought two large wide-mouthed thermos flasks in the bazaar and filled them with the most alcoholic booze we could find – local rum and brandy, Nasik gin and other horrors – lethal concoctions.

At last we were on our way. By rail down the Western Ghats to Ballard Pier in Bombay docks, well known to British soldiers since Victorian times. I'd already sailed twice from there and although I never imagined it at the time, was to do so yet again. There she was, His Majesty's Troopship *Multan*, an ex- P & O liner, named after a hot and singularly unpleasant city in the Punjab. Her sides were buckled – she'd been bombed in Port Said two years before, set on fire, burnt out, beached repaired and refurbished. No matter what she looked like, she was waiting to take me home.

We sailed on the 18th August 1944. First stop Aden to take on water and oil – no trouble from Jap submarines. Up the Red Sea, through the Suez Canal to Port Said where we joined a vast convoy assembling off Alexandria. After we'd carried out anti-aircraft drill by blasting off our weapons into the sky – there were also two 6-inch 'stern-chaser' guns firing aft – we took up our position in the centre of the front line of an armada stretching as far as the eye could see. To starboard was *H.M.S. Ramilles*, an elderly but enormously impressive 15–inch gun battleship, Headquarters Ship of the RN Commodore controlling the convoy. Over the horizon a screen of destroyers kept constant watch for submarines, we occasionally heard the rumble of their depth charges exploding. Although the *Ramilles* seemed quite close, she must have been half a mile away, surging silently through the water with a tremendous bow wave, not a sound to be heard, quite eerie, I watched her fascinated. I'd been aboard her in Plymouth in 1935 when I was with 1st Suffolk.

Off Malta we slackened speed to allow an RN pinnance to come alongside – tremendous excitement – there were Wrens (Womens Royal Naval Service) amongst the crew. The stampede to the rails to see these fabulous creatures made the ship list, the soldiers' shouting and whistling proved too much for the girls – they disappeared below decks in confusion!

Thankfully the Germans and Italians had taken such a hammering that we passed through the Straits of Gibraltar, across the Bay of Biscay and up the west coast of England unmolested. On the 17th September 1944 we sailed into the Firth of Clyde, disembarking at Greenock in Bonny Scotland.

Chapter 14

With Airborne Forces in England. Rejoin 1st Suffolk in Germany, 1945

I travelled by train, crammed with troops, to the Airborne Forces Depot at Chesterfield. After dumping my kit, I went to the mess for a drink, it was empty except for a young woman in uniform, wearing a Captain's badges of rank. I told her she was the first ATS officer (Auxiliary Territorial Service) I'd ever met. She no doubt thought I was making a pass at her.

Granted three weeks disembarkation leave, I set off for my parents' home at Bucklebury in Berkshire. As I stepped onto the platform at Reading, the nearest station, I heard the sound of aircraft. Looking up the sky was full of endless lines of aeroplanes towing gliders heading eastwards – a fantastic sight. Although I didn't know it at the time, they were part of the biggest ever but, alas, unsuccessful British airborne operation code named 'Market Garden' – the capture of the Arnhem bridge over the Lower Rhine in Holland. If I'd got back a week or so earlier I'd most probably been up there with 156 Para Battalion.

Arriving at Hatch Gate, my parents' small house, I found they'd both aged considerably and were rather infirm. My father was just eighty, my mother seventy four. She, poor dear, suffered terribly from arthritis in her right hip and was also pretty deaf; my father was suffering from glaucoma and loosing his sight – today my mother could have had a hip-joint replacement operation and the deterioration in my father's sight could be arrested.

It is difficult to appreciate the hardships elderly folk endured during the war and the first five years of peace, specially those without family nearby to help out with rations and transport. I'd not experienced rationing, and had no idea of its impact on food, clothes and petrol. My rations were some help to my mother, but even so the amounts of butter, cheese, sugar, tea, eggs and meat were minuscule, no wonder my parents had become so frail.

Uncle Charles Gibbs, as always, came up trumps by lending me his Austin 10 hp car, but getting petrol was a problem. I managed to get over to Newbury see my aunts Cicely Gibbs and Audrey Heywood (Mary Dudbridge's mother), and the Holding cousins at Kingsclere. Bucklebury was a hamlet with only a general store-cum-post office, a butcher and a pub, 'The Blade Bone', dispensing watery beer but no whiskey. I met two sisters there from a nearby village, the elder an attractive blond divorcee, we went to 'hops' in local village halls and saw quite a lot of each other, she was fun – my parents disapproved! There was little to do, all young folk were either working or in the Forces.

Instructions came through for me to join the Airborne Forces Technical Development Centre at Amesbury Abbey in Wiltshire, where I was to take up a staff job – evaluating developments in infantry weapons and tactics relevant to airborne forces. The Abbey was an imposing Palladian building, built by some Nabob who'd made his pile in Calcutta in the eighteenth century. The setting was magnificent, the river Avon flowed through the grounds, but the building was uncomfy, cold, draughty and cheerless, what's more, the Commandant was a Territorial Army Officer to whom I took an instant dislike – reciprocated no doubt.

While at Amesbury I got my friend Dicky Lonsdale, now a Lt. Col. (with a DSO and Bar) to give a talk on the Arnhem operation. I took the opportunity of telling him I wasn't happy in my job and would like to get back to soldiering with troops. A fortnight later I was summoned to HQ 1st Airborne Division to be interviewed by Major General Roy Urquhart. We got on quite well – he'd been on the North-West Frontier as a young officer. The upshot was that I was appointed Brigade Major to 1st Parachute Brigade under Brigadier Gerald Lathbury, based at Syston Hall, near Grantham in Lincolnshire.

This was a plum job, I was delighted, the Brigade HQ staff were pleasant and helpful. However, as they'd all been at Arnhem, and had taken part in other airborne operations, I felt a bit of an outsider; I wasn't familiar with the set-up, and knew few people in the Division other than 156 Bn. officers. Very different to soldiering in the Punjab with Indian troops, furthermore, Gerald Lathbury had never served in India, so he didn't appreciate my Indian expressions.

A Brigadier and his Brigade Major must work in the closest harmony; after four months it became obvious that Gerald and I weren't hitting it off as well as we should. It came as no surprise, therefore, when he called me into his office one day and said "Bertie, one of us has to go, and it won't be me." We had a bit of laugh, all most amicable, he was anxious to help and said he'd fix any posting I liked. Without hesitation I said I wanted to return to 1st Suffolk then with 21st Army Group in North-West Europe. This was an ironic turn of events – when approached by Bill Gough in Razmak in 1940, I'd had no hesitation in volunteering for parachute troops; now four years on, when given the push by Gerald Lathbury, my immediate reaction was to return to my Regiment.

So my time with Airborne Forces came to an end. In some ways I was sorry. I'd made lasting friends, had lots of fun and experienced some hairy situations. But I was first and foremost a 'Suffolk Soldier', and looked forward to serving under my friend, Dick Goodwin, CO 1st Suffolk, in the 3rd Infantry Division – famous since Waterloo – in action in Germany.

* * * * *

In early March 1945, after a few days leave at home, I boarded an ancient cross-channel ferry chock full of troops at Tilbury in the Thames estuary. We remained tied up alongside in great discomfort for three hours before sailing to Oostende in Belgium, then by lorry to a Reinforcement Holding Unit in barracks not long vacated by Germans at Bourg Leopold. On checking-in I was told that another Suffolk officer was there. Enquiring where I'd find him, I gathered he'd most probably be at the officers' club, an estaminet taken over by the army just down the road.

The club was crowded with officers from many regiments, of all ranks and ages; above the din I could hear a piano being played rather well, through the smoke-haze I just made out the pianist, a middle-aged captain. There was no problem in finding the Suffolk officer "Oh yes" I was told, "he'll be down there behind that curtained archway – with a girl." and he was! Major Malcolm Dewar and I hadn't met before; when he saw me he paused, then said "You're Bertie Bevan". Malcolm was an exceptionally fine athlete, a tremendous character, and no mean ladies' man. In the years to come the Bevans and the Dewars got on well together in many overseas stations, and in England too.

1st Suffolk, part of 3 Infantry Division, was then advancing rapidly in North Rhine Westfalar, heading for the great port of Bremen on the river Weser. I can't remember why, but HQ 21 Army Group at Bad Oeynhausn gave me a stop-gap job which delayed my reaching the Battalion for a week; this involved following the advancing formations and reporting on the conditions in the countryside. To do this I had a corporal, two drivers and a couple of jeeps. The roads were full of craters, bridges and culverts were mostly destroyed, but it was perfect spring weather.

We visited little towns and villages off the beaten track, some completely untouched by the Allied armies, others without a single building unscathed. Fruit trees in blossom lined the roads, the locals, hoping to curry favour, produced excellent German wine; if I hadn't been anxious to rejoin 1st Suffolk I'd have been more than happy to have prolonged this assignment. We came across a train-load of V 2 rockets on a siding in the open country, they'd been straffed by the RAF, I've got a photo of myself and my chaps standing on one. We spent each night wherever we could find accommodation, once in a camp of well equipped chalets amongst pine trees, deserted (unfortunately) except for the caretaker and his wife – I think it had been a senior German officers' brothel.

We'd planned to spend the last night near Luneburg, not far from the river Weser. In the late afternoon, driving past a group of Military Police standing outside a barbed-wire gate, obviously the entrance to a camp, we saw ghastly emaciated creatures inside the barbed-wire fence, dressed in sort of striped pyjamas. That evening, while having a meal at Rear HQ 30 Corps officers' mess in a commandeered house, I noticed two middle-aged officers in the Military Government drinking brandy from a demijohn. They told me they'd entered the camp we'd passed that afternoon – it was called Belsen. The only way they could banish from their minds the ghastly sights they'd seen was to get tight, which they were in the process of doing. Belsen was the first Nazi concentration camp to be liberated by the Allied armies – a name which became synonymous, worldwide, with Nazi atrocities.

I eventually extracted authority from HQ 30 Corps to join 1st Suffolk near Delmenhorst, just west of the great city of Bremen. Getting transport was a problem, however, having only a kit bag and pack, it wasn't too difficult to hitch lifts on the endless procession of military transport, surging along the main routes to the forward fighting formations. I reached 1st Suffolk at dusk. Bn.

HQ was in a cellar, constant artillery fire made conversation difficult. When the CO, Dick Goodwin, came in, I was shocked to see he'd turned grey. He paid me the greatest compliment I ever had during the whole of my soldiering days by saying: "Welcome back Bertie, not many chaps would have chosen to rejoin the battalion at this time, I know you could easily have got a staff job – delighted to have you with us again". My morale soared! He often referred to his incident in later years, when he'd risen to the rank of Lieutenant General, and a Knighthood.

The Company I took over was based in a large five-storey building with an un-interrupted view of the south of Bremen, two miles away. The intervening fields had been flooded and were dotted with the bloated bodies of dead cattle, their legs sticking up in the air. Lieut. General Horrocks, Commander 30 Corps, accompanied by Richard Dimbleby of the BBC, came to my HQ for a good view of the city. A Gunner Forward Observation Officer was controlling the gunfire from the attic. 'Yorrocks' (the General's nickname) unable to resist the opportunity, proceeded to direct the fire of the entire Corps artillery onto several 88s (the Germans's most lethal gun) just visible through binoculars, which were holding up the assault on the city. Delighted at knocking them out, for good measure he then called up the Typhoons, the earliest RAF jet fighter-bombers, who came over flying low at almost the speed of sound, their bombing accuracy was staggering. Considering he'd been terribly wounded and given up for dead in the North Africa campaign, I felt Yorrocks was entitled to get a bit of his own back. We advanced into Bremen along the only road above the flooded fields, encountering only token resistance – the Germans seemed anxious to surrender.

On Armistice Day a corporal in my company was accidentally shot and killed (I am ashamed at not remembering his name). We'd served together in India – Mhow and on the frontier. We buried him in a blanket in a roadside grave, marked by a makeshift cross bearing his name, rank and number. The excitement of the ending of the war was marred for me by this tragic death, of a comrade I'd served with for many years.

After the capture of Bremen the battalion moved south to the small town of Bramsche, just north of Osnabruck. Dick Goodwin then went on leave. As I'd been appointed Second-in-command, I had the unique distinction of commanding 1st Suffolk on VE Day, 8th May 1945. The area round Bramsche was full of camps for recently liberated POWs and DPs (Displaced Persons), the Communist flag flying over the Russian camps. Poles, Croats and scallywags of all sorts appeared from nowhere, hell-bent on terrorising the local German community and generally creating mayhem. I thought a show of strength was called for and ordered that at eleven o'clock on VE Day, everyone in the Battalion – then spread around the town – was to fire his weapon in the air. Major Shepperd of The Essex Regiment, an old friend of mine and a Small Arms expert who happened to be visiting us, helped by blanking several rounds of 17-pounder anti-tank gun ammunition. I fired the first shot, then there followed a tremendous burst of fire from all around the Battalion area. I like to think it had a salutary effect on our Communist allies in the camps.

Brigadier Eddy Goulburn, commanding 8th Infantry Brigade, a splendid, tall, Grenadier Guards Officer, given to walking about with his army braces over shirt-sleeve order, yet still managing to look immaculate, asked me to accompany him to the main Russian POW camp to meet a team of visiting Russian officers. He replied with aplomb, through an interpreter, to endless speeches and toasts drunk in what tasted like sump-oil – we surreptitiously tipped ours into convenient flowerpots.

Our next move was to Gutersloh, a large town just off the authobahn to Berlin, which had been smashed up by RAF bombing, but we made ourselves comfortable, taking over a large school for the troops and two pleasant houses for the officers. Every morning American lorries passed our billets apparently full of loot, including thoroughbred horses, en route to the Channel ports and the USA – we law-abiding British had no such luck. I spent much of my time with the Adjutant, Captain Alan Sperling, writing-up recommendations for awards. Alan, who'd been awarded the MC, was a schoolmaster by profession; he subsequently transferred to The Royal Army Educational Corps, rising to the rank of Colonel. A charming fellow, he still keeps in close touch with The Regiment.

The Battalion was on the boundary between the British and American sectors. Dick and I visited the Town Major, a Yank, to see if we could arrange a supply of beer for the troops from a brewery in Gutersloh. We found him ensconced in a deep arm chair, a full glass in his hand and a personable Fraulein hovering around. "Yes" he was more than willing to help, but not until we'd sampled his 'buzzard's boost', a vile concoction poured by his Staff Sergeant Lou, from a glass 'pitcher' into flower vases with serrated edges, acting as tumblers. An hour later we were still there, the Town Major asleep in his chair – I was feeling distinctly queer; I think Dick was too. Earlier on I'd noticed several civilian radio sets on the floor, as we hadn't got one in the mess, I saw no reason why we shouldn't presume on American generosity. Picking up a set, I passed it through the window to Dick's staff car driver outside. We left soon after – plus the radio.

On another occasion Dick and I discovered an optical instrument factory, deserted except for a storekeeper, who on being asked by Dick if there were any binoculars left, replied "Keiner Herr Oberst". At that moment a corpulent American major barged in demanding in forceful language, the expression 'bloody Kraut' featuring prominently, to be given a pair of binoculars 'Pronto'. When the storeman explained he had none, the Yank accused him of being a bloody liar, he said he could see some under the counter. The storeman reluctantly produced a pair, the Yank major snatched them and shot out, casting a scornful look in our direction as much as to say: 'That'll show you miserable Limies how to deal with Krauts'. The storeman shrugged his shoulders, producing another pair from under the counter and showed them to us – they had no lenses!

There was little entertainment, non-fraternisation with German girls being strictly enforced in the British Sector, not so rigidly by the Yanks. We heard of a camp for Romanian girls who'd been working as forced-labour in local factories, non-fraternisation apparently didn't apply to them; Dick told me to make enquiries. Brigade HQ raised no objections, so two parties of girls were collected in 3-ton lorries fitted with benches, and deposited at the officers' and sergeants' messes. The girls who had been living under appalling conditions for years, were overcome by our hospitality. Some could speak a bit of French, but language proved no obstacle, everyone enjoyed themselves tremendously. The girls were virtually destitute; we gave them army blankets to make up into coats – they were pathetically grateful. It was an eye-opener to discover at first hand, the treatment the Germans had meeted out to the East European countries they'd overrun. These visits became regular events, I kept them going after Dick had left to command a brigade when I was again temporarily in command.

Once more frustration set in, chances of promotion were receding, soldiering in Germany was becoming tedious. Tony Milnes had taken over command, he was a charming chap but we didn't see eye-to-eye in many ways, and it was clear we wouldn't get on. However, the war against the Japanese was still in progress, so I applied for a posting to South East Asia Command (SEAC). It was something of a relief when I was selected for 'a Pool of COs' in the Far East, and granted embarkation leave prior to setting off for India – yet again!

Leaving 1st Suffolk in Gutersloh on 15th July 1945, I set off with Lieut: Russell and a driver in a jeep for the Hook of Holland, a long journey on roads dense with military traffic, many bridges across the autobahn were still down. Apart from an argument with an enormous American lorry on the outskirts of Brussels, resulting in Russell having to have an eyebrow stitched up, we arrived at the Transit Camp in time for an evening meal. Next morning a rough crossing to Harwich, then back to Bucklebury by rail, arriving very late – my elderly parents, as always, welcoming me home.

Chapter 15

With Murna Again.
The Indian Military Academy,
Dehra Dun.

I got three weeks disembarkation leave – after the first week I felt at a loose-end. A lot of water had flowed under the bridge in the eight years since I'd last seen Murna. She'd been married and widowed – had a child, Richard, born four months after his father had been shot down in August 1941, in a leaflet-dropping operation over Flushing on the Dutch coast during the 'Phoney War'. I'd had a full life and numerous girl-friends, some serious and others less so. Murna had been in my heart all the time – my true love. I'd hardly allowed myself to think about her she seemed so unattainable. Now, with time on my hands, a desperate desire to see her swept over me – but would she want to see me?

Screwing up my courage I phoned her at Hill House, Stoke-by-Nayland in Suffolk. Marjorie Rolleston, Murna's mother, answered. She sounded taken aback, I heard her calling out "Murna – it's Silvanus, he wants to speak to you!". Then Murna's familiar husky voice came on the line saying how pleased she was to hear me. Overcome with relief, and almost tongue-tied, I somehow managed to blurt out that I couldn't wait to see her. She told me she was going to spend the next week with her sister, Kathleen, near Maningtree. As I was going to be at the Regimental Depot at Bury St. Edmunds, not too far away, I said I'd get over to see her.

Kathleen and her small son Philip Cragg (Kathleen was divorced) and Murna with Richard, aged three and a half, met me at the station in Murna's prewar Hillman Imp car. The years since we'd last been together rolled away, we were both completely at ease – as if we'd never been parted. She was as attractive as ever, with the added allure of a mature woman of twenty-seven – a tingle of excitement ran through me. Lovely soft wavy dark brown hair, the same devastating smile, smudgy deep blue eyes under dark eyebrows flying up at the ends – perhaps a bit thin, but then everyone was after years of rationing. She was wearing the obligatory countrywoman's dark blue 'twin-set and pearls', which accentuated her figure and suited her admirably. To me she was quite perfect – and what's more she knew it!

Having Kathleen and the two little boys in tow was a bit of a bind, but the house was old, with lots of corridors and odd little rooms, so I managed to get her on her own. She promised to come up to London for a couple of days, it wouldn't be easy, Richard could stay with friends; I was to make the arrangements and let her know the form. I fixed for us to stay at the Royal Court Hotel in Sloane Square which I 'd known from the days I'd lived with my parents in Sloane Street, Murna knew it too. We had two days together; adjoining rooms, it wasn't exactly platonic, but we didn't behave the way young folk do nowadays, perhaps because it was before the era of the pill.

Somehow things didn't work out as we'd hoped. We'd both changed and needed more time to get accustomed to each other, a few days in London wasn't long enough. With hindsight I'm certain Murna felt Peggy still had a hold on me – perhaps she was right. We were sad when we parted, I knew I loved her dearly, but my emotions were muddled – I'm sure it was my fault.

After three weeks leave spent at home and with Uncle Charles at South Stoke near Goring-on-Thames, I got orders to report to the London District Assembly Centre, a vast Victorian red brick building, previously a hotel, near St Pancras Station. Numerous delays ensued, but in due course, having reported to British Overseas Airways Corporation's (BOAC) offices in Victoria, I found myself in a first-class compartment on a 'Special' train to Poole in Dorset – very grand. Four other officers, all senior to me, were also travelling by Short Sunderland flying-boat to India. The next morning we boarded the plane in Poole harbour and took off for Cairo, our first over-night stop.

An uneventful flight, conditions were spartan, no stewardesses or fancy meals, but superb compared to webbing seats in the fuselage of an non-sound-proofed Dakota. We landed on the Nile, spending the night in a comfortable houseboat. The next evening we reached Bahrain, then on to Karachi, finally landing next afternoon on a lake near Agra south of Delhi.

Reporting to GHQ Delhi I was told I'd have to wait – no posting had yet been fixed for me. Needless to say I contacted Peggy who had recently returned to Delhi from Colombo where she'd been employed in the cypher section of Lord Louis Mountbatten's South East Asia Command HQ. Over the past six years we'd managed to be together in all sorts of places, mostly in Delhi, 'Pindi and Murree. I was still bowled over by her, but this was to be our last meeting in India. (Twenty-four years later we met again – her last letter to me was written in March 1988 when she was terminally ill – she died later that year).

I kicked my heels in Delhi for several days waiting for a posting, it was terribly hot, well over 100 degrees fahrenheit. Then the fantastic news came through – an atomic bomb had been dropped on Hiroshima – Japan's surrender soon followed.

In spite of the relief and joy of this dramatic ending of hostilities, it put paid to any hope I'd had of getting promoted. However, again knowing the staff officer in GHQ responsible for Second Grade (majors') staff appointments, I visited him in his office. After I'd explained my situation, he asked me where I'd like to go. I looked at his large wall-map while he read out the jobs that were vacant. I settled on the appointment of Deputy Assistant Quartermaster General (DAQMG) to 163 Lines of Communication Sub Area in Coimbatore, Madras District. I chose this firstly, because I'd never been to South India and secondly, as Coimbatore was near Ootacamund (Ooty) renowned for big-game shooting – it sounded a good bet. I held this appointment for six months. Life was very easy, we were mainly concerned with winding-down the huge bases set up for Operation 'Zipper', the invasion of Malaya, which never took place due to the Jap surrender.

While in Coimbatore I travelled all over Madras District, from Cochin on the Malabar Coast (where 1st Suffolk had been involved in the Moplah Rebellion in 1921–22) to Cape Comorin – the most southerly point of India – up to Nagappattinam on the Coromandal Coast where the Cauvery river flows into the Bay of Bengal. I spent a day at Tippu Sultan's great fortress at Seringapatam, near Mysore, where, on 4th May 1799, the 12th Foot played a distinguished part in the assault. Colonel Wellesley – later to become the great Duke of Wellington, made his mark during this campaign. An obelisk to the memory of the men of the 12th Foot killed at Seringapatam – a Suffolk Regt. Battle Honour – stood a short distance from the vast fort. Looking at it, I thought of the 'Old Suffolk Boys' in their tall shakos and red coats, who perished in the bloody assault, far from home, long, long ago – and shed a tear.

I spent New Year's Day 1946 on leave at Ooty in the Nilgiri Hills, staying with a 'grass widow' whose husband was commanding a battalion somewhere in SEAC. We had great fun, some form of entertainment was going on all the time. Being in the hills, large English-style houses with names like Arranmore had been turned into convalescent hospitals, they all held dances. There was an excellent club and the famous Ooty Hunt. Smaller hill stations – Coonoor and Wellington – both with good clubs, were not far away. I'd acquired a jeep, so I thoroughly enjoyed myself. Realising this idyllic existence wasn't getting me anywhere, hearing that the Indian Military Academy (IMA), the Sandhurst of India, at Dehra Dun in the United Provinces (now Uttar Pradesh) northern India, had vacancies for majors as Company Commanders, I applied, was selected, and arrived there on 2nd February 1946.

Dehra Dun lies over two thousand feet up in Himalayan foothills; a pleasant climate, green for much of the year. The Academy was in the process of reverting from a war-footing back to its original role of training Indian cadets for Regular Commissions in the Indian Army. Originally built by Indian Railways as a staff college, subsequently purchased by the Indian Government for the army, the Academy's impressive buildings were set in park-like grounds, with spacious officers' bungalows; quite the best accommodation I'd known in India.

The Imphal Cadet Battalion was commanded by Lieut: Colonel 'Pom' Power of the Dogra Regiment; he'd been a Jap POW in Rangoon goal, a superb officer, we became good friends. I took command of one of the two Companies of some sixty cadets each. My officers were: Captain Tikka Khan MBE, who'd been a Jap POW [later to become C-in-C the Pakistan Army]: Captain Inder Singh Gill, awarded the MC while serving with Special Operations Executive (SOE) in Greece, he retired as a Lieut.General – we still keep in touch: Captain Pat Stubbs MC, 2nd Gurkhas, who sadly died prematurely (he became my son's godfather). I also had six British Staff Sergeants. So, I can claim to have had some influence on the first post-war intake of regular officers into both the Indian and Pakistan armies – many of my cadets rose to high rank in their respective armies.

The Commandant, Brigadier 'Groppi' Balthrop, was pleasant but rather ineffective. The driving force was the Adjutant, Major

Jim Wilson, The Rifle Brigade (later to become Lieut: General Sir James). My close friend Lieut. Col. Ernest Gould, Royal Army Education Corps, was head of academic studies; he and his charming Icelandic wife Valgy moved to Canberra in 1965, where he was employed by the Australian Government.

Several Gurkha regiments had their depots in Dehra Dun cantonments, even so it was rather off the beaten-track. I was thirty-two and had lived a bachelor existence for over eleven years. The married officers had their wives with them, there was little social life for a single officer.

Fed up with mess life, I felt it was time I got myself married. The penny dropped – I realised what a fool I'd been in not proposing to Murna thirteen months before in London. I got into a panic – had she written me off, or worse, had she re-married?

I tore off a letter to find out. Her reply came two weeks later:

> "...I haven't married again..." and hoped I'd write again soon.

I shot off another letter on the 2nd May, asking her to marry me. She replied on 13th May 1946:

> "I have been hoping and hoping for this to happen. I've so often imagined myself married to you..."

At last we were engaged, sixteen years after we'd first met – I scarcely dared believe it was true!

Having at last got engaged, albeit at long range, I was determined to get a wedding ring on Murna's finger as soon as possible, the idea of a long engagement didn't appeal, I was steamed-up and wanted to get on with it. Her first reaction was to wait until I got home leave in eight months time, January 1947, when with luck. I might wangle a home posting, perhaps to Sandhurst, thereby eliminating the need for her to travel out to India – not my idea at all. I think her reason for wanting to wait was because she couldn't face leaving Richard in England.

A scheme had recently been introduced to enable people with long overseas service to fly home by RAF, spend several weeks on leave and return the same way – at HMG's expense. I applied, got leave and told Murna to expect me early in September and be prepared to become Mrs. Bevan a month later – adding that I hoped she'd return to India with me in December. If she wanted Richard to come too, that would be fine by me.

In early September I left Dehra Dun by train for Karachi via

Lahore, a hot dusty journey. A Reception Base had been set up at RAF Mauripur, a few miles north of Karachi, to handle the large numbers travelling under this scheme; accommodation was basic but no one cared – we were in sight of aircraft taking off for home. I'd been confidentially telling Murna to expect me about the 12th September, at the latest. When that date came and passed and I was still in Mauripur, I went almost berserk, others with a higher priority were always pipping me, frustrating to the n'th degree for an eager, lusty young man, thinking of nothing but his wife-to-be.

After what seemed an eternity, I got a place in an uncomfortable RAF York upper-wing monoplane. On landing at RAF Lynham – conveniently near Reading – its brakes failed; we trundled along the runway until eventually stopping – safely. I phoned Murna from Bucklebury that evening, 18th September. I didn't sleep much – far too excited!

My sister Elizabeth, who lived in Hampstead with her husband Otto, and three small daughters, proved a tower of strength. She arranged for us to be married by special licence on 5th October 1946, in Hampstead Parish Church, with a small reception afterwards at her house, grudgingly paid for by Murna's mother. Elizabeth was quite splendid, without her help we couldn't have coped. I was in uniform as was my bestman, Jack Prescott.

Murna's outfit from Harrods was a rust-red jacket with gold buttons and black trimmings over a matching dress, with a full flared skirt of the same colour and material, a black felt hat with feathers in the turned-up brim and a spray of orchids at her shoulder. How she got the clothing coupons was a mystery. She looked lovely, perhaps a bit scared, but her amazing blue eyes smiling at me from under the brim of her hat, told me all I wanted to know – I'd got her!

We spent the first three days of our honeymoon at Grosvenor House, a very swish hotel on Park Lane, we even danced in the ballroom – terribly sophisticated. We then crossed to Ireland from Holyhead and put up at the Royal Hibernian Hotel in Dublin for inside a week, followed by three days in a small hotel in the Wicklow hills. Murna was staggered at the profusion of food, especially meat – after six years of rationing she could hardly believe it was true. Our final night was back at the Royal Hibernian; when we'd first arrived the hotel management hadn't realised we were honeymooners, to make amends they insisted on giving us a very grand room with a king-size bed – at a reduced rate.

Before leaving the IMA, I'd put in an application for a return passage by sea; the Adjutant, Jim Wilson, promised to submit it as soon as he knew the date of the wedding. All went well, Jim had done his stuff, when we got back from Ireland, we were told we'd got berths on *The Queen of Bermuda*, commandeered for trooping, sailing from Liverpool early in December. The remainder of my leave was spent in visits and preparing for the voyage.

During our absence in Ireland, it dawned on Murna's mother that she would no longer have a daughter at her beck and call to run her house as an unpaid skivvy as had been the case for the past six years – the prospect didn't appeal to her. The ploy she adopted was to insist that it would be cruel to take Richard – poor little boy – to that dreadful unhealthy India, hoping thereby to make us feel guilty and hopefully change our plans so that Murna could remain at Hill House. Murna didn't succumb to this pressure and stuck to her guns. I'd never met, nor heard anything about Murna's father, other than that he was a rotter who lived in Australia. Apparently he'd left his ship, HMS *Renown*, in Sydney in 1919, during one of the Prince of Wales's (later Edward VIII) post-Great War tours of the Empire. I was intrigued, but realised the subject was taboo.

We embarked at Liverpool for the 'shiny' on 5th December 1946. *The Queen of Bermuda* was a comfortable ship – before the war on the Carribean run. Murna and Richard were in a dormitory with twenty other officers' wives and children, I shared a cabin for four officers – frustrating, to put it mildly, for newly-weds. She was a fast ship; we took on water and oil at Algiers, Port Said, Aden and Karachi, disembarking at Bombay on 22nd December. By Frontier Mail to Delhi, then the narrow gauge line to Dehra Dun, arriving at No.15 Bungalow on Christmas Eve. Everyone was helpful, hospitable and pleased to welcome us. Parties and all sorts of Christmas festivities were in full swing, a wonderful welcome for Murna.

My Bearer, Gul Mohamed, a Muslim from Punch District in the hills to the south of Kashmir (I hadn't been able to contact Babu, a great shame), had engaged a bawarchi (cook) and a chokra – a general dog's-body; our laundry was done by a dhobi, who also worked for three other officers' families; the garden was tended by a mali – an Academy employee. We quickly settled into our super bungalow, a vast difference for Murna from life at Hill House. Gul Mahomet looked after Richard; as there were a few other English kids to play with, much of his time was spent with his mother.

Having drinks on our verandah as dusk fell, looking across the Toms river valley watching the spectacular lightening flashing over the distant Himalayan foothills, was an unforgettable delight.

There were many species of birds in garden, especially in the evening when the dying sun caught the brilliant plumage of the scarlet minivets as they spiralled up chasing flying insects, also bee-eaters, hornbills, crested hoopoes, birds-of-paradise with long trailing ribbon-like tails, golden oriels and many others. English flowers did well – the Commandant held an annual flower-show in his garden when his sweet-peas were at their best. The C-in-C, Field Marshal Auchinleck, frequently came up from Delhi for a week-end's rest, staying with the Commandant and Mrs Baltrop. It was a lovely place, we were happy there, but alas – all was soon to change.

I see from our Visitors Book, which Murna kept religiously all our married life, that we had a succession of callers who came in for evening drinks, nearly all on the IMA staff, many Indian officers with their wives. At the end of March, Murna and I drove down in an IMA car to New Delhi where I bought her a snow leopard fur coat. At the end of June the three of us went in an IMA estate car to the small hill station of Chakrata, in the Himalayan foothills, then on to the more sophisticated hill town of Mussourie – very few British were there.

Silvanus and Murna Bevan.
5th October 1946

We followed the progress of the Viceroy's (Lord Louis Mountbatten) negotiations over Indian Independence with the Hindu and Muslim leaders – Mahatma Gandhi and Mr Jinnah respectively, with intense interest and apprehension. Early in July, Jawaharlal Nehru, leader of the Indian Congress Party and the outstanding Indian politician, came to the IMA and addressed the cadets in the Chetwode Hall, on the implications of Independence – the staff and wives listened in the gallery. He began speaking in perfect upper-crust English – he'd been educated at Harrow and Cambridge – then effortlessly switched into Hindustani – a memorable and profoundly impressive performance. A tea party was held outside the mess to afford Nehru an opportunity of meeting the staff. He had a word with many of us and spent some time talking to Murna, not surprising as he had an eye for a pretty woman – his devotion to Edwina Mountbatten, the Viceriene, was well known.

The Deputy Commandant, Colonel Stead, an Australian serving in the Indian Army, was replaced by Colonel Mhadeo Singh – (awarded the DSO in the Italian campaign) – a significant appointment. Mhadeo and I became good friends. After I'd left the IMA, when he was a Major General commanding an Indian Division in Kashmir, he wrote at length to me about the Indo-Pakistan war; stupidly I've destroyed his letters.

There were indications of trouble brewing. The bank manager in Dehra Dun said his vaults were full of valuables, deposited by wealthy Sikhs arriving from the Punjab. My Bearer became uneasy, saying it wasn't safe for him, a Muslim, to shop in the bazaar. The cadets remained staunchly loyal to the IMA and seemed genuinely determined to maintain close friendships with fellow cadets, irrespective of religion. However, tension between Hindu and Muslim officers, also between their wives, was daily becoming apparent. Nevertheless, it was a great surprise, when without warning, the Muslim cadets were flown from a nearby airfield to what is now Pakistan. They left amid protestations of enduring friendship from their erstwhile Hindu and Christian colleagues, many of whom found this traumatic turn of events hard to comprehend. No one would have believed, that within a year, some of them would be fighting each other.

Events then moved quickly. The whole of the Punjab was in a ferment. Akali Sikhs in Amritsar, who had more or less taken the law into their own hands, were slaughtering Muslims indiscriminately in thousands. Armed gangs of scallywags roamed the jungles round Dehra Dun, terrorising the villagers. Trains arrived at Dehra swilling with the blood of massacred Muslims. Mohammedan owned shops were burnt down; no Muslim dared show his face in the bazaar.

The IMA went onto a war footing. Cadets formed into platoons patrolled the extensive grounds; others assisted in a refugee camp for Hindus fleeing from the Punjab. I was appointed DAQMG, organizing the defence of the IMA. We were fortunate – apart from the inconvenience, life went on much as usual within the Academy, nevertheless, we were concerned and not a little apprehensive.

On Independence Day – 15th August 1947 – a parade was held at the IMA to celebrate this auspicious occasion, followed by everyone listening to Pandit Nehru, who'd become Prime Minister that morning, broadcasting a message to the new nation. In the evening a splendid drinks party was held in the Chetwode Hall.

Although the worst of the troubles in our area had subsided, the whole of northern India was in a state of complete turmoil, the Punjab in particular. Endless straggling columns of Hindus fleeing south, clashing with columns of Muslims fleeing north, both being indiscriminately attacked by hordes of Sikhs and gangs of

W S B and Murna at the Indian Military Academy, 1947

badmashes. Only the presence of British and Indian troops afforded any semblance of protection to the hundreds of thousands of terrified refugees – over a million were said to have perished in this holocaust.

An Independence Parade was held on the Maidan in New Delhi, below what had up to then been Lutyen's Viceregal Lodge. Contingents from India's Armed Services marched down the wide roadway, skirting the archway under which a statue of King George V, robed as Emperor of India, had stood. I took a contingent of a hundred IMA cadets to watch the parade. They looked smart, keen and determined. I've no doubt they appreciated the significance of the occasion; many of them must have remembered it when they'd risen to senior positions in India's army. It was a privilege to have been in charge of them on this historic occasion in India's history.

Due to the unrest, Indian officers were anxious to acquire personal and sporting weapons. On my 21st birthday my Uncle Charles had given me a good second-hand, side-lock ejector 12-bore shotgun with 28-inch Damascus steel barrels, somewhat ancient, but a first-grade gun nevertheless – I think he paid £25 for it, quite a lot of money at the time. I also had a Holland & Holland 12-bore gun, which he'd passed on to me when he became too old to shoot any more. An Indian Army doctor on the Academy staff made me a good offer for the older gun; I didn't really want to part with it, it had given me excellent sport for thirteen years, but I wanted the money, and I didn't really need two guns, so I sold it to him for a good figure. Today it'd have fetched perhaps ten times as much, if not more.

Officers and their families were being sent back to England, consequently there were staff changes. For my last three months at the IMA I was appointed Administrative Officer, with the temporary rank of Lieutenant Colonel, bringing a welcome increase in pay. We began planning for our departure; the problem was where to stay in England. Murna's mother was being difficult, so Stoke-by-Nayland was out. My parents were living in a hotel in Bath; my sister Elizabeth and family were in London, Ontario, Canada; Uncle Charles was too old to have us all for any length of time, so we wrote to Murna's sister, Kathleen Cragg, then running a Guest House in Felixstowe, to see if she could have us for an indefinite period as paying- guests – thank heavens she said she could.

Just before we left the IMA, the 2nd Goorkhas (the correct spelling) held a mammoth party in their mess in Dehra Dun cantonments – a sort of 'Waterloo Ball' – the regiment was shorty transferring to the British Army. We went in an IMA staff car with a Gurkha escort, passing houses on fire en route. Bill Gough, the original commander of 50 Indian Parachute Brigade was there, I was delighted to see him again, as he'd recently retired he was in white tie and tails which seemed incongruous (not long after he was tragically killed in an aircraft accident somewhere in South East Asia). The ball was a tremendous success, we danced, ate, and drank till the early hours. A magnificent show, the mess sparkling with regimental silver, shooting trophies on the walls, the Goorkha band as good and as smart as any in the British Army. I remember it vividly – especially my wife, who looked ravishing.

I'd arranged with a Gurkha Jemadar on the IMA staff, to have my Scotty terrier bitch put-down after we'd left the bungalow. This sounds callous, but there was no alternative, we'd tried to find a home for her, but in those uncertain times no one wanted the added responsibility of a dog. Our departure from No 15 Bungalow was consequently tinged with sadness.

Late in the evening of 25th October 1947, we set off in a convoy of four vehicles with a Gurkha escort for Delhi, via Meerut – a hundred miles in all. The Academy Sergeant Major, Mr McGarrity of the Irish Guards, and his family travelled with us. Arriving in the early hours at Delhi station we had difficulty in getting along the platform due to the swarms of refugees camping out, cooking food and doing all the unspeakable things lower cast Hindus always do on railway platforms. The Punjab Mail eventually pulled in, with Mr. McGarrity's help we piled, thankfully, into our reserved compartment.

We spent a week at the horrid Homeward Bound Trooping Centre at Deolali, near Bombay, moving to an officers' camp at Colaba Point for a few days, before sailing in the *S.S. Atlantis* on 11 November 1947 – almost twelve years since I'd first set foot in India. As we pulled away from Ballard Pier, although my mind was full of memories, I looked forward with confidence to the future with Murna. In a strange way things had worked out as we'd always hoped. The dreams we'd had sitting on Aldeburgh beach in January 1936 had at last come true. We were sailing home as man and wife.

Chapter 16

Soldiering in England, 1948–1950

The *Atlantis* called in at all the usual ports: Aden, Port Said, Malta (the first time for me), then on to Algiers, docking at Southampton on the 2nd December 1947. The voyage was uneventful, we were rather cramped in our cabin but the Indian stewards were good and the food excellent. The release from the tension we'd been under over the past six months was wonderful; having no troops to worry about was a relief.

After a night in a London hotel, we went by rail to Felixstowe, to stay with Kathleen in her Guest House until I'd got a posting. Christmas was almost upon us, Kathleen had asked her father, Charles Rolleston, a retired Commander RN, to spend Christmas with her. This put Murna into a dilemma. Whilst she had no objection in meeting her father, whom she hadn't seen since she was aged two, she had a sense of loyalty to her mother, despite the latter's disgraceful conduct towards us over the past two years. (Murna's parents were not divorced, in spite of living apart for over twenty-eight years, most of which he'd spent in Australia.).

When we were staying for a few days at the Junior Army and Navy Club in London, Murna asked me drop in without warning on her father. He was an Assistant Curator at the Natural History Museum in South Kensington, living nearby in a ground-floor flat in Thurloe Street. I went round in the evening of the 19th December – cold and drizzly – the flat was in a five-storied Victorian town-house, with a pillared portico and black and white chequered tiled steps up to the front door. I rang the bell, a light shone in the fanlight, a rattling of bolts, the door opened, a tall spare figure silhouetted by the light in the hall peered out at me. I said "I'm Silvanus Bevan, may I come in?" There was a pause, he stood there holding the door handle, then quietly said "You're Murna's husband; yes, please come in."

My heart was thumping, my mouth was dry, I felt like an intruder, but he soon put me at ease – I expect he was just as keyed up as I was. I explained the position about Christmas. He thought the best thing would be for me to report back on him to Murna, and if she agreed, the three of us should meet next evening in the nearby De Vere Hotel, opposite Kensington Park. He was already there when we arrived; he embraced his daughter, one could tell at once that he was taken with her. We had a drink, Murna showed him photos of Richard. Just before leaving, Murna said she looked forward to seeing him over Christmas. Later she told me she could only ever treat him as an acquaintance. I understood – sadly it was too late for her to feel any affection for him; seeing them together, anyone could tell the relationship at a glance.

I spent some time at the Suffolk Regimental Depot in Bury St. Edmunds awaiting a posting. Tony Milnes, who had taken over from me in Gutersloh in 1945, was the commanding officer. There as nothing for me to do; I was fed up and furious at being separated from Murna.

One evening four of us: Tony Milnes, Gerald 'Bossy' Heyland, Oscar Leach and myself, motored out to the Battle Training Area to have a crack at duck. Dusk was falling when we took up our positions round a frozen lake. I couldn't see any of the others, it was too dark and they were some distance away. I could hear birds on the ice in the centre of the lake but couldn't make out what sort they were. It was damned cold. Suddenly, to my right 'Bossy' fired, then further away Tony banged off, followed by a tremendous flapping of wings, honking, quacking and the unmistakable creaking sound of swans' wing-beats, I could just make them out as they pounded across the ice gaining speed; they took off heading in the direction of where I thought Oscar Leach had positioned himself. Swans on the wing are a marvellous thrilling sight, I wished they'd flown over where I was standing, so I could have got a glimpse of them silhouetted against the fading light. 'Bang', 'Bang', Oscar had loosed-off. A rotten shot, normally he couldn't hit a haystack at ten yards, then a sinister thud – he'd hit one ! Swans are a protected species, it's a serious crime to shoot one.

Bossy and I had almost got back to the car, when Oscar appeared carrying the bird by the neck on his back, its head just visible over his shoulder, wings flapping in the breeze. Tony Milnes, materialising out of the darkness from the other direction, said: "Oscar, what's that you're carrying?" Without batting an eyelid Oscar replied "Oh, only a snow goose." Considering snow geese hadn't been seen in Suffolk for many a year, it was amazing that Tony swallowed this blatant fabrication – or perhaps he didn't? We smuggled the bird into the men's cookhouse, the only place with a large enough oven; roast goose appeared on the menu three days later!

Eventually I received instructions from the War Office to proceed to Catterick Camp in north Yorkshire, to assume the appointment of second-in-Command of 7 Selection Regiment, Royal Signals. A few more days with Murna in Felixstowe, then off by rail to Richmond, the station for Catterick Camp – new territory for me. Murna had to remain with Kathleen as there was a long waiting list for married quarters.

My time in Catterick with the Royal Signals was most enjoyable. 7 Selection Regiment's role was to give large intakes of National Servicemen two months basic military training, before undergoing further specialist training. The CO had risen through the ranks – a 'Ranker' – we got on well, the instructors were infantry officers and NCOs from different regiments, the administrative staff were all Royal Signals. The Adjutant, Captain Peter Parker, and his wife Joan, became, and remain, close friends. I lived in the Headquarters Mess, everyone was most friendly.

It was just over two years since the end of the war; accommodation was desperately scarce. Scouting round I was lucky to find a house to rent eighth miles from the camp, called Ferngill in the village of Middleham, famous for its racing fraternity. The owner was Miss Doris Armstrong, who lived in Tupgill Park, a large racing establishment at the bottom of the track leading to Ferngill, and then on up to the gallops. The Armstrongs were, and still are, successful race horse Trainers. Doris's father, Bob, in his late eighties, was a well known character in racing circles. Her brother, Gerald, owned stables in the valley below Ferngill; his daughter later married the famous jockey, Lester Piggot. Doris became a good friend; I enjoyed listening to old Bob's stories of his early days when head stable-lad to the great Lord Lonsdale, of sporting fame.

It began snowing soon after Murna arrived from Felixstowe; deep drifts built up making the steep track through three heavy five-barred field gates to Ferngill almost impassable. Somehow I struggled daily into the barracks in Murna's old Hillman Imp car – it had no heating – so I often drove with my head sticking out of the window, the windscreen completely iced-up. The nearest grocer was in Middleham a mile and a half away, I shopped on my way home in Leyburn, a large village half way from the barracks; we did a big 'shop' on Saturdays at the NAAFI in Catterick. Doris's farmhand, Harker, brought us milk in a milk-can straight from the cow, generally with hay floating in it! Looking back on those days I don't know how we managed, it wasn't easy for Murna, but we were happy, specially when after I'd just got back one evening, she told me she was pregnant – I could hardly believe it.

Ferngill was a snug little house, in spite of only minimal central heating. The view across Coverdale valley was superb – the locals were friendly and hospitable. I got some rough shooting with Doris, who ran sheep on the surrounding moors. Strings of race horses, ridden by stable-lads of all ages, passed the house daily, morning and evening, to and from the gallops. Occasionally the 'lads' left notes for Murna, she showed me the first one, with the letters SWLK on the back of the envelope, which, she said – with a becoming blush – stood for 'Sealed with love and kisses'.

Arrangements were put in hand for the great event. A young midwife, Bessie Scarr, known as 'a monthly nurse', who lived in Wensleydale on the north side of the gallops, was engaged to come and live-in when needed; Alice Wardroper, a spinster of good birth, uncertain age and limited means, was recruited to run the house for two months; the doctor from Wensleydale came and kept an eye on the mother-to-be, no pre-natal clinics or nonsense like that in those days.

Alice Wardrope arrived on the 10th September, Bessie Scarr on the 13th. All looked set for a speedy delivery. But no – a false start. I spent the best part of a week pushing Murna over dry-stone walls, up hills, along winding lanes – to no avail. I gave up, and decided to take Richard with me into Doncaster, twenty five miles away, to have the Hillman's sunshine-roof repaired. We set off early in the morning of the 21st September 1948, getting back in the late afternoon to be greeted by a beaming Alice Wardroper – I vaguely wondered why. Going indoors I heard a sound soon to become very familiar – the penny dropped. Rushing upstairs, I found Bessie on the landing, grinning for all she was worth – and there was Murna – looking fantastically fresh and attractive, positively blooming, with my son in her arms – howling!

In January 1949 we moved into No.1 Whinny Hill, a married quarter in Catterick Camp. Married quarters were then unfurnished, we somehow rustled up a few bits and pieces, all very basic, mostly from a second-hand shop in the camp, but at least we had the silver cutlery and ornaments Murna had succeeded in retrieving, with difficulty and a certain amount of guile, although it was all hers, from her mother's house during a short visit we'd made for this purpose on returning from our honeymoon in Ireland. It had been stored with my parents, who had no idea of the contents of the boxes, while we we'd been in India.

Charles was christened in Catterick Garrison Church, followed by a party in the Officers' Club attended by all our Middleham and Royal Signals friends. He lay in a side room in his 'Moses Basket', letting everyone know he was there. We both felt very proud. I was delighted with my clever, beautiful wife.

There was always a lot going on in Catterick; dances at the club, regimental sporting events, drinks parties – very social. Having a babe to cope with was a problem, but we managed to get baby-sitters, and often took him around with us in his basket. I succeeded in getting a 'gun' in the highly sought after garrison grouse shooting syndicate, organized by the club secretary, a retired Indian Army brigadier. First class sport at a trifling cost, on moors owned by the army; soldiers acted as beaters, we never lacked volunteers.

In March 1949 there was an unfortunate incident involving the Quartermaster and his staff, resulting in a Court of Inquiry and a Courts Martial. The upshot being that the CO was removed – unfairly in my opinion. The Garrison Commander, a Major General, formerly in the Royal Signals, who knew me well, said he'd like me to take permanent command of 7 Selection Regiment, he'd recommend my promotion to Lieut. Colonel. This was very flattering, but I knew it was impossible. The Adjutant General's Department would never agree to an Infantryman taking over a Royal Signals unit – in any case I'd no wish to change my cap badge. The matter was resolved by my being posted to The War Office, AG 2 Branch, in Lansdowne House, Berkley Square, London. I'd commanded for over three months, and drawn a Lieut. Colonel's pay – a help as we were very tight for cash.

Again we were faced with the problem of where to live. Murna and Charles stayed on at Catterick; Richard was at boarding school; I lived in the War Office Officers' Mess in Woolwich, south-east London, and searched for suitable accommodation.

Meanwhile my Branch had been moved to new hutted buildings in Stanmore, north London.

Realizing we'd never find anywhere suitable to rent – the only answer was to buy a house reasonably close to Stanmore. Between us we scraped together £4,000 (mostly Murna's) with a small mortgage (at 4%) sufficient to buy No.12 Deacons Hill Road, Elstree, Herts, a comfy early 1930s house, with a pleasant garden (the previous owner's son had been at Sherborne with me). We gradually acquired enough furniture, but it was hard finding the cash – we got no help.

In May we engaged a nanny for Charlie, Bobby McGuire, a Roman Catholic, tricky as Murna was a bigoted Protestant, but we got on well enough. We enjoyed our time at Elstree, a bit lonely for Murna as we had few friends nearby, but it was a start in house ownership which stood us in good stead in years to come. Charlie's nanny left after a year and a half.

Peter Parker had been posted from Catterick to a job in the main War Office building in Whitehall. They were having difficulty in finding accommodation they could afford, so we agreed to share our house with them. It was to our mutual financial advantage (they paid us £10 a month). Sometimes we had meals together, but otherwise were more or less independent. Whilst with us Joan produced her first-born, Christopher ('Toffer'). All things considered, sharing the house worked out remarkably well – we remain friends.

Chapter 17

With 1st Suffolk During the Malayan Emergency, 1951–53

When my posting to 1st Suffolk in Malaya came through, Joan and Peter Parker were still living with us at Elstree, it was comforting for me to know that Murna would not be on her own when I left. We'd heard that married quarters in Kuala Lumpur were scarce, it was ghastly having to face another period apart, but that was normal in the life of a regular army officer – no use moaning about it.

I sailed from Liverpool for Singapore on the 5th July 1951 on the troopship *Empire Pride*, two days before Murna's thirty-third birthday. She brought Charlie with her to see me off on the troop special from Liverpool Street Station. There was a lump in my throat as I watched the little fellow walking away quite unconcerned, holding his mother's hand, Murna didn't take it so calmly, she was terribly upset – poor darling – we'd endured many separations during the four and a half years of our marriage, all mercifully reasonably short, this time it was likely to be a long one.

The voyage was uneventful, the sixth time I'd passed through the Suez Canal – we docked at Singapore on the 7th August. The military special train to Kuala Lumpur (KL) left that evening; as it was occasionally shot-up by Communist Terrorists (CTs) while chugging along the single-line, bordered for most of the way by thick jungle, it had a Gurkha escort in armoured wagons at the head and tail, who periodically fired a few bursts from their Bren guns as a deterrent. Pat Hopper, a keen young subaltern not long out of Sandhurst, who'd been on the *Empire Pride,* shared a compartment with me; I suggested we put our bedding rolls against the side of the carriage to stop any stray bullets – he thought this was an excellent idea!

1st Suffolk, after a difficult time acting pig-in-the-middle between Jews and Arabs in Palestine as the British Mandate came to an end, followed by a spell in Greece keeping the warring political factions from each other's throats, landed up in Malaya, where an Emergency had recently been declared, with the job of preventing the CTs from ousting the British from the Peninsular and establishing a Communist regime. Since its arrival the Battalion had been outstandingly successful under Lieut. Colonel Ian Wight. The number of 'kills' it had clocked-up already approached the record for any British regiment. Morale was superb, many officers and Other Ranks had been decorated for gallantry. Ian had finished his period of command not long before I arrived.

The new CO, Lieut. Col. Philip Morcombe, an Australian, commissioned into The Suffolk Regiment from Duntroon – the Australian equivalent to Sandhurst – had joined 2nd Suffolk in Madras in 1929. As a young subaltern I'd served with him in Mhow. During WW2 he'd been with East African troops. Some of the older, stuffier officers in the Regiment didn't take kindly to a 'Colonial' commanding the Battalion, I had no such reservations, indeed I found his uninhibited attitude stimulating and a welcome change.

Battalion HQ was in an attap and bamboo hutted camp at Wardiburn, on the outskirts of KL. Advanced HQ was in a commandeered school at Kajang, a small town twelve miles further south off the main Johore Bahru and Singapore road. The four rifle companies were based on rubber plantations up to twenty miles apart. Our job was to track down, engage and eliminate groups of the so-called Malayan Races Liberation Army (MRLA) operating in the KL area, in particular those commanded by Lieu Kon Kim, a ruthless bearded Chinese bogeyman, who terrorised the local villages, forcing the peasants – known as Min Euen – to provide information, food, medical aid and assistance to the CTs in their jungle hide-outs.

I took over A Company, about a hundred and twenty men all told, based on the Bukit Darah rubber estate, twenty-five miles from KL, enclosed by serried ranks of rubber trees interspersed with taller trees to provide shade, oil palm plantations and secondary jungle – impenetrable in places without cutting a path with a parang, a long bladed machette. It rained for a few hours daily, the humidity was high. We slept in tents, corrugated iron huts for cookhouse and stores. I had four officers: my second-in-command Captain Hugh Taylor, a very pleasant chap with family connections in the Regiment; Jimmy Kelly, who'd been awarded a well deserved MC; Pat Hopper and another subaltern.

About half the soldiers were National Servicemen, although they only served with the Battalion for eighteen months at the most, they soon became excellent jungle fighters, who could be relied on to take the correct immediate action in the event of a 'bump' with the CTs. Two-thirds of the Company was always out patrolling, sometimes for up to five days at a time, carrying rations, water, ammunition and a bivouac sheet on their back, no porters or pack-mules, one quickly learnt that a full tube of tooth paste weighed a lot more than one a quarter full.

In mid-August I attended a three-week course at the Far East Training Centre in Johore Bahru, just north of Singapore Island – CTs were very active in this area. It was a grind for an old chap of thirty-seven, however, considering my age and groggy knee, I think I acquitted myself quite well. On a five-day exercise we were to be re-supplied by helicopter; hearing there was whiskey with the rations, we made a quick job of clearing a landing place in the jungle. The third night a few shots were fired into our camp, no one was hit, but in the excitement a sergeant hurriedly pulling on his long canvas jungle boots, was bitten by a scorpion which had crawled into one of them; he was evacuated by helicopter next morning.

On returning to the Battalion I was appointed second-in-Command, alternating weekly with the CO between Kajang and Wardiburn; whenever a major operation was mounted by 18 Infantry Brigade, to which we belonged, I was back flogging the jungle. Our run of successes continued, but inevitably we suffered a number of fatal casualties.

Although the security forces were gaining the upper hand, the CTs were quick to take advantage of any opportunity that presented itself. This was dramatically demonstrated on 6th October 1951 when Sir Henry Gurney, the High Commissioner for the Federation of Malaya, was shot and killed when travelling with his wife in his Rolls Royce, which was ambushed returning from Frasers Hill, a lovely hill station seventy-five miles north of KL. The Battalion was alerted to track down the bandits, but was not called out. We had the sad duty of providing the Firing Party at the funeral.

Murna and Charles set off from Southampton on 17th January 1952 in the troopship *Empire Windrush*, reaching Singapore on 17th February. She made friends on board with Jill Hall, the attractive young wife of a major serving with the Worcester Regiment in Malaya. From what I later gathered, they were both 'chatted-up' by handsome, eager, young subalterns, who fell for them – Murna said they thought she was only twenty-five which pleased her – they came in useful looking after Charles – 'Where's Charlie' was a constant refrain. I flew down to meet them, returning after two days in Singapore. As there was a long waiting list for married quarters in KL, Malcolm and Maureen Dewar kindly made room for us in their bungalow in Ampang Road.

On 13th March we all travelled by troop-train to the bandit free island of Penang off the north-west coast of Malaya for 'Rest & Re-training'; the Battalion moved in two parties, I was in charge of the second one. Officers families stayed in the Runnymede Hotel right on the foreshore. It was a marvellous interlude and a wonderful introduction for Murna; being together again was all that mattered.

Back again in Wardiburn Camp I found that an officer in the Essex Regiment, Paul Clementi-Smith, slightly senior to me, had been posted to 1st Suffolk for six months as he required a report on his fitness for command. District HQ told Phil Morcombe that Paul was to take over as second-in-command, I wasn't best pleased.

I took over D Company, based a long way from KL, only accessible along a highly ambushable road. Each Company Commander had a Ferret armoured scout car, so the likelihood of getting shot up was slight, but it was a dicy place to get to after dark. I managed to get into KL about once a week. Mercifully, throughout the Emergency, when in KL we were able to discard our weapons and move around normally. The Mess had joined the Lake Club where we could swim, have a meal and go the occasional dance. The Golf Club had a super pool, much patronised by Charlie. There were lots of excellent Chinese restaurants and a few European ones, interesting shops full of things we couldn't afford; however, we did buy a traditional Chinese carved teak chest lined with camphor wood. I also bought Murna a ruby, amethyst and diamond triple half-hoop ring from a reputable English jeweller.

We bought a second-hand tiny Fiat Topolina covertible, just big enough – at a pinch – to take the three of us and Ah Choy, our young Chinese amah. We were allotted quarters in a married officers hostel, The Istana, previously occupied by the Sultan of

Selangor's wives. Our accommodation was cramped, but as I was away such a lot it didn't matter; Murna had no catering worries and it was relatively cheap. We knew we weren't going to be in Malaya long, so in some ways it was a satisfactory solution.

The Battalion was still having successes. A major triumph was when Lieut. Raymond Hands, a National Service Officer, led his platoon with great dash and spirit, along fallen tree trunks right into Lieu Kon Kim's camp in the heart of a dark, dank, swampy forest, the Ulu Langat South, where the trees reached up well over a hundred feet, with roots like enormous buttresses, the branches high up forming a canopy shutting out the sunlight – everything below was gloomy and sinister. A shoot-out followed. Raymond wounded Lieu Kon Kim, who crouched behind a fallen tree and returned fire, but he was hard-hit and Raymond finished him off. Only a few of Lieu's group escaped, most were shot as they fled from their bashas. There was a fine haul of weapons including Lieu's Sten gun, now in the Regimental Museum, and bundles of paper money, partially eaten by white ants – the Hong Kong and Shanghai Bank obligingly accepted the notes without question. General Sir Gerald Templer, the High Commissioner, came out by helicopter to congratulate Philip Morcombe, Malcolm Dewar B Company Commander, Raymond Hand (who was later awarded the MC) and his platoon. A large number of troops had taken part in this operation lasting several days; my Company, although not far away, was not so lucky. However, I later got a 'Mention in Despatches' – for distinguished services!

Not long after this excitement, Murna, Charlie, Ah Choy and I set off in the Fiat, in convoy with Malcolm and Maureen Dewar and their small daughter Melanie, also Frank and Vera Lockett and young son Nick, for a week-end in Frasers Hill. We were escorted the last twenty-five miles up the hilly section, by a troop of armoured cars from the Twelth Lancers. I was afraid our little car might find the steep road too much for it, and didn't fancy getting stuck near where Sir Henry Gurney had been killed, but all went well. Apart from an elderly brigadier and his wife, we had the place to ourselves. During the Japanese occupation, it had been an officers' leave centre – young Chinese girls no doubt had proved very obliging. We all shared a Swiss-type chalet, played hilarious golf on a well kept, beautiful nine-hole course, drank in the small club-house-cum-pub and thoroughly enjoyed ourselves. The evening before leaving we heard that a British Police Sergeant had been ambushed and killed on his way up, a sombre ending to an otherwise splendid short break.

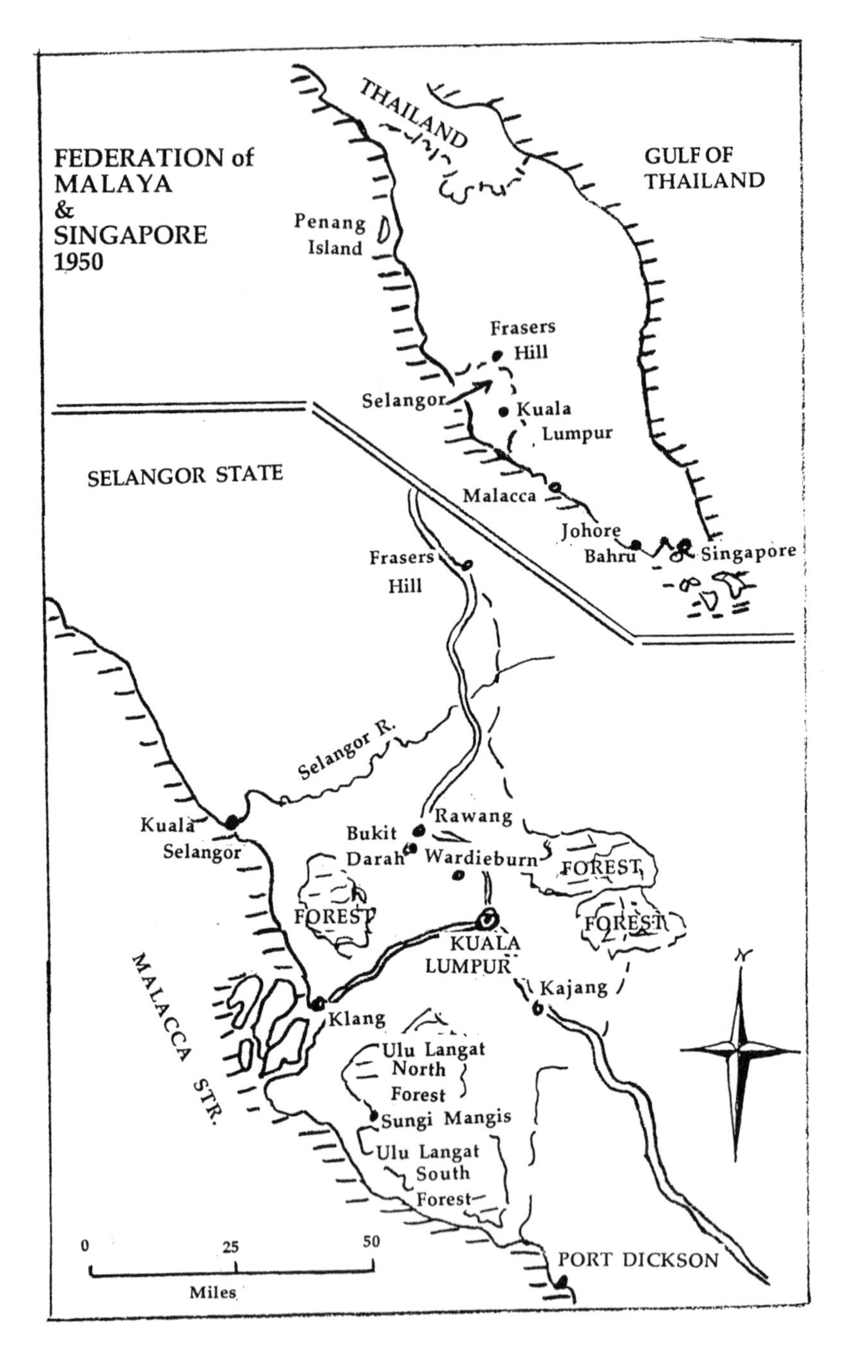

Selangor State and Federation of Malaya & Singapore, 1950

In July I flew down to Singapore to collect Richard, who'd flown out in a BOAC Constellation aircraft at our expense – no free travel for Service children in those days. I was due for leave, so the four of us drove in our new Vauxhall Vanguard car to a Leave Centre in the Cameron Highlands in the State of Pahang, a hundred miles north of KL, again escorted part of the way by the Twelth Lancers. Unfortunately, there was little for the boys to do, rather dull for them, but an ENSA troupe (Forces Entertainment) gave a couple of enjoyable shows. The cool hill air, and lack of terrorist activity was a relief.

Paul Clementi-Smith was posted away, so I again became second-in-command, holding this appointment for the rest of my time with the Battalion. Rumours about our departure began to circulate. Late in the year we heard we were to be relieved by the Somerset Light Infantry and embark for England in early 1953 – stage in Meanee Barracks, Colchester, followed by leave, prior to moving to Trieste. Time flew by, it didn't seem long before we were on our way home.

As our Band had returned to the UK some while before, we were played down to KL station by the Somerset's Band, the Battalion marching, with fixed bayonets and Colours flying, from Wardiburn Camp down the Batu road lined by smiling Chinese and Malays, past the High Commissioner and the Sultan of Selangor, the latter took the salute outside the Government buildings – Murna and Charlie standing close behind the dais. Before entering the station, Philip Morcombe laid a wreath on the war memorial, in memory of our fallen comrads.

A great crowd of friends and wellwishers had assembled in the station to see us off. Planters and business people, as well as Government Officials, Service Officers and their families. The Sultan, The High Commissioner General Sir Gerald Templer, and many others walked along the platform chatting to the soldiers leaning out of carriage windows. Dusk had fallen, Murna and Charlie were already in our reserved compartment when I joined them; General Sir Hugh Stockwell, GOC Malaya, who knew us well, came into the compartment for a word or two. There was much cheering, quaffing of beer and general bonhomie. A fantastic and well deserved sendoff – after all we'd accounted for more CTs than any other British battalion during the Emergency.

In the gathering dusk of 8th January 1953, the train pulled slowly out of Kuala Lumpur station, to the haunting strains of 'Auld Lang Syne'. A memorable farewell to the 1st Battalion The Suffolk Regiment – The Old 12th of Foot.

Murna Bevan. Wuppertal, Germany 1956

Chapter 18

The coronation Parade in London and the Emergency in Trieste, 1953–55

On arrival at Singapore from KL, officers' families were accommodated in The Rex Hostel, not very comfy but adequate. We explored the island, went on excursions in army launches in the beautiful harbour, and were made temporary members of the Tanglin Club, which had an excellent swimming pool – an enjoyable interlude.

Our Vauxhall Vanguard car was driven down by a Regimental Driver, and put aboard an aircraft carrier – one of the few perks I ever wangled in my army career. We collected it five weeks later at Portsmouth – total charge £1!

On the 20th January 1953 we embarked on Her Majesty's Troopship *Georgic*, 27,000 tons. As we sailed out of Singapore harbour the RAF saluted the Battalion with a Fly-Past – most exceptional – a great compliment. The Battalion occupied most of the ship so the voyage was very much a family affair – Murna and I certainly enjoyed it, I'm sure the other families did too. Plenty of entertainment: competition shooting at balloons over the stern of the ship, a fancy dress dance, the ship's daily distance raffle, endless Tombola (Bingo), boxing and tug-of-war competitions, outdoor cinema shows, and all sorts of deck-sports. The time raced by, soon we'd changed out of jungle green drill into serge battledress and were steaming up the coast of Spain in glorious sunny weather.

After we'd docked at Liverpool on the 12th February, a large

Regimental Reception Party came aboard. The Colonel of the Regiment, Brigadier Bertie Backhouse, gave an address over the Tanoy to all ranks, saying how proud everyone in Suffolk was of our successes in Malaya and so on. The ship's owners laid on a drinks party in the saloon and beer for the troops – we were all somewhat overwhelmed by the warmth of the reception, but if the truth were known, most of us were anxious to get started on our leave. We went by train – First Class – to Reading, and spent four nights in the Great Western Hotel, before going to our house, 12 Deacons Hill Road, Elstree, Herts, just vacated by American Airforce tenants.

In March I rejoined the Battalion in Meanee Barracks, Colchester; Murna remained at Elstree. The Battalion had a full programme of welcoming visits to towns in Suffolk, including Ipswich, Sudbury and Bury St. Edmunds. The procedure was generally the same – an addresses by the Mayor, a reply by the CO, a march through the town followed by a good 'blow-out' laid on by the Civic authorities. The highlight was an officers' ball in the Atheneum in Bury St. Edmunds.

While the Battalion was in Colchester, Philip Morcombe handed over command to 'Tiny' Heal – I remained second-in-command. I'd first met 'Tiny' (so called because of his imposing figure) in Blackdown in 1933, when I was in the Supplementary Reserve doing my annual attachment to the 1st Suffolk; we'd not served together since February 1936 in Plymouth, when I left to join 2nd Suffolk in India. We got on well enough, but there wasn't the same easy rapport between us as I'd had with Philip. I'd only met Moy, his wife, on odd occasions, and was doubtful whether she and Murna would hit it off.

With everyone back from leave, the Battalion moved to Trieste in April. Tiny detailed me to command the detachment representing the 1st Suffolk in Queen Elizabeth II's Coronation Parade early in June, so I remained in Colchester; Murna was still in Elstree arranging for the house to be let again. We'd collected our car from Portsmouth, and planned to drive to Trieste immediatly after the Coronation Parade.

The detachment consisted of Lieutenants Alan Horrex and Bob Godfrey, both of whom had been awarded the Military Cross in Malaya; Mr. Duffy, the Regimental Sergeant Major; two Colour Sergeants and two Sergeants; a Corporal and Lance Corporal. We remained in Colchester, practising for the parade, quite a sweat. Bob and Alan carried the Colours, the oldest still carried by any regiment in the army; six foot square, they had been presented in

1849, taken by the 1st Suffolk to Australia, and carried in action in New Zealand during the Maori Wars of 1861–1867. Apart from being historic, they were made of beautifully embroidered silk, the Regimental Colour in particular being an unusually attractive shade of yellow – both were extremely frail.

The great day the 6th June arrived. All units taking part in the parade had been billetted in Olympia for two days, we set off very early in the morning in a drizzle – more rain forecast. Being 12th in seniority in the infantry, we were near the head of the Regular Army infantry detachments. A wonderful sight, the Colours of every regiment in the army on parade – never to be seen again. We marched the five miles to Green Park near Buckingham Palace to the music of bands spaced throughout the column, where we halted, fell out, 'eased springs' as we say in the army, had a cup of tea and a sandwich, then fell in again and continued the march. During this break the Coronation Service was taking place. It was still drizzling.

We continued round the Palace, down Birdcage Walk, past Westminster Abbey, up Whitehall, through Trafalgar Square and along Piccadilly, where we came to a temporarily halt opposite The Ritz Hotel. It was then raining steadily, the fabric of the Colours was soaked – the weight of water caused them to slip down their poles! Bob and Alan effected emergency repairs by securing them with their tasselled cords; we were very worried and hoped they wouldn't disintergrate completely. It didn't help seeing people in The Ritz tucking into caviar and quaffing champagne, they even had the nerve to wave to us while we were steadily getting wetter – my new Blue No.1 Uniform (which had cost me £35) was already soaked through.

Murna took up a position just inside Hyde Park near Marble Arch with my sister Elizabeth and two of my nieces, Brita and Corinna. I spotted them as we turned down Oxford Street and waved – I'm not sure whether they saw me – they said they did. By the time the column returned to Olympia we'd covered thirteen miles, not all that far, but we'd been on our feet for eight hours and my knee was giving me hell, it was a tremendous relief to get my boots off. Each infantry battalion was allotted only eight Coronation Medals; Tiny reckoned I'd already got enough medals, so I didn't get the 'gong', a pity, it would have rounded my collection up to ten.

We'd arranged to lease our house in Elstree, again to American airforce people; our heavy baggage had already been sent ahead to Trieste by the Military Forwarding Officer. On 12th June we set off,

Charlie ensconced on a platform of cases across the back seat. We crossed the Channel by ferry from Dover to Calais, spent the first night at the Bristol Hotel in Reims; the next night in Victoria Hotel, Basle, Switzerland; the third night in the Unter Bergen Hotel, Innsbruck, Austria; reaching Trieste on the 15th June. A long and tiring journey, we took turns at the wheel – Charlie lasted out well. In Trieste we'd been allotted rooms in the Excelsior Hotel, slap on the quayside, taken over as an officers' hostel.

1st Suffolk formed part of the British Element of the Trieste Force (BETFOR). The Battalion shared the large imposing Rosetti Barracks with another British battalion. The ownership of this beautiful city at the head of the Adriatic, connected to Italy by a single road along a narrow coastal strip, had been contested for centuries; up until the end of WWI it formed part of the Austro-Hungarian Empire. The population was predominantly Italian, but the Yugoslaves held all the hinterland and the escarpment overlooking and surrounding the city; not a very happy situation, trouble was always simmering just below the surface. BETFOR's job was to prevent the Italians and the Yugoslavs from stealing a march on each other by a sudden descent on the city.

In August we moved into a flat in the Piazza Dalmatia, and were allotted a pleasant young Yugoslav woman as a daily help. There was lots to do and see – super sea bathing, picnics, lots of Regimental and Service functions, open air opera in the castle, excellent restaurants and tratorias; a complete change from Malaya.

Bill Brinkley, of the Royal Norfolk Regiment, was posted to 1st Suffolk; being senior to me by service, Tiny had no option but to make him second-in-command. Yet again I found myself ousted by an outsider, very galling and hard to stomach, but there was nothing I could do except grin and bear it – I reverted to Company Commander. I liked Bill, Murna got on well with his wife Jean, who was a dear.

Owing to lack of facilities in Trieste, British battalions went in turn for a month's Rest and Retraining to a camp at Schmelz, in the hills of south eastern Austria. In July the Battalion moved by road through Italy, up a pass in the eastern Alps into Austria, marching the last few miles up a mountain track to the camp. Kit was ferried up by a primitive unreliable cable hoist – individuals sat in tiny two-man wooden goldolas, frequently getting stuck swinging about half-way up. It was a lovely remote area of soaring mountains and valleys, with alpine flowers, lakes and trout streams. We slept in log huts, built originally for the German army. Although constantly soaked through, we did a lot of training and enjoyed the change and freedom, after the restrictions of urban life in Trieste. Back again in Trieste, Minden Day was celebrated on 1st August in the traditional manner; the American General commanding the U.S Element in Trieste inspected the parade and took the salute.

Richard had come out for the summer holidays, so we motored up to Austria for a week at the Golf Hotel, an officers' leave hostel, near Klagenfurt on the Worthersee Lake, convenient for interesting places such as the fairy-tale Hochocterwitz castle, and the Gros Glockner glacier (12,400 feet) – thankfully in those days there were virtually no tourists.

Incidents between the Italians and the Yugoslavs had been increasing, one could feel tension in the air. Even so it came as a complete surprise when General Jack Winterton, GOC of Trieste Trust Forces, who lived in the medieval Duino Castle outside the city, speaking on the Forces Radio on the evening of 24th October, gave the startling news that all British families were to leave Trieste within the next twenty four hours; I think the American families were evacuated by the US Navy. There was a mad rush to get the wives and children organised.

In the event Murna and Charlie left early on the 26th October in our car with as much stuff as we could cram into it; they joined other Suffolk wives and children – Maureen and Melanie Dewar, Vera and Mike Lockett, Prue Fairholme and Betty and Colette Boycott – a convoy of four cars – heading for Wuppertal in North Rhine Westfalar, where the Battalion was to move to when the situation in Trieste allowed; they managed to keep together for much of the journey.

Murna, with Charlie, motored through Italy up into the Austrian Tyrol, spending the first night in Hotel Krone, Bad Gastein, having put the car on a railway flat through a long tunnel under the Alps; the second night at Hotel Roseraie, Augsburg, in the south of Germany; then right across Germany to Darmstad, staying the night at the Hotel Aur Taube; the final day they crossed the Rhine, arriving at the married quarter we'd been allotted, 32 Ost Prussenweg, Wuppertal, on the 29th October. Considering she had to keep Charlie a small boy of five amused all the way, while concentrating on driving through three countries she'd never been to before it was a stout effort – she was a most competent driver. All our married families were given a splendid welcome by 2nd Battalion The Durham Light Infantry (DLI) who were tremendously hospitable, the Suffolk wives were fussed over and had a wonderful time. Bill Brinkley was sent to Wuppertal to take charge of the rear echelon administering the families, and preparing the barracks ready for our eventual arrival; consequently, to all intents and purposes, I again became second-in-command.

The situation in the city was daily becoming uglier, there were several killings; Italian flags hung out of windows on one side of a street, Yugoslav ones on the other. The dockers in the large shipyards, mostly Communists, were waiting on the sidelines. It was rumoured that an armoured Italian force was poised to crash through the Frontier Post and head for the city; clearly a storm was about to break.

Meanwhile, on the diplomatic front, Anthony Eden, the British Foreign Secretary, was pulling out all the stops. We in Trieste knew nothing about these goings on being fully occupied trying to keep the lid on a simmering cauldron assisted by the Trieste Police, an excellent body of men trained on London Metropolitan Police Force lines even down to the shape of their helmets, with senior ex-British police officers in charge.

Tiny Heal decided to prepare for the worst. Knowing I'd been involved in Internal Security (IS) situations in India, he told me to train each Company in IS drills. The next day I ran a series of short courses on the parade ground, no one really believed we'd ever have to put them into practice. However, the training had barely been completed than Malcolm Dewar's Company was rapidly clambering into four clapped-out grossly over-loaded 3-ton lorries, all that could be rustled up, wearing steel helmets, armed with rifles and fifty rounds SAA per man. There had been rioting, resulting in a number of shootings and deaths in the Piazza Unita, the central square in the city. At the top of the piazza was an imposing Town Hall, flanked by large buildings forming a hollow square, with a road along the harbour edge at the bottom. Malcolm's Company de-bussed in a side street, formed up in column four abreast (as I'd taught them), charged their magazines, fixed bayonets, and with rifles at the high-port marched off smartly round the corner into the bottom of the Piazza Unita with Malcolm – a tall, gaunt, wiry figure, his steel helmet clamped down at a slightly jaunty angle – in the lead.

At the top of the piazza a crowd had gathered round a burning Royal Navy staff car; apparently a senior RN officer had blithely driven into the square; when forced to stop by the crowd he'd got away, but the car had been set alight. The communist flag was flying above the Town Hall. When Malcolm with his Company suddenly appeared, the sight of a disciplined body of determined British troops was enough for the rioters, the Piazza was soon empty and the entrances sealed off; a subaltern and escort entered the Town Hall and pulled down the Red Flag. An excellent photo of Malcolm with his Company entering the Piazza Unita, rifles at the high-port, appeared on the front cover of the 'Soldier' magazine captioned – 'Centuries of experience in maintaining law and order' – or something like that. Another plus-point for 1st Suffolk.

A day later I took my Company down. By then US troops had taken over, the Piazza was jammed with an impressive array of military hardware. Vehicles sporting heavy calibre machine guns, enormous radios – the lot. GIs in full battle kit, cameras at the ready, smoking Lucky Strike fags – 'Total War – Yes Sir'! They put our four ancient 3-ton lorries to shame – but they hadn't succeeded in quelling the rioting.

The American Major in command informed me that there were machine guns in the Lloyd-Trestino office building opposite to where I'd decided to establish my HQ; when he'd cleared all his vehicles and clutter from the Piazza I sent an officer over to investigate – no MGs were found.

For the next ten days or so the Battalion maintained a presence in the city; there were only a few minor incidents. It was dull and uncomfy, reminding me of my days in the Police Station in Chandi Chowk in Old Delhi during the Gandhi troubles of 1942, but it wasn't so hot – and there weren't any mossies.

To our great disappointment, we heard that we were to remain indefinitely in Trieste. Our baggage had been moved to Germany, all barrack furniture and fittings had been sold to local contractors, we were in effect camping in empty barracks, and it was cold, very cold. There was one telephone line for use at specific times for calls to Wuppertal; we each had a few minutes. I spoke to Murna, not very satisfactory, but at least I knew she was alright because she'd held a party, to which she invited all the 'deserted' wives and Rear Echelon officers: Bill Deller, Harold Wiggington and Richard Wilson.

By the middle of December the situation had eased considerably. I got a week's leave, travelling by the military MEDLOCK train to Wuppertal. I found all well at our new home, a modern, comfortable house in a development, known rather disparagingly as 'The Cabbage Patch' occupied entirely by officers' families; the Boycotts were next door, the Dewars Locketts and Lummises not far away. Murna and the boys had a good Christmas with lots of parties. Heavy snow fell, so she bought them each a toboggan, which kept them occupied. In Trieste, apart

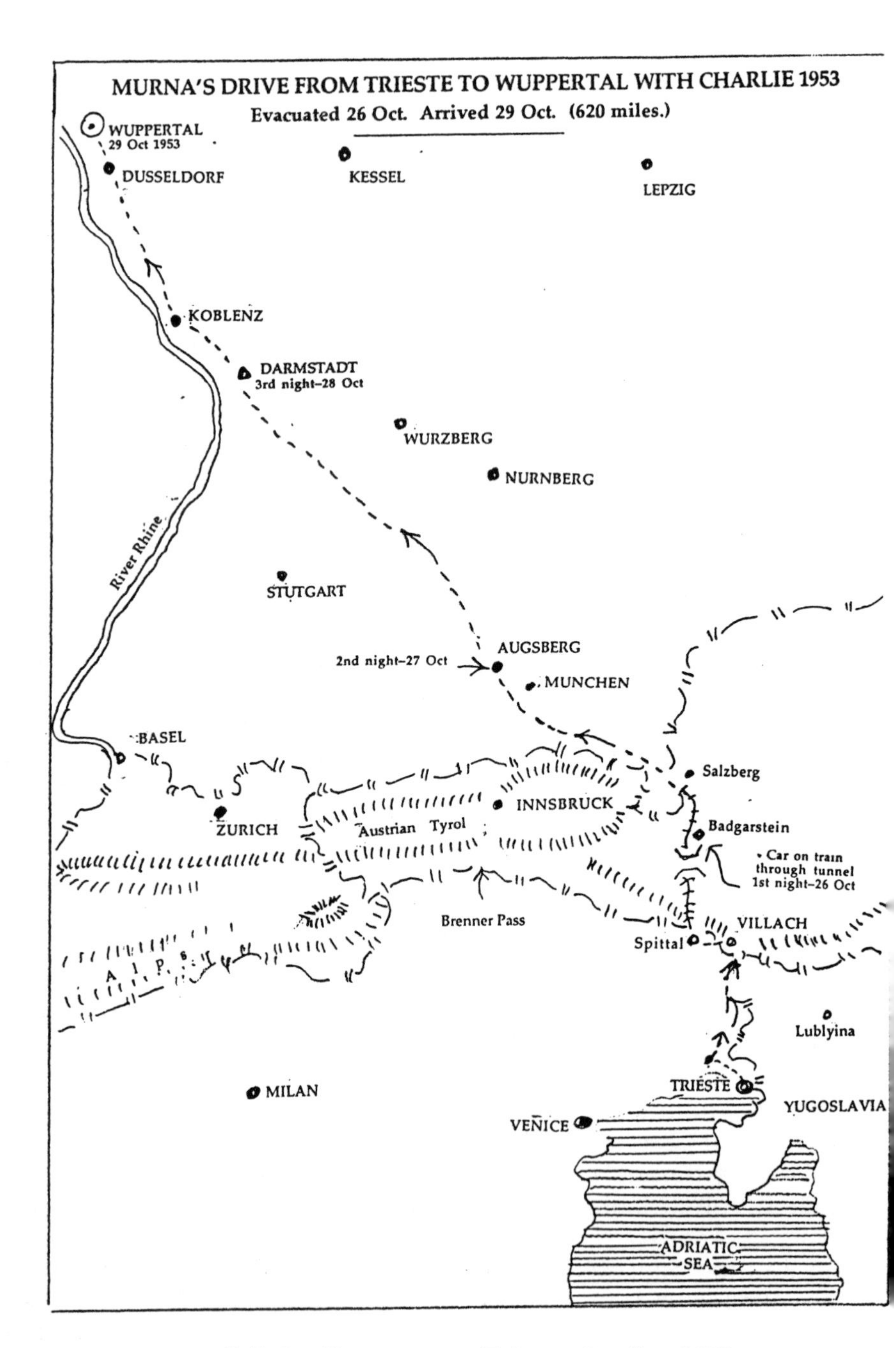

1st Suffolk families evacuate Trieste, October 1953

from missing our families and being uncomfortable, we enjoyed ourselves, as the British Army invariably succeeds in doing – under all conditions.

Bill Brinkley was posted away, so Tiny Heal sent me to Wuppertal on the 15th January 1954 to replace him which suited me excellently. This was my farewell to Trieste; it had been an interesting, and at times an exciting episode although hankering to get back to Murna I left with a tinge of regret. When released from Trieste the Battalion was due to join 6th Infantry Brigade, 2nd Division, British Army of the Rhine (BAOR) in Wuppertal, the Brigadier, Cosmo Nevill, and his wife Grania, were charmers, we became good friends. The other two battalions in the Brigade were 1st Northamptons and 2nd DLI – we all got on extremely well.

In May I took a week's leave. We went to The Kuthaus, an officers' leave centre in the Hartz mountains, near Winterberg, almost on the border between West and East Germany. A pleasant change but rather dull for Charlie, the only other children were Canadians based at Zoest – Murna and I enjoyed the marvellous forest scenery. Soon afterwards I left for a six-week course at the Senior Officers' School, Erlstoke Park, near Devizes in Wiltshire. I hated being away from Murna but we both knew that it was important that I got a good report – which presumably I did.

We stayed in Wuppertal until August, then I took up a staff appointment in the Military Training Directorate at the War Office at Chessington, Surrey. Once more we faced the problem of where to live. Our house in Elstree was let, anyway there was no point in going there as it was too far from Chessington. Eventually we got an army hiring, a large maisonette in Reigate, belonging to an elderly couple, Colonel and Mrs Battensby who became good friends. We were happy and fairly comfortable there for the next twenty months. Meantime Charlie started at a small day-school nearby, Richard left his Prep school in Redhill and started at Wellington College, the famous public school in Berkshire, his fees paid by the RAF Benevolent Fund. We hadn't any friends in the area so it was rather lonely for Murna – but we'd acquired our first TV!

The War Office job was boring in the extreme, but I did manage to wangle a week's visit to Canada in March 1955. First Class by BOAC Strato-Cruiser from Heathrow (still wartime huts and tents) to Montreal, then on to Ottawa, where I and another chap from the WO stayed in the Lord Elgin Hotel. Endless conferences, heavy meals and too much booze. I don't think we achieved anything worth while, however, I saw quite a lot of Ontario, but deep snow made getting around difficult.

Maureen and Malcolm Dewar spent the odd night with us in Reigate, he was then attached to the School of Artillery at Larkhill in Wiltshire. We arranged to go with them and their children Melanie and Michael, for a ten-day holiday to Brittany, staying at a convent, L'Abbaye St. Jacut – they'd been there before and recommended it to us. Primarily for French families, it was pretty basic, the food was entirely French, wholesome but the portions somewhat meagre. By-and-large we enjoyed it, despite the fleas, which attacked both Richard and Charlie mercilessly. It was always fun when Malcolm was around.

Towards the end of 1955 I got a letter from the War Office, telling me that I'd been selected to take over command of 1st Suffolk the following May. Tremendous news – at long last I wouldn't have to play second-fiddle any more. Murna was delighted; I was quite as pleased for her as for myself. She'd 'followed the drum', coping wonderfully with many moves, making a home wherever we were, never complaining, always supportive and attractive – I was still very much in love with her.

With promotion to Lieutenant Colonel assured, and the challenge of commanding the only regular battalion of The Suffolk Regiment ahead, I felt my future was reasonably assured. Time flew by. I crossed from Harwich to the Hook of Holland on the ferry *Vienna* on 20th April 1956, arriving by train in Wuppertal the next day. It was all very familiar. However, I knew I wouldn't be there long – 1st Suffolk was to move to Cyprus (of all places) in August 1956.

The Battalion occupied a fine prewar German army barracks. Tiny and Moy Heal were due to vacate the CO's house, 107 Adolf Vorverkstrasse, the most imposing quarter in 'The Cabbage Patch' within a few days, in the meantime I lived in the Mess. At an impressive handing-over parade on the 28th April, I addressed the Battalion, saying how proud I was to assume command. Next day the Heals were bid farewell – their car towed out of the barracks in the traditional way by the Warrant Officers and Sergeants. Then I was on my own, in charge of some seven hundred soldiers, many of whom I'd served with and knew well, indeed seven officers and NCOs had been with me in 2nd Suffolk on the North-West Frontier. There were also the wives and families – no mean additional responsibility.

Murna arrived on 8th May in our Ford Zephyr estate car, she soon got things sorted out in our well furnished quarter. We had a batman, a driver and a German women to help in the house, so she wasn't everlastingly in the kitchen.

DIVISIONAL ROUTINE ORDERS
by
MAJOR GENERAL CAR NEVILL, CBE, DSO
GENERAL OFFICER COMMANDING
SECOND INFANTRY DIVISION

HILDEN 11 June 1956 DATE OF ISSUE

SPECIAL ORDER OF THE DAY

1. The successes achieved by units and individuals of 2nd Infantry Division in the BAOR Rifle Meeting 1956 warrants this Special Order of the Day.

2. I congratulate the following on their achievements:

CHAMPION SHOT BAOR

Sergeant C. CHAPMAN 2nd Infantry Division column RASC

RUNNER UP CHAMPION OFFICER BAOR AND THIRD CHAMPION SHOT BAOR

Lieutenant Colonel W.S. BEVAN 1st Battalion The Suffolk Regiment

Within a week we motored up to the All Arms Training Centre at Sennelager. I was in the Battalion shooting team competing in the BAOR annual rifle meeting, we stayed with friends in Paderborn nearby. In those days BAOR numbered some seventy thousand, there were also Canadian, Belgian and other allied formations. Shooting was taken very seriously, the standard of marksmanship high, competition fierce. Over the years I'd done a good deal of competition shooting at Bisley and with civilian clubs during my time at the War Office. However, having only just arrived, I was very out of practice. Nevertheless, to my surprise, I succeeded in getting excellent scores, ending up on the third day of the meeting Runner-up Officer Champion Shot – pipped in a shoot-off by a Canadian – and third overall.

On the 1st July 1956, the Battalion marched with the Band and Drums at its head, and the band of 1st Buffs in the centre, from Harding Barracks to Wuppertal station where it entrained and set off for the UK. We'd attended a succession of farewell parties during the previous fortnight, so were somewhat jaded and quite relieved to be on the move again, although, as we'd heard that married accommodation in Cyprus was extremely scarce, the prospect a further spell of separation from Murna lay like a dark cloud on the horizon. The physical separation from her was bad enough, but accommodation, and schooling for the boys, posed the usual ghastly problems.

I travelled with the troops, Murna came over with Charlie on the ferry *Amsterdam* from the Hook of Holland to Harwich and drove to Ardleigh Park, a guest house near Colchester, were we stayed for a week. The Battalion de-trained at Colchester station – well known to Murna and me – and after a welcoming address by The Colonel of the Regiment, Brigadier Bertie Backhouse, marched up North Hill, past the Town Hall where the Mayor took the salute – Murna and Charles again standing behind the dais – thence three miles on to Roman Way Camp, where we were staging before sailing to Cyprus.

Shortly after our arrival in England, I was summoned to Clarence House to meet Princess Margaret, The Colonel-in-Chief of the Regiment. Her ADC, Francis Legh, a major in the Guards, ushered me into a small private sitting room where she greeted me, and asked me to sit down next to her on a sofa. She was a petite, beautifully dressed, exceptionally attractive young woman, with lovely eyes and a flawless complexion – still unmarried. I was anxious to do the right thing in what was for me a completely new situation – after all she was the Queen's sister, but I'd no need to worry, she quickly put me at my ease. We discussed Regimental affairs, in particular how the families remaining in England would manage; she was well clued-up, I was sure she had the interest of the Regiment at heart. After three quarters of an hour I felt it was time to leave, but she insisted that I stayed on a bit longer. Although I had to adhere to strict protocol, she didn't make me feel awkward – it was quite an experience. I was to meet her again on several occasions, each time was a pleasure and an honour.

During the summer holidays Murna and the boys stayed in the garage flat at Uncle Charles Gibbs's house, Stoke Abbas, in the small hamlet of South Stoke, Oxfordshire, on the Thames. Not exactly the lap of luxury, but it was free and my uncle enjoyed having them; being August, they were able to get out and help with the harvesting on nearby farms.

I stayed at Roman Way Camp, where feverish preparations were in hand for a visit by Princess Margaret. Despite constant rain, the parade went off well – I made a short welcoming speech to which the Princess replied. She then visited the messes, met the families and spoke to some of the soldiers.

After lunch in the Officers' Mess, which Murna attended, the Princess drove off to the cheers of all ranks. A large number of guests attended the parade, including my sister Elizabeth, and my eldest niece Brita. The visit was voted a great success.

Murna at South Stoke, Goring-on-Thames, 1955

Chapter 19

C.O. 1st Suffolk During the Emergency in Cyprus, 1956–1959

On the 10th August 1956 1st Suffolk embarked at Southampton on the troopship *Dilwara*. Also on board was the 1st Oxfordshire and Buckinghamshire Light Infantry, commanded by Tony Reed (subsequently to reach the rank of Full General). After a pleasant voyage, we arrived at Limassol on the 21st August, to the welcoming sound of the Band and Drums of 1st Royal Norfolk, playing on the quayside as we came ashore in lighters. We then set off in civilian buses on a hundred mile journey to Aberdeen Camp, Xeros, on the north west coast of the island, taking over from the 1st Gordon Highlanders.

The return to the island of my birth, after a lapse of almost thirty-four years, was a nostalgic experience. In the bustle of disembarkation and getting on the move, I hadn't time to take in much, but somehow everything seemed familiar. The smell of wild thyme, the colour of the sky, the goats and donkeys, it all suddenly struck me in a rush – I thought of my parents and hoped I wouldn't let them down.

For operational purposes I was responsible for twenty-five square miles of sparsely populated mostly mountainous country, with cultivated areas along the coast and round the small town of Morphu, where my father had set up an experimental farm thirty-five years before. The population was mostly Greek, except for the large Turkish village of Lefka. Colin Thom, the Assistant District Commissioner, Lou D'Olivera the Superintendant of Police and I, formed the Lefka District Security Committee. We met daily, reviewed the situation and decided on action to be taken. I came directly under the Chief of Staff in Nicosia, but for administrative purposes relied on 50 Independent Brigade, also in Nicosia, commanded by Brigadier Ramsay Bunbury, who became a close friend.

As this is not a Regimental History, I don't intend dealing with my time in command in great detail. However, as my family has been so closely connected with Cyprus since my father arrived in 1901, I feel some explanation of the emergency is necessary. I'm going to quote a passage from the excellent History of The Suffolk Regiment, written by my friend Bob Godfrey:

> 'The situation on the island of Cyprus, after simmering for several years, had blown up into a major crisis towards the end of 1954. For a long time there had been a movement among the Greek Cypriots who made up four-fifths of the island's population (the remainder being largely Turkish) for union with Greece (Enosis) and when the British Government announced in June 1954, that it intended to transfer the Headquarters of its Middle Eastern Forces from Egypt to Cyprus, the statement triggered off an instant response from the supporters of Enosis, led from the pulpit by their champiom, Archbishop Makarios.
>
> The Greek Cypriots were not alone in seeing their chances of union with Greece fading with the arrival of the British HQ from Egypt. The Greek Government itself immediately appealed to the United Nations to consider its claim to the island. In December, 1954, the UN General Assembly refused even to debate the request, thereby triggering off an outburst of violence in Cyprus.
>
> But worse was to come. A guerrilla force calling itself Eoka had been formed by young Greek Cypriots. Led by George Grivas, a former Colonel in the Greek Army who adopted the legendary name of Dighenis, its activities were to become a serious menace to the Government of Cyprus and led over the next eighteen months to a major build-up of Army units in the Colony.
>
> Eoka operated in two ways. Its agents stirred up trouble in the towns on the one hand, while its gangs of armed guerrillas ambushed security forces and attacked Police Stations in rural areas on the other, aiming to weaken the resolve of those Greek Cypriots who served as Policemen and Government

> Officials. Once an action was carried out, the terrorists, as they were known by the security forces simply faded away. Those in the towns were quickly lost among the general population and the armed gangs had the rugged terrain of the Kyrenia Mountain Range in the North and the main central Troodos Mountains, dominated by Mount Olympus, in the heartland of the island, in which to hide.'

Although the country was completely different, the tactics I adopted were similar to those we'd employed with such success in Malaya: ambushes; cordoning-off and searching villages for known terrorists, based on Special Branch information supplemented by our own local knowledge; road checks and above all, constant patrolling to dominate the area and deny Eoka any opportunity to take the initiative.

While we were in Xeros, much effort and sweat was expended on large and small operations of this type, they rarely proved rewarding and were generally frustrating and time-consuming. Patrolling along the crests of the foothills, or climbing steep rocky re-entrants in the heat of a Cyprus summer, was physically very demanding. However, we suffered few casualties, which I attributed to the forceful action taken by all ranks, specially junior officers and NCOs. The terrorists soon realised that to ambush a Suffolk patrol or vehicle was to court a rapid and vehement response, for the most part they decided discretion was the better part of valour and gave us a wide berth.

We had our successes. One in particular was when a night patrol ambushed and killed Marcos Dracos, second-in-command of Grivas's Eoka organization. The Governor, Field Marshal Lord Harding, flew out by helicopter early in the morning and congratulated me, Arthur Campbell the Company Commander, and the men of the patrol. Although only a minor military engagement, the psychological impact on the locals was immense, as had been the case in Malaya when Lieu Kon Kim was killed. It was undoubtedly a considerable triumph and featured prominently in the UK national, and East Anglian newspapers.

I flew home on the 4th October to attend a course at the RAF School of Land/Air Warfare at Old Sarum near Salisbury. Murna met me and we stayed at my sister Elizabeth's flat in Hampstead which fitted in well as the Edholms were away. The course only lasted five days, so we had a wonderful few days together afterwards. I flew back in an RAF aircraft, stopping at El Adem near Benghazi. In March 1957 I attended the Infantry Com-

1st Suffolk – Winners Cyprus Dist. Shooting Competition, 1958
Sitting (left to right) Sgt. Ridout, Lt. Morton, Capt. Starling, Lt Col. Bevan, Capt. Cobbold, CSM Lyon, CSM Hazelwood, CSM Evans

W S B being presented with a shooting prize by Brigadier Bunbury. Cyprus, 1958.

manders Conference at the School of Infantry, Warminster, Wilts, then took leave before returning to the Battalion.

Commanding a battalion in a non-family station is always easier than having to cope with all the problems associated with married families, while simultaneously coping with urgent operational matters. Without doubt I was fortunate in not having this distraction during the first nine months the Battalion was on operations in the island. I pined for my wife as much as the next chap – rather more I reckoned – but I knew there was no possibility of getting families out while we were in Xeros – anyway there was nowhere for them to live.

In May 1957 there was a general change round of units within the island, as a result 1st Suffolk was moved from Xeros to a tented and partially hutted camp on a dusty windy bit of land, not a tree or blade of grass, on the outskirts of Nicosia known as Kykko Camp – not all that far from where I was born. The move meant families could join us. I immediatly set about finding a house which had to be near the camp. I heard of a family shortly returning to the UK occupying an army hiring – 13 Achaeans Street, near enough to Kykko. I settled on it and made preparations for Murna's arrival with Charlie.

Since the beginning of December Murna had been living in a rather pokey little house at West Mersea, a sort of island not far from Colchester. Vera Lockett, who was always helpful and fun, was living close by with her two boys, her husband Frank, a considerable character, was with me in Cyprus. On the 14th May, Murna and Charlie sailed from Liverpool aboard the *Empire Pride*, a comfortable old troopship. I went down to meet her at Limmasol on the 24th May, she looked absolutely blooming, quite perfect – she lost no time in telling me that she was pregnant.

The Battalion stayed in Kykko camp for the next two years, maintaining law and order in the old walled-city inside the moat, and in the immediate surrounding country. No easy task during periods of tension, which increased or decreased according to the success or failure of the political machinations at Westminster to resolve the Cyprus problem. Eoka's methods ranged from murder and thuggery to carefully orchestrated riots and demonstrations, especially by students, frequently ending in bloodshed. Patrolling the narrow streets of the old city was an unenviable duty, but the soldiers took it in their stride – just another job, never losing their nerve or their tempers in spite of constant provocation. For long periods we were fully stretched and constantly on duty; then Grivas would call a truce for a week or so, ostensibly to enable negotiations to take place, actually to gain time to reorganize his forces. During these truces we were able to lead a more normal existence, and get over to Kyrenia for sea bathing at 'The Slab' a reserved area immediatly below Kyrenia's crusader castle's massive walls – where I used to fish for crabs when a boy.

In early November 1957 a Colonel from HQ Cyprus District and I attended Iraqi Army manoeuvres as Observers. We spent the first night in Bierut, the next day on to Baghdad, putting-up in the Semiramis Hotel, considered grand by Iraqi standards but actually pretty grotty. We were under the wing of the Military Attache and his Assistant, Bill Lawson (who later put up a 'good show' – displaying considerable personal courage in the dicy situation in the Belgian Congo – he retired as a General). After a few days we motored up to Rawanduz, a large Kurdish village in the hills close to the Iraq-Persian border, where a camp for Foreign Observers had been pitched. It was wet, windy, muddy and cold. We each had an ancient bell-tent, everything was rudimentary, especially the sanitary arrangements.

It was an interesting experience. The Iraqi troops seemed keen and fairly hardy, but their officers, with a few exceptions, didn't impress me. Our party attracted the attention of the Commandant of the Iraqi Staff College, an Anglophile and pleasant chap. He came round of an evening to our tents to get our opinions on the day's manoeuvres. I didn't see him go to the American's tents, in spite of their large party and impressive high-tech cameras and so on.

One evening we were invited by King Hassan to a 'feast' in his private camp a short distance away. I had a few words with him, taking the opportunity to pass on best wishes from one of my officers, Richard Wilson, who had been at Harrow with him. The King was clearly pleased at being able to talk freely with no political overtones. He enquired eagerly: "How is Richard?", he was clearly under stress. A few months later, he, and his family, were a brutally assassinated.

I was the only one in our party to have a camera, a pretty ropy one at that. I took as many photos of Iraqi officers as I could without being too obvious, later passing them to the Intelligence people in the War Office who showed little interest, they wouldn't even pay for the film. I was understandably somewhat disgruntled. The photos, although out of date, might perhaps have been useful during The Gulf War.

No sooner had I returned to Nicosia, than I set off again for England to attend an Amalgamation Conference at the War Office, called to decide how best to amalgamate and rename seven infantry regiments: The Royal Norfolk, The Suffolk, The Bedfordshire and Hertfordshire, The Essex, The Royal Lincolns, the Royal Leicesters and the Northhamptons – a daunting task. Each regiment had given distinguished service over hundreds of years, evident from the Battle Honours emblazoned on their Colours. They all had peculiarities, and jealously guarded traditions – each regiment considered itself superior to all the others. They formed a very important part of the country's heritage, to monkey-about with them would most certainly cause a furious outcry throughout the land.

After three days of deliberations – not acrimonious but a good deal of in-fighting, a decision was arrived at which was put to the Army Council for confirmation. The upshot was that The Royal Norfolk and Suffolk Regiments were to amalgamated and become the East Anglian Regiment; in all seven regiments were reduced to three. A traumatic experience, especially for the oldest: the Royal Norfolk and Suffolk were both raised in 1685 by King James II. For two hundred and seventy three years they had served King and Country, a very impressive record.

Whilst in the UK I was again summoned to Clarence House, to report to Princess Margaret our Colonel-in-Chief. The procedure was the same as on the first occasion. She was still unmarried; a most attractive young woman.

I got back to Cyprus on 5th December, a fortnight before Murna was due to give birth. When she'd first arrived we had a Greek Cypriot woman to help in the house, but after a bomb had been discovered in the Governor's bed (Sir John Harding) in Government House, Cypriot servants were banned. From then on my Batman, Corporal Laws, my Driver and a Radio Operator slept in the house. This worked alright until Murna went into the BMH on 29th December, remaining there till 8th January. Alice was born on the 30th December 1957. We managed without any help in the house, but it wasn't easy, especially when the boys came out for the holidays.

My sister, Elizabeth, visited us at the end of February, unfortunately the situation in the island was rather tense, so we weren't able to get around as much as we'd have liked.

Alice was christened on the 28th April by the Regimental Padre, Tom Metcalfe, in St. Paul's Church, Nicosia, where I'd been baptised forty-four years before. Afterwards we had a big party in the Officers' Mess. Mercifully Eoka weren't too active, so there was a good turn out.

Time passed quickly. Sir Hugh Foot replaced Sir John Harding as Governor. As a young man Hugh Foot had served in Cyprus and remembered my father, so we had something in common. He accepted my invitation to take the salute at our Minden Day parade on 1st August, and gave a very complimentary address. He visited us again with Lady Foot when Brigadier Dick Maxwell, the Colonel of The Regiment, came out in February 1959. Murna and I had lunch at Government House on two occasions. When I'd been there as a boy in Malcolm Stevenson's time, it had been an unimposing wooden building. Burnt down by rioters in 1930 and replaced by an attractive building in honey-coloured local sandstone.

The British Government eventually became exasperated with the continuing demand for Enosis by Archbishop Makarios, abetted by the Greek Government in Athens. It was obvious no progress could be made while he was able to stir-up trouble, and provide Grivas and his Eoka henchmen a rallying point. After much head-scratching, the Colonial Secretary, Duncan Sandys, screwed up his courage and ordered the Governor to exile Makarios ('Black Mac' to the soldiers) to the Seychelles, a group of small islands in the Indian Ocean – a turning point in the Emergency.

It became unpleasantly hot in Nicosia in July, so I took Murna and little Alice up to Pine Trees Leave Camp on Troodos where it was cool and we could relax. In August, when Charlie and Richard came out for the school summer holidays, we stayed in the Villa Carlotta in Kyrenia, rented for officers' use. We did a lot of bathing, visited Richard Coeur de Lion's Crusader castle of St. Hilarion in the Kyrenia hills and the beautiful Bellapaix Abbey – I'd been to both these places many times as a small boy with my parents and Betty, riding on a donkey. Richard, Charlie and I swam out to Snake Island, a rocky islet a hundred yards off the coast, I recalled doing the same in about 1922, clinging on to my father's shoulders.

I'd now been in command for over two and a half years and was thinking about my next posting. Having been commissioned through the Supplementary Reserve I'd lost at least a year's seniority, this was now catching up with me and proving a handicap. I was well over forty-four and hadn't yet held a 1st Grade Staff job (as a Lieutenant Colonel), a further obstacle to promotion, especially as the army was being run down – I knew the Suffolk and Royal Norfolk Regiments were soon to amalgamate. I had a wife and three children to provide for, my future prospects were beginning to give me concern. I'd always had good Annual Confidential Reports; for the last five years being graded 'Above Average' – essential for further promotion. About this time I was appointed an Officer of The British Empire (OBE), presumably indicating that I'd made a success of my time in command.

Towards the end of 1959 I was selected for the appointment of Assistant Quarter Master General 'Q' Operations and Plans, a 1st Grade Staff job, in HQ BAOR, Rheindahlen, near Munchen Gladbach, Germany. I was delighted, but later, on considering it dispassionately, I had misgivings. It was flattering to have been selected for such an important job, entailing planning the logistic back-up for BAOR, but I only had a very slight understanding of nuclear warfare. I'd actually hoped for a job at the School of Infantry or something similar, where my experience in infantry tactics and my shooting skill could be usefully applied. However, I was fairly confident I'd be able to cope alright at HQ BAOR.

In October I again flew back to the UK, this time to visit Infantry Record Offices to sort out promotions and postings resulting from the impending amalgamation, visiting Bill Murray-Brown, CO 1st Royal Norfolk in Iserlohn, Germany. Before returning I collected Charlie, who'd had a nasty operation for a suspended hernia whilst at school, he'd recovered sufficiently to travel back to Cyprus with me. In January 1959 Murna flew with him to see him safely back to school, returning straightaway to Cyprus.

My time in command was almost up. We had a large party in our house on 31st March, followed by a farewell Guest Night in the Mess. The Sergeants' Mess presented me with a silver salver and beer mug. Finally, after a farewell parade, Murna and I were towed in the traditional manner out of Kykko Camp. After just under three years as CO, it was a wrench to leave the Battalion; I knew I'd never serve with the Old Twelth of Foot again – an emotional departure for both of us.

Chapter 20

Last Years in the Army, 1959–61

We sailed on the 2nd April 1959 from Famagusta in the troopship *Devonshire*, arriving at Southampton on 14th April, yet again facing the inevitable problem of where to stay. We found the Burningfold Hall, a quiet hotel in the country near Godalming, Surrey. At the end of May I set off for Germany, crossing by the car-ferry Harwich to Hook of Holland, arriving at 'A' Mess (senior officers) HQ BAOR, Rheindahlen on 27th May where I stayed till Murna came out with Alice in mid-June.

There was a long waiting list for married quarters, so we were accommodated in 'C' Married Officers Hostel; we had three rooms and fed communally, not exactly lavish but adequate. We'd engaged a nanny for Alice, a young English girl who proved utterly useless – she didn't last long. In October we got a married quarter – 5 Salisbury Walk, and a German 'Batwoman' to help in the house – things were looking up.

Rheindahlen was a vast complex for several thousand service folk, mostly British, in a pleasant wooded setting. There was an excellent Officers' Club run by NAAFI, a good cinema with up-to-date films, an Olympic standard swimming pool. We either already knew, or soon got to know lots of people; altogether very social, we liked it. The rate of exchange was favourable – DM12.60 to the £ sterling – (BAOR had its own currency – BAFS) petrol was subsidized and there were other worthwhile perks.

I won't dwell on my time in 'Q' Ops & Plans. Suffice it to say I was ill-suited for the job. Never having been a 'Planner' before, and lacking experience in the deployment of nuclear weapons, I was out of my depth. More importantly, I didn't hit it off with my immediate superior, a Brigadier with a fine war record (he became a Full General and a member of the Army Council), we had little in common – I wasn't sharp enough for him. Just my luck to get such a tricky appointment at a critical juncture in my career.

In January 1960, Murna, Charlie, Alice, the nanny and I travelled by train to St. Anton, a winter sports resort in Austria, staying ten days in the Hotel Post (Princess Beartrix of the Netherlands was staying there at the same time). It was terribly cold, not much fun for Alice who was only just two, nor for me, I couldn't skate or ski due to my gammy right knee. Murna skated gracefully impressing the onlookers, she hadn't lost the skills she'd learnt at Villars when as a girl she'd won numerous competitions; it was almost the first time I'd seen her perform on the ice, I was very proud of her. Charlie had his first skiing lessons.

Whilst in Rheindahlen I made two duty trips to the War Office. On the second, in February 1960, I hired a car and visited our house in Elstree. Driving back to Hampstead where I was staying with my sister Elizabeth, a baker's delivery van drove into me whilst I was almost stationary. My car was badly damaged, I was severely shaken up and taken by ambulance to Stanmore Orthopaedic Hospital not far away; Elizabeth came up in the afternoon to see me, very good of her. I was collected by an army ambulance that evening and taken to Queen Alexandra's Royal Military Hospital, Millbank, on the Thames Embankment, where I remained for four days before returning to Germany. I was very bruised, but mercifully suffered no lasting damage. Two years later there was a Court case to apportion blame – a lot of money was at stake. After four hours of wrangling by three barristers, the wise old judge, to my great relief, accepted my version of the events and awarded me damages.

The time came round for Annual Confidential Reports. My Brigadier only graded me 'Average', which of course put paid to any further promotion. I felt I this was unfair, and asked to see the General Officer Commanding HQ BAOR – a Gunner. He interviewed me but he was unwilling to change the grading to 'Above Average'. As an army officer it was second nature to accept orders and not to bellyache; this may sound rather corny, maybe I took it too lying down? Both these two officers are no longer with us, at least I've the slight satisfaction of outlasting them.

Hindsight is dangerous, nevertheless, I feel that if I'd been reported on by infantrymen, they might have been more considerate; perhaps a further report in six month's time, or a posting to a job more in keeping with my experience. Promotions to Full Colonel were made by a War Office Selection Board, guided by Confidential Report gradings. I knew many very senior officers who, if I'd approached them, might have put in a good word for me. To do so never occurred to me – perhaps it'd have been worth a try. Just my luck to come up for promotion at a time when the Empire was being run down with consequent reductions in the armed forces. During my service I'd done a number of somewhat unusual jobs satisfactorily, had been an early volunteer for parachuting duty, had proven shooting ability, been a successful operational battalion commander for three years, appointed an OBE and Mentioned in Despatches. I felt I deserved one rank higher.

In the event I was posted to the Ministry of Defence to arrange a high-powered conference of Commonwealth Defence Scientists, to be held over a period of a week in late July 1961 at the Royal Military College of Science, under the sponsorship of Sir Solly Zuckerman, the eminent scientist. The sop being that this would provide me with an opportunity to find civilian employment before being compulsorily retired two months after the conference ended.

After a week at the BAOR Leave Centre at Winterberg in the Hartz Mountains, we left Rheindahlen at the end of September 1960. I felt depressed and hardly done by, the prospect of leaving the army and finding a civilian job was frightening. How was I going to support my Murna and our family? My army pension would be small – I'd only got in just under twenty-seven years service. I was forty-seven; I'd hoped to serve till I was fifty-five and reached the rank of Full Colonel. With three children to educate, and no worthwhile civilian qualifications, what was I going to do? I viewed the future with considerable foreboding.

Confronted with the usual difficulties in finding accommodation – we couldn't go to Elstree as our house was let – we were eventually allocated an army quarter in Bushey, Hertfordshire, just north of London, moving in early in November. A few friends were living in this 'patch' including the Goulds, which was a help, but it was an awful long journey to my office in the Treasury Building, Westminster.

Murna had been having pain in her right wrist for some months, eventually diagnosed as carpel tunnel syndrome requiring an operation. She was admitted to Queen Alexandra's Military Hospital at Millbank on 2nd March, and was operated on by

The Author – 1960

Colonel John Watts, a highly thought of RAMC surgeon whom we'd known in Cyprus. We engaged a housekeeper for a month, she wasn't much good, and what's more had her ghastly young daughter with her – Alice was understandably very upset, but there was no alternative.

Realising that when I would be out of the army in September, the location of our house in Elstree would be inconvenient, we decided to sell and find a house in a more suitable area. After much deliberation we picked on Camberley, Surrey, where we had many army friends and hopefully we'd find a good school for Alice. It would be handy for Richard who'd left Wellington College and was about to enter Sandhurst with a view to getting into my old Regiment, and also reasonably easy to get to Charlie's school in Sussex, moreover there was a good rail service – essential if I found a job in London.

We motored down; an estate agent showed us a house in the early stages of construction, which we thought would suit us. We contacted a solicitor, John Hand, of Stevens & Bolton in Camberley, and made an offer. We'd put our Elstree house on the market, it took quite a time to sell and we didn't get much more than we'd paid for it twelve years before, so we needed a small mortgage. Somehow we managed to find 'the necessary' using up all our capital in the process – we'd no parents or relatives to help us out. The 'golden handshake' I got from the army was a measly £5,000, pretty rotten by today's handouts. We moved into Hadleigh House on 2nd June 1961 – choosing the name to remind us of when we'd first met in Suffolk.

My job bored me. Preparations for the Conference were eventually arranged satisfactorily, in spite of the overseas delegates behaving like prima donas, all expecting VIP treatment. Sir Solly Zuckerman, who was always most helpful, opened the Conference at The Royal College of Military Science where I and my staff – a Sqn. Ldr. RAF, a Lt. Cdr. RN and a Senior Civil Service Executive Officer – were accommodated in a Hall of Residence. It ended on the 27th July with a morning meeting in Lancaster House, near Buckingham Palace, chaired by the Chief of the Defence Staff, Lord Louis Mountbatten, with an evening reception hosted by the Secretary of State for Defence, Francis Pym MP. When I'd tied up the loose ends after the conference there was nothing else for me to do, so I quietly took myself off into retirement.

I received a few official letters thanking me for my service, noting my achievements and so on, all pretty impersonal. That was that – rather a flat ending to my army career. As from the end of September I would be out, no time to be sorry for myself – I'd got to find a job!

Chapter 21

'Civvy Street'

When I left the army many officers were being 'axed', so there were lots of chaps in the same boat as myself – looking for civilian jobs. The army arranged a Business Familiarisation Course at the City of London University which was helpful, but produced no concrete results. I wrote endless letters enclosing my Curriculum Vitae, but got few replies and fewer interviews.

After a month I was becoming desperate. Not having any specialist qualifications I'd little to offer other than integrity, commonsense, enthusiasm, and what the army called 'Man Management'. I'd written to, or contacted personally, everyone I could think of who might possibly help or give advice, no matter how slightly I knew them or how long since we'd last met, including Murna's second cousin, Geoffrey Eley, Chairman of Richard Thomas and Baldwins, leading steel manufacturers. I was offered a rotten job by Rolls Royce in Derby, which in any case was out of the question as accommodation would have been impossible. Nothing else came up – what was I to do?

I was almost at my wits end, when one morning a totally unexpected letter came from Geoffrey Eley (subsequently knighted), written on British Oxygen Company headed paper, saying he'd arranged for me to meet Dr. Augus Roy, the Group Personnel Officer, in the Company's Head Office at Bridgewater House, St. James's, London, near Lancaster House. We knew Geoffrey was a Deputy Governor of the Bank of England, but had no idea he was also a Director of British Oxygen.

This was terrific news. I was interviewed by Dr. Angus Roy, a stocky little Scot, on the 9th June. He explained that the position of Bursar at the Company's Staff College at Chartridge Lodge, near Chesham, Bucks, was vacant. The Principal was one Tommy Cochrane, also ex-army, who would like me to visit Chartridge the next week. I went by train to Amersham, where Tommy met me. From the moment we shook hands I knew I'd get along alright with him. We set off through lovely country the six miles to Chartridge. The weather was wonderful, the sun was shining, my spirits rose every mile of the way – perhaps this was going to be my lucky day? Chartridge Lodge, a large early twentieth century house, stood in fifteen acres of well-tended lawns and garden in the heart of the Chiltern hills. Tommy, a much decorated ex-Sapper officer, about four years my junior, had retired eighteen months before to start up the college from scratch. Without any doubt he'd have made General's rank if he'd stayed in the army – he'd retired early for family reasons.

I met the staff: five domestic assistants – attractive young women, the secretarial girls and the garden and maintenance employees, quite an outfit. Three Tutors, all in their thirties, helped Tommy on the instructional side – I liked them all.

My job would be to run the administration, including the accounts, wages, salaries, maintenance of the house and grounds, transport and so on. I was offered a cottage adjoining the Lodge, but I explained that to live there would upset our schooling arrangements and anyway we'd only just moved into a new house. The distance from Camberley was a problem, but Tommy said I could sleep in an empty student's room two or three nights a week, if that would help.

While driving me back to the station that afternoon he said the job was mine if I'd like it. Starting salary would be £1,250 a year, rising to £1,500 after three months – he was kind enough to say he hoped I'd take it.

I couldn't wait to get home to tell Murna. She'd put up with such a lot of moves, and the operation on her wrist had set her back. Her love, support and reassurance over the last two difficult years had been a great comfort – I was terribly lucky in having such a wonderful wife. She thought the salary rather measly, and pointed out I'd have to do an awful lot of motoring, but accepted it was at least a start. She was delighted for me – at last it looked as if our path would be a bit smoother. A second car was essential, so we bought a new Mini Minor van for £500 – Minis were still quite a novelty. We'd got Alice into a small private school close by in Camberley (the Miss Leese's), where she was happy and making progress.

I started at Chartridge Lodge on 21st August 1961, a month before I'd officially retired from the army which pleased me – in spite of the somewhat humble position I felt this was quite an achievement. My salary, together with my miserable army pension – I'd commuted half mainly to buy the house – would just about enable us to keep our heads above water, but making ends meet would be a struggle.

As the college had only been going for a short time, there was considerable keeness amongst British Oxygen management to attend the four-week courses of twenty-two students. The Directors and senior managers from within the UK, and from overseas companies too, never missed a chance to visit the college, including the Chairman, John Hutchinson, a dour, monosyllabic Glaswegian, and Lord Reith, the megalomaniacal Vice-Chairman (of BBC fame), who was feared and disliked by everyone.

I found I could cope with the work and made friends with all the staff, in particular with the head gardner, George Hance, a splendid man who'd been employed at Chartridge Lodge since a boy; he came to Camberley with me once to advise on our garden and was very taken with Murna. My Assistant, Cindy Holmes, was an attractive young woman from Yorkshire, we became, and remain, good friends; she stayed with us at Camberley on several occasions. A few years later she married Leslie Smith, the Managing Director, later to become Chairman, a wonderful man whom I greatly admire – she's now Lady Smith.

I enjoyed my three years at Chartridge. Tommy Cochrane worked long hours and expected us to do likewise; we gave of our best and were a happy team. The constant driving to and from Camberley was a ghastly sweat and expensive on petrol, but I hated being away from Murna for more than two consecutive nights, so there was no option. Mine was a comparatively painless introduction to industry. I got to know all the senior management in the Company, everyone was friendly and helpful, the only exceptions being a few senior ex-service officers, who found it difficult to forget their previous rank, although everyone was addressed as plain 'Mister'. At that time British Oxygen had some twenty-seven thousand employees worldwide – an enormous corporation.

The Labour Party was in power, Harold Wilson, the PM, had instituted 'pay freezes'. As a result, after three years at Chartridge, my salary had only increased by a few hundred pounds – inflation was biting deep. Our family expenses were heavy; Richard was off our hands, but we still had Charles and Alice to educate. To make ends meet, we sold quite a few pieces of silver, and a beautiful 'mille fleurs' glass paper-weight I'd inherited from my father – I hated parting with it – Murna sold some jewellery, which we lived to regret, but there was no alternative, or so we thought at the time; with hindsight we could have raised a loan, but I was scared of doing so.

Realising I'd never make much progress financially if I remained at Chartridge, I let it be known that I'd like a job at Head Office, recently re-located in Hammersmith House, West London, reasonably accessible by car from Camberley. I wanted a change, not only to improve my salary, but also because Tommy Chocrane was leaving for another job within the Company, I didn't fancy working under his replacement. Furthermore, and most importantly, both Murna and I were fed up with being away from each other such a lot.

The position of Group Personnel Officer had recently been taken over by an old friend, Harold Kitson, an ex-Sapper Brigadier, he and his wife Sybil had travelled out to India with us on the *Queen of Bermuda* in 1946. Harold considered the Company's chaotic salary structure required rationalising, and offered me the new job of Salary Administration Officer at the princely salary of £2,250.

I started off at Hammersmith House in October 1964. Harold explained what he had in mind, but no one had really any idea of what it would entail – it was up to me to work out a plan of action. As can readily be appreciated, anything to do with salaries was a very sensitive subject, people were extremely cagey about their remuneration and reluctant to discuss it with a stranger from Personnel.

Over the next three years, I visited the Company's regional offices, production plants and installations. With Works Managers I compiled job descriptions of their staff, and graded them into salary brackets. The work was interesting and gave me a good insight into how industry worked. I soon got a fair knowledge of the various processes and was able to weigh up one job against another with some accuracy; a formidable task in a corporation of such size and diversity. Having met most of the senior management while at Chartridge, and having the Managing Directors's authority behind me – although I don't think he attached much importance to the exercise – I was invariably made welcome, and given full co-operation. I became something of an authority on the subject and well known throughout the Group.

During this period we'd got ourselves established in Camberley. Richard had been commissioned and was a Second Lieutenant in The East Anglian Regiment the successor to The Suffolk Regiment. Charlie was at Bloxham School in Oxfordshire, Alice was Head Girl at her small private school. We'd discovered the attractions of The Scilly Isles where we hired a flat and had many happy holidays, we also ventured to St. Brelades in Jersey, and spent a week in Paris with our Regimental friends the Lummises.

The time was approaching for Alice to move to a school where she could stay until she'd finished her education. The only suitable one in the area was St. Nicholas's, in Fleet, seven miles away. Murna said she was too old to do a daily 'milk-round', so there was nothing for it but to move closer to Fleet. We were lucky in finding a late Victorian house almost backing onto St. Nick's – 36 Victoria Road – which we bought very reasonably. However, as property sales were sluggish, Hadleigh House took the best part of a year to sell. We eventually sold it, but only after letting the purchaser have an extended period to pay.

36 Victoria Road required considerable improvements including rewiring, a new roof, new plumbing, central heating and so on. We found a Master Plumber in his late sixties, Mr. Hunt, who carried out the work with a team of bricklayers and plumbers. By the time the alterations were finished there was little left in the kitty, but we all liked the house and garden; Richard erected a pre-fabricated double-garage entirely on his own. We moved in on 12th October 1966.

Our house was in the long-established part of the little town of Fleet with many substantial Victorian houses roundabout standing in large gardens – rhododendrons and fir trees proliferated. Up to the beginning of WW2 Fleet had been popular with comfortably-off gentle-folk, especially retired Service people. Victoria Road rose gently to the highest point of the town, but it was only a short walk down to the high street and shops. My job entailed my being away pretty often, but Murna managed alright, she had Alice and our dog Caesar, a black Labrador-Collie cross, (like Rover) for company.

I started off by driving up to Hammersmith House in a Mini, but developed cervical spondilosis in the neck and left arm, so I bought an old bicycle for £5 from a nearby farmer (which I still use daily) and rode the mile to Fleet station, chained the bike to the railings and caught a train to Waterloo, then by Underground to

Hammersmith. If all went well I could be in my office in an hour and a quarter, but with the Labour Government there were constant rail strikes, making the journey horrendous. I hated it, such a waste of precious time, it became a strain, especially in the winter.

I was still working on salary administration, and had an assistant, an ex-Commander RN. My friend, Harold Kitson had been replaced by a recently retired Rear Admiral, James Walwyn, at the superior level of Chief Executive. A Dame, previously Director of the Womens Royal Naval Service, had been appointed Supervisor of all female employees – so the Royal Navy was in the ascendancy. James was an unlikely chap for a senior naval officer, – amongst other things he had the infuriating habit of working late after all sensible people had left, which meant us underlings couldn't take-off till he'd gone home – most inconsiderate.

My salary had increased a bit, also in 1968 all Service Pensions were indexed to make up for the effects of inflation (one of the few good things Ted Heath did as Prime Minister) so we were marginally better off and could afford the odd overseas holiday. Murna, Alice and I motored to Chateau D'Oex in Switzerland; we visited the pension in Villars where she'd stayed as a girl – very nostalgic for her.

Early in 1968 Murna went down with a severe attack of laryngitis and was in Fleet hospital for three weeks, followed by a fortnight in a convalescent home on the south coast at Hove; she hated it there and longed to get home.

In March I took her and Alice to the comfy Tregarthen's Hotel in St. Mary's, Isles of Scilly. As always in the Scillys we enjoyed the friendly atmosphere, the boat trips to the neighbouring islands and the unspoilt rugged environment. By the time we left she'd regained much of her strength – she'd also given up smoking which delighted me – I'd done so not long before.

At the end of July 1968 we decided to hire a caravan and go over to Brittany for a couple of weeks – not really a success. Murna wasn't taken with caravanning, I was rather too long in the tooth to do it for the first time and it was a bit boring for Alice. However, we got around, visited Mont St. Michael and saw the Bayeux Tapestry – the weather was good which made it worthwhile.

By this time Richard had left the army – he was never cut-out for a soldier's life. His hearing had deteriorated, so he was pronounced unfit for further service on medical grounds.

I'd realised for some time that all wasn't well, but it was a blow to all of us when he had to chuck it. He succeeded in getting taken on by the BBC, starting in the Record Library, and living in digs in London. Realising he'd never get far in his job, he applied for a passage under the Australian Government's £10 emigration scheme. We took him to Southampton docks on 15th May 1969, where he boarded the Greek liner *Ellinis*, and sailed off for Sydney. Although he and I had had our disagreements, nevertheless, I was, and still am, extremely fond of him – to me, in some ways, he is more like a son than a stepson. It was hard for Murna, Richard was her firstborn, he had a special place in her affections. She put on a brave face, but I knew she felt his departure deeply – she was never to see him again. To buck her up, I took her and Alice to the island of Elba, off the west coast of Italy; we hired a car and enjoyed discovering this interesting Italian island.

My career at BOC (as British Oxygen had become) took another turn. James Walwyn called me into his office and told me I'd been chosen for a new job – Internal Communications Manager – in the Public Relations Division, under Mr. Alan Eden-Green. James was uncertain what it involved, but assured me it was in my best interests to take it – perhaps he was keen to off-load me? My task would be to communicate to management the implications and reasoning behind major directives or changes in policy initiated by the Managing Directors (there were three of them then). The problem was how to glean this information, and assuming I succeeded, how much should I divulge? Alan Eden-Green was a charming man, I'd had no contact with him before. He was a Past President of the Institute of Public Relations, his background had been in Local Government – I got to like him very much. I wasn't a type he'd come up against before, nor was I as quick-witted as perhaps he'd have liked, but he always treated me courteously – on balance we got on well. It was stimulating working under a real professional.

I got to grips with the job. Prompted by Alan, I started what was called 'The 1500 Club' (a play on the letters MD, the Latin numerals for 1500 – MD for Managing Director). A select number of senior managers were sent a letter by the Managing Directors, inviting them to join the club. Membership soon carried quite a cachet – people approached me hoping to get invited to join the club. Meetings were held in the MDs's suite on the top floor of Hammersmith House. An outside speaker, often a personality in the public eye, was invited to address the meeting; afterwards there was an excellent buffet, over which the MDs got a chance to chat informally with their senior managers. The speaker usually stayed on for dinner with one of the MDs, myself and one or two others. Not only were these occasions enjoyable, but I also met many interesting people. On one occasion I asked Martin Bell, the BBC TV Reporter, to give a talk, this was many years before he became well known for his reports from the Gulf War and Bosnia. He'd done his National Service in The Suffolk Regt. under me in Cyprus, I promoted him to Sergeant in the Intelligence Section – he still frequently wears the Regimental tie when speaking on the 'Box'.

We carried on steadily at Fleet, but both Murna and I were beginning to feel our years. Charlie had followed in his half-brother's footsteps and left to try his luck in Australia, again on the £10 emigration scheme in the Greek liner *Ellinis*. Alice had settled into St. Nicks. We went annually for two weeks to the Scillies which we loved, staying in the Penlee Flat. One year Pat and Gay Thursby, with Clive their younger son, joined us; another year Malcolm and Maureen Dewar came over for ten days which was fun. We motored up to Scotland and stayed with Mary Eley (Pat Eley's widow) at Appin, and also up to Suffolk for Fiona Lummis's christening – Murna was a godmother.

On the 7th November 1971, we had a belated Silver Wedding Party (it should have been on 5th October). There was a good turn out – my sister Elizabeth Edholm and her three girls, and my cousin Mary Dudbridge, were my only relations – there were none from Murna's side, but many friends turned up, mostly ex-army. We missed not having either Charlie or Richard with us.

Murna and Alice went to the Austrian Tyrol in January 1972 for a fortnight's skiing and skating and in August we took our usual holiday in the Isles of Scilly, my sister joining us in the Peenlee flat for a week. The next year, 1973, we didn't go to the Scillys, I forget why, but on the 27th September our lives changed dramatically – I suffered a severe heart-attack!

I'd driven to the office instead of going by train as I was expecting to be late getting home. I didn't feel well the whole morning, so at lunch time reported to the Nursing Sister in Hammersmith House. She took my blood pressure, then told me to wait while she fetched Dr. Geoffrey Matthews, the Group Medical Consultant, he was having lunch in the restaurant. Geoffrey, who knew me well, came in, sat down at his desk and looked at me. After a few questions he said, "Come on Bertie, I'm just taking you to the Charing Cross Hospital down the road for tests which I can't do here". His car was waiting outside, I got in front, Sister sat behind, we set off. Within twenty minutes, perhaps less, from the time I'd reported to Sister, I was in the intensive-care ward. Without a doubt they saved my life, I'm deeply indebted to them, they were absolutely first class.

Murna and Alice came bustling up the next day. I was Okay but pretty dopey – it was quite wonderful to see her. At first she was distraught, but was reassured when she realised I wasn't going to konk-out. I stayed there till 16th October, then was taken home by John Cole, a splendid chap in PR Division, a tower of strength and a great support to Murna at this difficult time. I spent a fortnight at home – a strain on Murna who wasn't on top form; she and Alice then drove me to Osborne House, the Officers' Convalescent Hospital on the Isle of Wight, where I remained for six weeks. (Originally Queen Victoria's country home where she died). In the meantime, after and absence of almost three years, Charles had returned from Australia and New Zealand, where he'd travelled extensively and done all sorts of unusual jobs; he'd got on well with the Aussies, and learnt how to cope with their rather brash ways. It was clear to Murna and me that he hankered to return there. He drove over to the Isle of Wight, collected me and took me home.

By this time I was back to normal, apparently none the worse. Amazingly, I've never had any further trouble on this score – I've really been most extraordinarily fortunate. I put it down to clean living, plenty of exercise and a burra-peg every evening.

Chapter 22

The Unbelievable Happens

Having come through my heart-attack so well, I started doing three days a week, gradually working up to full time, but was able to arrive late at the office and leave early. I'm certain it was due to this considerate treatment by BOC that I'm still around.

While I was building up my strength, the opposite was happening to Murna. Since my return from hospital she'd seemed off-colour and listless. She'd put on weight – strange as she didn't have much of an appetite – and was a bad colour. I thought it might perhaps be jaundice; I became alarmed. Our local GP arranged for her to have tests at the Cambridge Military Hospital in Aldershot, seven miles away. We expected she'd only be in for a day or two – after five days I became worried and asked to see her doctor.

Arriving at the hospital in the afternoon, I was told that the Royal Army Medical Corps consultant surgeon looking after her, would see me as soon as he'd finished operating. After a few minutes, he came out of the theatre in his green operating gown and head-scarf – a stocky thick-set Scot. Taking me by the arm he led me into the Theatre Sister's office, sat down at a desk and fished his pipe out of his pocket. Standing opposite him on the other side of the desk I asked if he could tell me the result of the tests. He took some time lighting his pipe, when he'd got it going he looked up at me and said – "Your wife has got cancer." I replied "I think I'll sit down." He said she'd got a tumour on the pancreas, a by-pass operation would give her a year's life – there was nothing else he could do. Colonel Coakley operated on my darling Murna on 1st February 1974.

On the 4th March 1974 Alice and I took her to a Convalescent Hospital in Brighton for three weeks – she hated being there. From then on we our activities were restricted. Charles got a job as a 'Roustabout' (jack-of-all-trades) with Shell North Sea Oil Exploration Co. on a rig (Staflo) far out in the North Sea. He worked fortnightly shifts so was able to get home to see his mother quite often. Bill Francis, Charlie's great friend whom we all liked and knew well, stayed overnight now and again. Murna's Aunt Una, (Lady Albery) in her late eighties, came down for the day with her daughter Sheila Jackson. In August Murna, Alice and I motored up to Shropshire and spent a couple of nights with our old friends Joan and Peter Parker at Castle Pulverbatch – the last long journey she was to make.

As each month passed I knew Murna's life was slipping away, she did too, but we never talked about it. She wasn't in pain but looked sad, and was a travesty of what she'd been a year or so before. She never complained, but I knew she was bitter at not having been to Australia to see Richard and her first grandchild, Hugh Thomson, and meet her daughter-in-law Leonie.

There was a sort of numbness over all of us – waiting for the worst to happen, rotten for Alice who was devoted to her Mum and at the difficult age of seventeen when a girl needs a mother's help and guidance – I felt inadequate and useless. I still went to Hammersmith House daily, which helped by keeping my mind occupied with things other than Murna's illness.

In the early hours of 18th December she woke me up in great pain. I took her straight to the hospital. She was able to return home over Christmas, which was wonderful as Charlie had brought his girlfriend, Tania Nakoneczna, an Australian, down for Christmas. I think Murna knew they were in love – it was wonderful that Tania just met her, even though so briefly.

The morning of the 10th January 1975, when I took Murna for the last time into The Cambridge Military Hospital in Aldershot, was bright crisp and sunny. A few early daffs were poking their heads through the soil, the osmanthus bush beside the front door was giving off a sweet lemon scent, a robin was hopping around cheeping. She knew she'd never come home again – so did I.

She had a small ward to herself and was well looked after by the RAMC staff – she felt at ease in an army environment, the Orderlies all thought the world of her. Alice and I went over every evening to see her. Her room was full of flowers, our friends rallied round, but there was nothing anyone could do. She lingered on, undaunted, sustained by her deep Christian faith, and comforted by the Sandhurst Padre, who visited her.

The end came in the evening of the 20th February 1975, about the only evening that Alice and I hadn't visited her. We hurried over, but it was too late – I'll never forgive myself.

Murna

Epilogue

Much has happened in the twenty years since Murna died. Soon after her death Charles got a job in Alberta with an oil-well servicing company, a subsidiary of BOC. He had little money and no suitable clothing for the freezing conditions on the leeses, in the foothills of the Rocky Mountains. The senior manager was 'agin' him for some reason; perhaps he'd got a grudge against the Brits ? Anyway Charlie stuck it out; I was relieved when he phoned to say he'd managed to get his pay and was coming home soon, I told him to keep a low profile.

After a short time in England he decided to go back to Australia. However, as he'd been away for more than six months the Australian authorities refused him a Work Permit. There was only one thing for it – to get engaged to Tania. This would enable him to get work, and provided they got married within six months he'd be able to remain permanently. It worked out wonderfully well. They married, now there are three Miss Bevans, my granddaughters, the eldest, Alexandra, having Murna as her second name – which gives me enormous pleasure.

Before Murna's death, Alice spent six weeks with Richard and Leonie in Queensland during the summer holidays and fell in love with Australia. After leaving St. Nicks, she worked hard and obtained – to my pleasure and surprise – a good secretarial diploma; she also got a diploma in Cordon Bleu cookery. These qualifications satisfied the Australian emigration authorities, so she decided to join her brother and half-brother in Australia. She sailed in the Russian liner, *Mikhail Lermontov*, from Southampton on the 4th January 1977 – she'd just turned nineteen. I went down to the docks with our neighbour, Rhona Bancroft, to see her off. A cold bitter wind was blowing – one of the saddest days in my life. She's now Mrs. Kouznetsoff, with two small half-Russian/ Australian daughters. Like her mother, whom she resembles in looks, she has an obstinate streak – but also great courage.

I'd decided to put 36 Victoria Road up for sale, it was too big for me on my own and held too many memories. A BOC friend told me about a flat he'd just bought in a large still unfinished development called Camden Hurst at Milford-on-Sea, on the south coast opposite the Needles – the western extremity of the Isle of Wight. Shortly before Alice's departure we motored down together to view a flat overlooking the sea; we thought it would suit me; I put in an offer and got it.

I moved in on 15th February 1977 – a wet, grey, windy day. I was entirely on my own, lonely and miserable, with all my possessions dumped around me. The door bell rang – there was my friend and solicitor, John Hand! I hadn't realised he owned a holiday bungalow in the village, he cheered me up, I felt less sorry for myself and got down to sorting things out.

In July I made my first visit to Australia, where I spent three months visiting Richard, Charles and Alice in turn. Not long after my return I was asked to lunch by Molly Allott who lived in one of the Camden Hurst flats (she'd been the Director of The Womens Royal Air Force before retiring as an Air Commadore). Molly had also invited two friends, one was Jill Lawrence. I was the only man.

Jill and I met again at the end of the year, we became friends and saw a lot of each other. Through her I met many local people and began to feel I belonged, especially when I joined the Royal Lymington Yacht Club. I was again in Australia when Jill wrote and told me the semi-detached house adjoining her's was shortly to be sold – she'd got first refusal, was I interested in making an offer before it went on the market?

By this time we'd more or less decided to get married. I didn't like living in a flat – missed a garden and somewhere to do a bit of carpentry. So I made an offer. The vendor's solicitors pushed me up, but I got the house very reasonably indeed. I realised it needed a lot of alteration, but hoped I'd have sufficient left over from the sale of the flat to do what I had in mind and a bit to invest. It worked out as I'd hoped, in spite of the flat taking longer to sell than I'd expected. I invested the balance from the sale in early 1982 when share prices were low; from then on equities took-off – the flat did me proud.

Jill's daughter Elaine, who is a dear, and son Russell, welcomed me into their family – they were pleased we planned to marry. Elaine, her husband and small son Tom, soon emigrated to New Zealand; whenever I visit her she's always anxious to make me feel at home. Russell – the only one of our five children (including Richard of course) in the UK – can invariably be relied on for help and wise advice. His wife Valerie, has very kindly helped me with this book.

We married on 5th August 1981. My friend Jack Prescott told me he thought Jill was "very elegant" – an apt description – she's also a wonderful wife. How lucky I was that Molly Allott decided to ask me to her lunch party!

Index

(Note: Ranks shown are contemporaneous with the narrative)

INDEX

INDEX

INDEX